To Linda,

May you live in an Up Spiral always.

Barbara

Dr. William Kent Larkin

Is Director of the
Applied Neuroscience Institute

He is a researcher in the applied neuroscience of happiness and well-being: how the brain and the person operate more efficiently and economically on positivity. His research shows that people and organizations trained in an UpSpiral of positivity are happier, more successful, more productive, and healthier. Positivity dramatically increases well-being and productivity.

Dr. Larkin was educated at Yale University, and holds a doctorate from Harvard University. For 10 years, he was the voice of psychology for the Armed Forces Network broadcasting to 72 countries.

Dr. Larkin is the author of five books, the most recent being <u>Growing The Positive Mind</u>. His new book, <u>A New 12 Steps for a New Millennium</u>, will be released in October.

Dr. Larkin shares the principles of this research with individuals, groups, private business and the government sector using positivity to increase productivity and effectiveness.

www.GoToANI.com

12 NEW STEPS
For A New Millennium
The UpSpiraLife Group

Finally, there are 12 steps to well-being, to feeling good, and to meaning and vision in life that don't depend on having to be an alcoholic or a drug addict to use them. What they do depend upon is the kind of growth that happens when people work together in groups and provide a sub-culture of trained positivity and clear and focused reinforcement for each other. The Up Spiral Life group, shortened to UpSpiraLife or USL, is as life-changing for "normies" (people without addictions) as the other 12 steps are for people who have some addictive behavior to overcome. Unless you consider negativity an addiction, it is the thing you grow beyond into an UpSpiral of Positivity. Face it. Your negativity is the root of addiction.

The power of positivity in a human life can be not only the difference between living and dying. It can be the difference between living and being alive or flat lining your way through life, living your life for others.

The goal of this group is innocent enough. It's "feeling good." However, the power of feeling good is life changing once you decide you will and set your sights on finding what it is for you. Ultimately in this group, it means that you will have to consider what it means to live from your heart and to discover what your hearts longs to live and love for. You can't be in the group, stick to it, and not find out what that is.

This is the ultimate experience in recycling. It is recycling human beings who have lived their lives according to the norms, succeeding, meeting production deadlines and sales goals, or getting by the best they could, trying to love themselves and maybe doing ok. This is a group for people who are successful and who are not happy or those for whom success has been elusive. You will recycle yourself with the love and challenge of what makes your heart sing.

This isn't about finding bliss or ecstasy or religious fervor, or even spirituality unless that means that what you find already dwells within you as the essence of your dream for you.

A NEW 12 STEPS FOR A NEW MILLENNIUM
The UpSpiral Life Group

Neuroscience Press books may be found on the Applied Neuroscience Institute
website and purchased in bulk through arrangements there. www.gotoani.com.
Please put Special Markets Department in the subject line of your email.

First Edition January 2012

Manufactured in the United States of America

Cover Designed by
Al De Ramos
Sir Speedy Whittier

Larkin, William Kent
A New Twelve Steps for a New Millennium: The UpSpiral Life Group
William Kent Larkin

Includes bibliographical references.

ISBN 978-1-4507-8296
ISBN (eBook) 978-1-61061-720-8

This book is dedicated to:

Dr Martin E.P. Seligman

With great gratitude

And to
The Positive Psychology Movement

Acknowledgements

The UpSpiraLife group and movement could not have happened were it not for the pioneers who took my lead and started to lead the first groups. They were some of our first trained coaches and they brought forth what would work and what would not. Mostly they brought forth the assurance that it worked. The process and the idea worked and it worked well with the wide variety of their leadership styles. They did a great job and they had a lot of courage. So I give special thanks and acknowledgement to Andy Hamling, Mary Garvey Horst and Ken Horst, Margo Nelligan, Mary Ann Cullens, Mark Anderson, and Suzanne Grace.

An enormous amount of credit goes to the field manager of these first groups, Dr. Donald Johnson, the Associate Director of ANI. He did a masterful job of both managing the group leaders as well as leading and inspiring his own superb group. He has been an enormous support in both the original groups and in the preparation of this book: his guidance, his great critical eye, and his deep devotion and zeal in this process. He buoyed me up on any number of occasions when my enthusiasm and faith in the process lagged, and I will be forever grateful to have him as both a business partner and dear friend.

I want to also say how important the traditional 12 step groups around issues of addiction have been. While this is not the same thing and this process in no way claims, attempts or wants to be a replacement, they were an inspiration to the evolution of this process. These treatment groups are essential and these 12 steps in no way are any kind of a replacement for the work they do. These steps are an extension. The original 12 steps cannot do everything, and there is tendency to make them and their communities an answer to everything. Those expectations are unfair and misplaced.

I also want to thank Bill Wilson and Dr. Bob. I was inspired to do this from a play I saw in Los Angeles that was about the origin of AA. There was a particular scene when the two first met and they began to share with one another on a "heart to heart" level, and that is what I think is the basis of the whole 12 step recovery movement. It is that heart to heart sharing that creates growth and freedom from the isolation from one's self and others that addiction creates. It can do it with recovery from addiction and it can do it with recovery from negativity, which I happen to believe is also an addiction for many.

When I formed these steps and promises, I started by doing what can seem to be like a rather "out there" thing to do. I sat down and prayed and asked them to inspire me wherever they were and however they were. I sat down at the computer and a short time later, I had both the steps and the promises pretty much in the form they appear now. I believe that they didn't conceive then of addicted people who would have 20 and 30 years of sobriety. I think they would be coming up with something more now if they saw the needs of these healthy, recovered people, so mature in their growth and their lives. In a humble way, I hope this carries on their tradition by being inspired by it and adding to it.

Finally, I thank all the members of UpSpiraLife groups who jumped into experience this and gave us the nitty-gritty feedback and data we needed to see if it would work. And has it ever worked! The stories abound from these wonderful folks.

Table of Contents

Part III: The Twelve Promises

Part IV: The 52 Guides

The 52 NeuroPositive Quick Guides

INTRODUCTION

An Up Spiral Life group, trademarked UpSpiraLife©, is a positive 12 step group. These groups are not designed for addiction treatment (unless you consider persistent negativity an addiction), but rather for growing and deepening what we call "neuropositivity being" and well-being. This is more than simple "positive thinking" or positive emotions, but it includes them.

UpSpiraLife groups create and sustain a culture and fellowship of positivity that has come to be called "The UpSpiraLife Sanctuary." If you haven't already done so, please read "The UpSpiraLife Sanctuary." Why a new 12 steps in a group? The social context of the group is the most powerful way to learn and apply these 12 strategies and to grow into them. We call this journey "NeuroPositive©" and it is the trademark of the work of the Applied Neuroscience Institute. That is the journey: to change the neuropathways in the brain to create a lean, a stronger and stronger lean toward positivity. This is the handbook for the UpSpiraLife positivity group.

We have tried to solve life's problems by addressing the problem and finding a solution. We have had 60 years and more of research on illness. Perhaps we have learned all we need to know about suffering to at least search for another way. This is the new way that looks at what is right and what works about the person and builds upon that. As simple as positivity sounds, if not a little too simple, it's not. The research is profound and so are the results. I am going to ask for your trust. Experience the process of these 12 steps with others and then ask yourself the same questions you are asking now. This is a "game changer." You cannot feel better and become happier, you cannot increase the level of your well-being, without big changes occurring in your life, changes for the good. And I would wager that these changes are going to be so significant that when you finish the first journey through these steps, you're going to wonder how you lived in some of the ways you did, without this learning and without the support which your group can provide. The UpSpiraLife group is a "calling." You are called to it by some event or series of events. If you're not, don't stay, but come back again when you are.

These group meetings provide the opportunity for sharing insights and effective strategies for living the well-lived life, for growing into an UpSpiral, characterized by well-being and personal renewal at even a cellular level. The strategies you will learn in these groups increase and strengthen well-being. You will become stronger in many ways. The group is not religious, although there are those who regard this as a "spiritual" experience. The group is not intended to foster conversion or spiritual experience.

An UpSpiraLife group will do these things in your life if you work the 12 step process:

1. You will increase your capacity to experience positive emotion by working out in "The Emotional Gym."

2. You will experience increased engagement in every aspect of your life.

3. You will enlarge and deepen your personal relationships.

4. You will find deeper meaning in your life.

5. You will find goals that lead to a sense of vision and personal significance.

We call the effect of all of this learning "neuropositive" growth because, in the process, the neuropathways in your brain change from a tendency toward the "DownSpiral" to a greater tendency to be in an "UpSpiral" in your life. Neuropositivity being is a *way of life* that is dedicated to growing an increasing UpSpiral of "feeling good," enabling individuals to experience a sustained sense of well-being and easier and more sustained positivity and happiness. However, "feeling good," as essential as it is, is only one part of the journey.

You can have a happier and more flourishing life! Your "positivity being" is like a magnet of engagement that draws to you the hopes and desires of your life and increases your experience of happiness and a well-lived life by giving you greater access to your real strengths. It is more than healing. It is living a life marked by greater thriving and personal flourishing.

How does the UpSpiraLife Group work? There are 12 steps that guide you in the process of experiencing this growth. Working these steps with others is of great benefit. In fact, it is the key to the success which individuals in these groups have experienced. The experience of sharing this growth is enriching and fulfilling, and you learn more easily with others when you can observe their experience and bounce your concerns off of others. Sharing with others deepens and enriches the growth process.

The group is one hour in length with a prescribed format that allows for a short presentation by the facilitator and a shared reading. Members of the group then share where they are in their own UpSpiral and how they have used the positivity tools they are learning in living their everyday lives.

Through the mutual support and the shared experience of others, members learn to "identify" in a positive, heart-to-heart way with the experiences of one another. Through this experience of identification with what works, with positive emotion, and the content of each of the steps, members grow significantly in their own well-being.

You can participate from anywhere in the world. While some groups meet physically together, others meet on the ANI secure telephone bridge line.

UpSpiraLife Groups are led by facilitators that are trained by the Applied Neuroscience Institute.

This is the handbook of the first positive 12 step group in the world and the first positive 12 step group in history. It has 3 parts.

The **12 Steps of NeuroPositive Growth** (how to do it)

The **12 Ways and Means** (the guidelines or rules)

The **12 Promises** (what you can expect to experience)

The **12 Ways and Means** are the broad rules, guidelines, and understandings that are necessary for the group to move smoothly over time. They constitute the "spirit" the glue that holds them together.

The **12 Promises** are the results that you can expect from working the program to the fullest of your ability. They are also, in a way, goals for what can happen. They are what others have experienced and what you can aim for.

Please be sure to read the section called "The Sanctuary of Positivity." It is important and significant to beginning this journey. Before you read this book or begin this experience, please take "The Positive Mind Test." Take the test at the beginning of this experience and take it when you have finished Step 12 for the first time. Then take it after you complete each journey through the steps. You can never get the whole process in one time through.

The UpSpiraLife Sanctuary

Creating a Sacred Space For Neuro-Positivity Being

A sanctuary is a place of reserve, of preservation, and of safety. We find safety in a sanctuary that is a place for the preservation of something highly significant, like **personal freedom** or **rare birds**.

A sanctuary of positivity is a wholly new concept because we haven't yet revered positivity. Positivity is something we squander, waste, and disregard as something like a fleeting experience we hope we might get, perhaps, so long as it doesn't get in the way of several other things on our schedules of trying to make life interesting.

The Zeigarten principle in psychology tells us that we have a lean of 9:2 toward the negative. We have come to learn that this is because of evolution, because of our development as a human species. Think about that for a moment. We have nearly conditioned out, in our evolution, the capacity for positivity. Yet it has persistently remained in our DNA. Not only has it remained, but it is responsible for the creative, ongoing, emergence of the progress of the human species.

Positivity is a primal essential to ongoing creation and evolution. Without it, we die. Without it we die not only sooner, we die less well, with greater misery and loss of meaning.

Think about it. This precious human resource responsible for the evolution and progress of inventions, great art, great music, great social movements, is the natural human resource that engages, emerges from and allows the flow of creativity. It is this precious resource that we have nearly succeeded in bringing to extinction, and yet it has survived. It is hard to imagine the human race without positivity, even though we have paid really so little attention to it. Positivity is the ground of flourishing.

How is it that such a great natural resource has gone so unnoticed and taken so for granted? We have done it with animals, we have done it with the rain forests, we have done it with energy resources, and we have done it with human life. The fact that our evolutionary lean is 9:2 in favor of the negative is a staggering realization that we could have come so far. Yet it was not so long ago that one American president said that we would land a man on the moon in 10 years, and we did. Had that not been said and done in what positivity is, there would have been no man on the moon.

Could we say with great intention that we will change the world in 10 years dedicated to posititivity, bringing such sanctuary to its presence that it becomes revered as the force that puts a man on the moon and ushers in a new world of consciousness not possible in a ratio of 9:2? In our lifetimes, we intend, by making a sanctuary for positivity, to change that ratio to a positive 3:1 at least, and 5:1 ideally. There is no imagination capable of knowing what that would mean.

If we think of our own lives, it is not difficult to remember when we have nearly extinguished it there. And for sure, we know people have pretty much extinguished positivity in their own lives. The statistics of suicide and depression are staggering. What does the current epidemic of depression tell us about where we may be headed?

But positivity seems so frivolous over and against the really serious issues in the world. So does a tiny tree frog coming to extinction until it dawns on us that it is a signal of a world in a crisis of survival. 9:2 is not frivolous.

We know so little about the concept of keeping a positive space and that its implications are greater than putting a man on the moon. It is not enough to meditate, go inward and find peace. Peace, as important as it is, can put you to sleep, just as it does to many who try to meditate.

The importance of meditation is that it sets the stage for the appearance of positivity, it makes way for it. Meditation sets the stage for gratitude, love, joy, hope, and peace. Inner peace alone does not sustain on-going creation and evolution. Positivity does. The purpose of meditation is to bare the human stage for the emergence of those inner states of positivity that live and create and evolve. It is meditation that sets the stage for positivity and it is positivity, essentially, that enables flourishing to happen.

Peace is part of it, but the larger space embraces the elevation of higher states that we can simply call positivity. This is a sanctuary that renews and motivates us to live and to create. We need positivity to create, to evolve, now even more than ever. It is time that this 9:2 ratio change and that our very human DNA change along with it. This sanctuary of positivity is about nothing less than evolution.

UpSpiraLife sanctuaries are spaces in human life that we are just beginning to understand. Positivity isn't associated with a sanctuary because we don't yet believe all of this is so important. But the research isn't just mounting exponentially, the research is already there. Slow to be translated to human experience, but the research is there. The UpSpiraLife group is the first positive 12 step group experience to emerge from that research, if not in fact, the first significant on-going group experience.

UpSpiraLife groups are sanctuaries of an evolving awareness that we are wired for positivity and we need it to flourish. As important as meditation can be, it is only a predecessor to the sanctuary of the UpSpiraLife group.

In meditation we shut out a noisy, busy world to find peace. In an UpSpiraLife group, we shut out negativity and dwell in the positive. Shutting out negativity, in a space of time, is as essential as shutting out noise and distraction. It is something like getting on the new high-powered antibiotics. If you cannot shut out negativity and reduce it, you cannot experience flow and you cannot flourish in your own way in your own life. You cannot create from inside a field of negativity. The creative act is the first step out of the negative field.

The experience of positivity, in an extended UpSpiral of positivity, means inevitable growth into and through transitions of knowing self and other, the roots of consciousness. The old ego will work harder in the face of positivity than it will to distract the meditator with a barrage of thoughts. The growth of positivity in an UpSpiral of life means leaving a deadening ego behind and creating a new one. Positivity knows more of what it deeply wants and moves more quickly and powerfully than the meditator who has enough peace to get through the day. The tired ego of negativity will fight positivity with a greater ferocity than it fights meditation with distraction. But the experience of positivity is so empowering and non-linear that it will not give up if it is reinforced, sustained, and supported over time.

Good meditation will always eventually lead to the inner states of gratitude, peace, love, joy and hope. But it is a long road to these internal realities from meditation. It is with these states that the UpSpiral sanctuary begins.

We have to create these weekly one hour spaces where we do something that we do not do anywhere else in our lives: be positive with others and share that consciousness for one hour. We have to create these spaces and know how important these one hour sanctuaries are. We just don't get it yet, but if we persevere we will get it. What we don't get is that what these groups do in creating neuropositivity, positive neuropathways in the brain, doesn't just happen. We have to be reminded in a space of shared consciousness that changes how we think, that changes the very structures of our brain and its consequent structures of reasoning.

This sanctuary of positivity does not exist anywhere else in our lives. It is a wholly unique sanctuary that over time alters what is like an addiction to negativity. It is not something that we can do alone. We need the shared consciousness of others because the power of positively shared consciousness is enormously powerful in affecting how the brain works, especially the balance and inter-relationship of the left and right hemispheres.

This is an experience of positive emotions that is an experience of brain integration. Positive emotion equals brain integration. Emerging neuropositive brain integration equals positive emotion. In this sanctuary of positivity, from week to week, we will come to realize that positive emotion equals mental integration.

We are changing our DNA, we are changing the negative lean of the 9:2 to 3:1, and then to 5:1, positive to negative, and one day Losada's butterfly of chaotic creation and novelty will be let loose, one UpSpiraLife group at a time.

We are creating sanctuaries that are preserves of positivity that we don't get anywhere else in our lives. Because positivity and the UpSpiral is so challenging and so threatening in its simplicity in changing our lives and threatening the old ego and a million neuropathways of negativity, we will want to leave before the miracle happens, but we will stay if we realize that if we can put a man on the moon, we can change the negative 9:2 ratio.

These UpSpiraLife groups are sacred spaces of "**freedom**" for "**rare birds**." Treasure them and fan these small flames into fires of positivity that will burn around the world.

"There is never a crowd on the cutting edge."
-Esther Hicks for Abraham

Applied Neuroscience Institute

The USL Preamble

The UpSpiraLife Group is an outreach of the Applied Neuroscience Institute, and its purpose is to create a culture and a fellowship called a "Sanctuary of Positivity." Our aim is to encourage the optimally well-lived life. We do this by providing an opportunity for sharing insights and learning tools and strategies for a happier and more fulfilled life.

UpSpiraLife Groups are not politically oriented, and are not aligned with other groups or affiliations. The UpSpiraLife group is not group psychotherapy. Healing disorders, illness, or personal problems is not the purpose of the group, even though it may be a benefit of group membership.

As members of this group, we commit ourselves to grow an UpSpiral of the positively lived life, characterized by an increasing sense of well-being. We dedicate ourselves to learning the tools which will guide us to the well-lived life, both for ourselves and for others.

The UpSpiraLife Group Format

1) **Preamble** (Read aloud by a participant chosen by the Group Leader)

2) **The Ways and Means** (Read aloud by a participant chosen by the Group Leader. Read one **Ways and Means** statement from the 12)

3) **Introductions** (First name only. Introductions are never skipped even if group members know one other well)

4) **Shared reading from ANI literature.** This may come from **Growing The Positive Mind**, from **A New 12 Steps for A New Millennium**, an ANI blog entry, or other ANI material)

5) **The Leader presents a 5 minute Share** (This is the initial sharing portion of the meeting from which the leader speaks from the "I" about relating the material read to his or her own life)

6) **Individual Shares** (3-5 minutes, maximum length. Each member gives his/her name and UpSpiral score at the beginning of the share. In their share, members are encouraged to identify something personally significant from the reading and share how they are using the tools they are learning in the Group)

7) **Homework and Appropriate Announcements**
   a. Appropriate homework
   b. **Do The Big Three (Blog, Boost your partner, Gratitude exercise)**
   c. Appropriate announcements

8) **The 12 Promises or the 12 Steps are alternated** (Read aloud by a participant chosen by the Group Leader)

9) **Pearls** (What was most significant in the meeting for each group member in 30 seconds or less)

10) **Closing Affirmation (recited in unison)** "I have an abundance of health, wealth, happiness, and love. I live in an UpSpiral of love, peace, gratitude, joy, and hope. I grow in my giving, and I open to see and receive the goodness that comes to me and is all around me."

The UpSpiraLife Group

The 12 Steps

1. Made the decision to experience positivity as often as possible.

2. Made the decision to stay in an UpSpiral regardless of events outside of us.

3. Dedicated ourselves to knowing, growing, and living our strengths.

4. Found, over time, five personal heroes that would act as guides to the use of our strengths.

5. Made the decision to know what we wanted personally by remaining, over time, in an UpSpiral and became open to letting a Source greater than ourselves guide us to our knowledge of them.

6. Committed to grow in our belief in a personal VibeCore - that we could have what we wanted in life.

7. Became increasingly open to the diverse and multiple ways that what we wanted in our lives could come into being and used these steps to build and increase a core positive vibration that became the "flow" of our lives.

8. Became increasingly generous and reciprocal with ourselves and our "means" in life.

9. Formulated five malleable five-year goals and three actions steps every four months to move toward these aspirations.

10. Allowed these goals to lead to the emergence and development of a vision for our lives.

11. Allowed this vision to navigate us and to attract to us others whom we allowed to be guides and sources of wisdom, who became the experience of MasteRevelation for us.

12. Shared this program and these steps with those who, demonstrated by their lives and interest, showed a readiness to hear them.

The UpSpiraLife Group

The 12 Ways and Means

1. The core and soul of the UpSpiraLife group meeting is "heart to heart" identification. "Positive Identification" is the signature feature of the cohesion of the group. It is the central way learning happens. When people identify with each other, it creates oneness and instant learning.

2. All groups must adhere to the prescribed format of the UpSpiral Life Group as set forth by the Applied Neuroscience Institute. Do not change or vary the parts of the format of the group. They are there and in this order for a purpose. So, adhere to the format.

3. What will help everyone is if you share from your heart and from your gut. Nix the "teachy-teachy," "let me teach you from my experience" talk. Tell your story to tell your story for own self-expression. The Universe will know exactly who needs it, why and where to take it. Most of the time, you may never know. Share the negative, share your struggle. But focus on solution-finding.

4. "I" is the pronoun of the group. "You" is rarely every used because you are taking about "I", your own experience, your own insight, and your application of growth in neuropositivity. "We should" and "you should" and "I have a suggestion" is off-base language and is not permitted at any time. The only "shoulds" and "suggestions" are for one's self, never for another group member.

5. Bring the gift of what your 'I' has to share with your personal "voice." And then bring its companion - a listening heart. Open

your heart and listen. Really hear what people are saying or trying to say but can't. Be the ears that make everyone in the group "feel" and have the experience of being "heard," without comment, suggestion or evaluation. Just being able to talk with your own voice and be heard is a great, great gift.

6. Cross-talk, advice and suggestion-making are stopped mid-sentence. Just put your hand, palm outward, and say "hold on," or "use the I." You will find your ways of stopping cross-talk, but you must stop it from the beginning.

7. The definition of a weed is a plant that is growing in the wrong place. A rose bush could be a weed in a corn field. So it is with questions. No matter how good they might be, they can choke out and divert the intention of the meeting. Questions are not a part of the format and they need to be asked at another time other than the meeting.

8. "Subtle cross-talk" is sharing something that is your experience, not because you need to share it, but because you think someone else we be helped to hear your experience. You have no idea that may be true. You are in the group to say what you need to say about you from your own experience, not to be an aid to any else's learning.

9. Other resources are wonderful in other places, but not in the UpSpiraLife group. Outside resources may be directly relatable and reinforcing, but so that each group leader does not have to be put in a position of judging, keep it simple by using only ANI resources in the UpSpiral group meetings.

10. Anonymity may seem desirable but is it not guaranteed. People will want to share the good you share with others. If you wish to have a guarantee of anonymity for something you share, it might be best not shared at the group level unless that degree of discretion is developed and practiced by your group. Information that requires anonymity should be shared with the group leader in a confidential capacity.

11. Some of what is said won't "hit" or "connect" until people are three days away from the group. Never assume people are getting exactly what they need to get in the way they need to hear it or at the moment they hear it. The power is in "the process." The

one mind of the group will order the group in perfect synchrony and establish group harmony. There is rarely a need to judge the effectiveness of a group session. Let go.

12. Group leadership is not an easy task. The social brain must process a billion bits of information over the course of a single meeting. Leadership can be exhilarating but it can also be exhausting. Be good to your leader and let them use the skills they have spent a good deal of time developing in order to fill this function.

The UpSpiraLife Group

The 12 Promises

1. You can feel the positive emotions that you choose to feel if you lean your consciousness consistently and gently over time in that positive direction.

2. Positive emotions will increase for you in three dimensions. You will be able to get to them rapidly, you will be able to make them last in duration, and you will be able to increase their intensity.

3. You can stay in the UpSpiral 100% of the time and by being there raise both your happiness and emotional set-points and "feel good" most of the time.

4. Negative feelings, over-reacting, and the sense of the fear of oppression will decrease. Unnecessary anger and anxious over-reactivity will eventually be replaced by expecting and seeing the best in others and outside events.

5. By knowing and using your strengths everyday you will become happier, more content, and increase your sense of personal competence.

6. You will come to know that every negative event is an experience that can take you to your strengths, providing, over time and with practice, solace and solutions that are empowering and build personal confidence.

7. Your VibeCore is at the heart of you and can grow. As it increases, you will, over time, get more of what you want.

8. You will live your live in a flow, more and more one with the music of life.

9. Your goals, expressed over time in writing, will give you a sense of direction in life.

10. Your goals, malleable and given written expression over time, will lead to an inspired vision.

11. You will find and define the vision of passion for your life.

12. Your vision will give you a sense of personal significance and meaning, and attract to your life vital sources of revelation and support.

12 NEW STEPS FOR A NEW MILLENNIUM
The UpSpiraLife Group

PART I

The 12 *Steps*

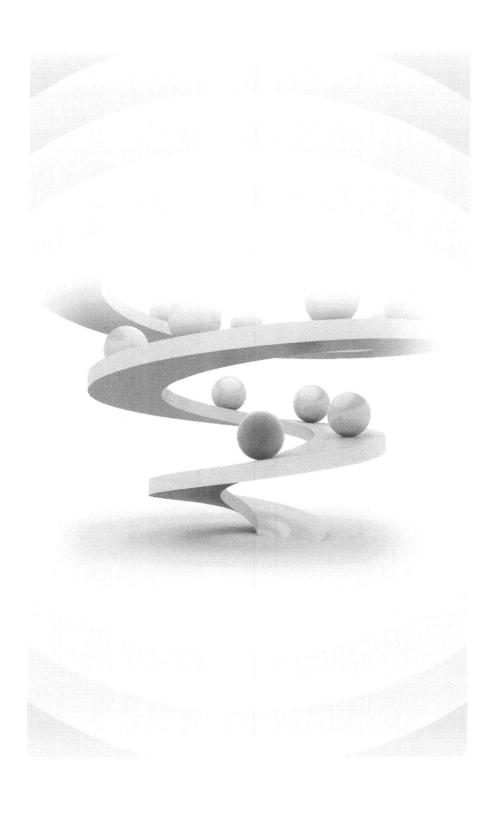

Step 1

**Made the decision to experience positivity
as often as possible**

**"A man is about as happy as he has decided to be."
-Abraham Lincoln**

This quote, from the man who symbolizes great liberation, called the shots very simply here. We are about as happy as we intend to be. If you are ready to decide to be happy or to be happier, you belong here. If you are undecided about the legitimacy of the "pursuit of happiness" or about "life" or "liberty," you may be in the wrong place at the wrong time.

It's alright if you're not 100% sure of all this. All of that will grow. But it does start with the decision on some level that you want to be happy, and that you have the right to your life, to your liberty, and to your pursuit of happiness. Why "freedom" if you can't experience this? As the decision to be happy deepens, the happiness will for sure come to you. It will be helped here, because of the other people who constitute this group. Coming together with them will raise your "consciousness," a word and a reality that will become increasingly important to you as you grow here.

Step One- in fact, all of the 12 steps- are about "positivity being." This will also be referred to in these steps as "neuropositivity." It is the hallmark of this growth that the very neuropathways of your brain have to change, over time, from how they are presently constructed in your brain to new structures of making greater meaning out of your life. These Steps are about "positivity being" because it is so radically important to us. You might ask: Why, then, if it is so important to us, is the world in such a mess? Precisely because we have not realized the importance of "positivity being" for our evolution. Positive emotion and affect have evolved within us because they have been so important for our ongoing survival, especially the great bursts of growth in evolution and culture. If positivity were not so very important, it would by natural selection become less and less as we have evolved. To the contrary, positive emotion has become increasingly important to the survival of the species. Positive emotion has remained around precisely because it is the creative source of ongoing evolution. Negativity and fight-flight is a warning system that has kept us protected, but it is the positive emotional states that are responsible for unfolding, ongoing creation.

Here is the short case for "positivity being." You either live most of the time in an UpSpiral of positivity, in a DownSpiral of negativity, or, like most people, yo-yoing up and down. The goal here is very simple. It is to enable you to get yourself into an UpSpiral and its benefits, and to get *you* to keep *you* there, at a high level of "feeling good," most of the time. Sound unrealistic? Then your idea of what is real will need to change! We aren't aiming for bliss or ecstasy; just "feeling good" most all of the time. You will learn how to manage and have great agility over positivity in such a way that you will develop positive emotional muscle and have a mastery over the use of positive emotion. Do the work and the work will work for you. Simply put, you can be a happier person and your emotional set-point can grow and become constant in a higher level of positive emotions. Your neuropositivity can increase as a reality in your own brain.

Here are just a few of the benefits of positive emotions from the emerging research in the field. Positive emotion enlarges the scope of attention. It broadens your personal access to strengths and increases your choice of options and behavior from your own larger repertoire. Negativity creates a sense of being trapped with no choices because it narrows focus and attention. Positive emotion increases intuition and creativity. Positive emotion changes our body systems and speeds up recovery from cardiovascular surgery. It alters the nature of frontal lobe asymmetry and increases immune system response. Positive affect predicts good mental and physical health outcomes. It is predictive of increased happiness, stronger resilience to the negative, psychological growth and lower levels of cortisol, as well as reduced inflammation in response to stress. Positive emotion is correlated with resistance to sinus infections and reductions in stroke. Positivity predicts how long people will live. Positive affect means that you will solve problems more easily, be more creative, and have greater access to the higher functions of strengths and to their range. People stronger in positive emotion score higher on every test of well-being, every test of life satisfaction, and there is an increase of healthy functioning at a cellular level. Positive affect is negatively correlated with generalized anxiety disorder, obsessive compulsive behavior, agoraphobia, and social phobia. The list could go on and on.

And with all of these research results firmly in place, we still have a great investment in negativity, in illness, in negative core beliefs, and we have sold out to a notion of "healing" that focuses on the negative, misguided spirituality and the supernatural, the idolization of modern medicine, and the largest pill-popping culture in history. We are brainwashed at looking at the problem and finding solutions to problems. We are steeped in the co-dependency that fixes and rescues. If there is such a thing as negativity addiction, it is the culprit here. We believe that we need negativity to perceive accurately, to be smart, to be clever, to appear intelligent and insightful, and to protect ourselves against our own imagination and our power to create and be great. We believe that we need negativity to be "balanced."

If it is your desire to be well-balanced, go find a group of well-balanced people and put your time there. See how positive you are after spending a few hours with boring "well-balanced" people, if you can find them. Finding them is as difficult as finding a functional family in a world of dysfunctional ones. We do not need to be negative and we do not need to be balanced, nor is it helpful to think that negativity is the balance for us that we believe it must be. Everything that negativity or pessimism are supposed to provide for you, all of its protections, will be better provided for you by your real strengths, which we will spend a great deal of time with in this process. Anything you can do by being negative, you can do by using your strengths much better and with much less personal cost. Anything your negativity protects you from will be far better protected by knowing, using, and growing your strengths.

The well-balanced person is a myth. No such person exists. Being well-balanced is a way of a reducing people's uniqueness to a rounded, manageable level so no one stands out too much. What you learn here will balance you in your own unique way very well, and you will know because you will be happy and you will feel good. Trying to be a well-balanced person is to put yourself in a position where someone else can tell you what your weaknesses are and how you should correct them to be more balanced. Get away from them and let them balance their own lives and not meddle in yours. No one will ever understand what balance is for you - but you. Well-balanced people are usually boring. They are boring because they have cut off part of themselves in order to appear in control and self-regulated.

If there should be a 12 step group for well-balanced and well-rounded people, let them go now and begin that group and not bother with this one.

The decision to be happy is radical. The decision to live in an UpSpiral of "positivity being" is radical. The decision to allow "positivity being" to root you and ground you and be your truth is radical. It means that you are going to believe more in the power of your own strengths, desires, hopes, thoughts and emotions than you are going to believe in negativity. It is not that negativity is wrong or useless; it has its job to do as long as you don't live there. The job of negativity is to tell you that you are not moving in the direction of your own happiness and your own heart.

Most people believe that if they were not negative, they could not protect themselves. That's why the decision to be happy is so radical. Along the way you give up negativity as a way of personal safety. Actually, you won't even want it.

Giving up negativity is a hard thing for people who have spent a lifetime learning to be cynical and cleverly catty in just the right incisive and cutting ways. It's hard to give up the laughs and the fear it creates in others when you can just really, really be cutting. As wise and clever as negativity may make you feel, and as much of an addictive escape as it is from finding real solutions, it undermines the power of the decision to be happy. As you become happier, you will give up negativity more and more because it will just not work for you. You will discover and live your strengths, and they will always deliver for you. If they don't, it is because you do not know them well enough, and have not practiced them long enough, but we will get to that.

Is it possible to be addicted to negativity? Yes, it's an extreme, but most people who find their way to an UpSpiraLife© group are usually not addicted to negativity. Usually people who are addicted to negativity have brought along a companion like drugs, alcohol, shopping, sex or something that disguises what is the root of all addiction, and that really is negativity. They are doubly bound and they will find this process of growth doubly difficult because there will be too many masters demanding their share of the brain's real estate and attention. But they can succeed if they deeply and increasingly decide that happiness is what they want.

Being happy is a tough call because it is not nearly as realistic and sophisticated as some people seem to need to be. If being very realistic and sophisticated as a result is important for you, then you need to spend more time being realistic and sophisticated while that works for you. When it doesn't, come back. You will always be welcome if your desire is to be happy and to live in the UpSpiral of "positivity being."

You will find that these tools will work. There are 12 tools here that will seem like magic to the degree that you work them. While they are simple, they are not superficial. When you work them for you, and you really work them, you will find an elegance that leads you and steeps you in higher and higher levels of happiness and permanence in an UpSpiral of positivity. The goal is not as lofty as to feel like you are in a zone, blissed-out, or in a mystical state, but rather, simply to "feel good" and to begin to feel that you are flourishing. These other states of bliss may happen, but they are not the goal here of becoming happier and feeling good consistently, day after day after day.

There are those who will argue that we need the contrast of sadness to be happy, that we need to feel misery to be able to feel joy. That is not true. Gratitude is gratitude and you can feel it anytime you want to and you do not have to experience ingratitude to do it. The same is true with peace and love. These are all states that you are meant to experience in and of themselves. If you have to take a journey to experience their opposites in order to appreciate that they exist, then that's a journey that you will have to take, but not everyone must take that route. It is not a requirement of being human. It is not an essential or required journey. Experiencing gratitude, love, peace, joy, and hope is a choice. What it takes to get you to make that choice is your journey, but the day will come when we actually teach our children to feel, experience, and grow these emotions. The day will come when we educate and train our children to be happy, and when we do, our ideas that suffering is so necessary will have changed. But it is very difficult to let go of suffering and how important we think it is, and then to find out that it isn't as necessary as we thought. There are people who have been happy most all of their days, without a great deal of suffering. They do exist.

We do not suffer so much because opposites are such a necessity. We suffer because we don't know a better way. This is a better way, and it begins with the decision to be happy. Suffering may have gotten you here, and may have been essential for you, but please do not pass that onto your children or the next generation, because they do not need to learn that to be happy. The world has already learned everything it has to learn from suffering. It is now time to learn from happiness and joy. That's why you have made the decision to be here.

The great personal myths of the importance of our negativity and the legitimacy of our suffering do not have to fall away or be left behind to make the decision to be happy. But the happier you become and the more agility you develop with positivity, the more your notions about all of this will change and fall away. The happier you become, you just will not need your old story in the same way. It will slip away like a snake that is shedding, over time, one skin after another.

What of the importance of healing negative core beliefs in making this decision to be happy? Don't they have to be out of the way? No. Forget them. If you have not changed enough of your negative core beliefs to entitle you to decide to be happy, then go and heal some more of your negative core beliefs, and when you are tired of that, come back and you will be welcome. Negative core beliefs are not healed by pulling them out by the roots either quickly, gently, or with a rip. Negative core beliefs are healed by the growing mastery of positive emotion, a neuropositive[©] state of being, life in an UpSpiral- all things that you will learn as you move from this first step of the decision to be happy.

Years and years of a focus on problems and weaknesses, sin and guilt, diagnosis and healing, have so heavily slanted our brains that we have grown patterns of thought that create according to what we have thought. Limited notions of humility and modesty, creating an endless rounding of well-balanced people, has created an enormous imbalance of defenses like intellectualization and compartmentalization, along with the sharpest increase in depression we have seen in history. And all the while we have not yet discovered what happiness and positivity can create, absent of the need to cap them because they "feel good," and we have become afraid we don't deserve good feelings for very long. Some have even believed that "feeling good" is a harbinger of bad things to come, because "this too shall pass." And sure enough it does, when you believe it all of your life. Because of the "wet-blanket" ways of attempting to protect ourselves, we have dampened, again and again, the very positive emotions and affect that could heal us and sustain our well-being and feeling good. All of this creates the opposite of the neuropositive mind. These are the neuropathways that program negativity.

And so we are not only looking at, in this step, the importance of the decision to be happy and to live in an UpSpiral of positivity. We are literally standing on the threshold of joy. Could it be that the world and "our own little world" are getting ready for joy?

The decision to be happy is a decision to experience positivity as often as possible. That is the first step. We begin to build a neuropositive mind. How is it done here?

Positivity does not necessarily begin with positive thinking, although that is a helpful and important part. Thinking is only a part of this. We begin neuropositivity by beginning to exercise and develop positive emotional muscle. This emotional muscle is a set of skills that helps you go inward to realize that these same emotions or "states of being" exist inside of you and always have. You are just made that way. Emotional muscle developed on the outside is for connecting up and moving in on the same states that exist on the inside.

Let's take a look at the concept of "emotional muscle." On the negative side, it does not take much to know that we are able to get to negative emotions in an instant. We can go there in less than a second. We also know that we can stay there, nursing a negative emotion and obsessing over the negativity for a long time. That is the "duration" part of emotional muscle. And for sure, we all know people who can intensify a negative emotion and make it bigger and bigger and bigger. We know they are over-reacting and that we do the same, but we don't think much about it because we don't realize the enormous cost of being so competent, capable, and agile with negative emotions. These are the measures of positive emotional muscle, as we work with them here. Neuropositivity© promises that you can get to positive emotions instantly (immediacy), you can stay there for a long time (duration), and you can increase the feeling at will (intensity.) As agile and skilled as we are at doing this with negative emotion is very often as limited as we are, to some extent, in doing it with positive emotion. Most of the time we haven't even considered growing positive emotion. That would seem unrealistic, but being an ass with negative emotion is much more familiar. The workouts of the Emotional Gym© are reducing the blubber of excessive negative emotions and growing the muscle of positive ones. The Emotional Gym is the set of exercises that runs throughout this book, and that teaches you how to flex, build, and maintain your positive muscle to a stronger degree than you have already done with your negative emotion. It is neuropositivity© in the gymnasium of your brain.

Why haven't we ever done this before? Why weren't we taught this in school?

It's just too simple, and sophisticated, negative, cynical people think that being positive is being superficial –like Pollyanna. We will talk more about Pollyanna and what she was really all about in Step 2.

In this Emotional Gym, your goal is to grow neuropositive emotional states in three measures- develop the mastery to get to them instantly, gain duration and neurologically make them last, and gain the agility (and courage) to intensify them. That sounds pretty simple, and it is, over time. And that will be no small amount of time. Changing neuropathways in the brain takes time. Just consider the time it's taken for you to develop the ones that presently determine your emotions and behavior. Here are the measures of positive emotional muscle:

1. Immediacy- you can get there in seconds.

2. Duration –you make a positive emotion last over time.

3. Intensity –you can increase the positive emotion to a higher level at will.

Here are the directions for your first work-out in the Emotional Gym.

On a scale of 1-10, if 1 is a little and 10 is a lot, try feeling a little bit of gratitude at 1, 2, or 3. Just a small amount to begin with. One hundred hits of gratitude a day are more valuable than a single, large, great hit in a week or a month. Now, as if you were chanting, or better, pulsing with energy, feel the emotions of gratitude 25 times at a 1, 2, or 3. Feel a little of the emotion, just touch it and feel it again. You are pulsing "gratitude, gratitude, gratitude, gratitude." If you are so far away from your feelings that you just can't feel it, then think it; it will come to you and that's a promise.

Next do the same things with each of the following emotions: joy, love, peace and hope. You can choose any emotion and put them in any order. Usually one or two of the emotions are hard to feel at first. If you can't feel the emotion, then just think it. What you think, with the intention of feeling it, will emerge as a feeling after a while, if that is your intention.

Every morning before you start your day, the first thing in your day, try smiling very broadly when you wake up and then do each of these feelings 25 times. It takes a very short time. If you don't do it when you first get up, do it as often in your day as possible. But doing it when you start your day puts your intention "out there" and you tell your brain what you want it to do. You have to keep telling the brain what you want it do. Throughout the day, use anything negative as a cue to go the Emotional Gym and begin to pulse, within you, a positive emotion. If a negative thing is too difficult as a cue, choose something like stop lights or something positive like pets. Eventually, after you practice, you will be able to use negatives as a cue to go to a positive emotion and, when that happens, you find that you have developed much more control over your life.

What you are building is a new ambient soundtrack in your life. You want the positive emotional setting to become your default setting - a place you just normally go to, rather than worry, fear or dread.

You are building psychological capital. You are building a kind of reservoir of positivity that will cause negative feelings to last a much shorter time. You also building a buffer zone against negativity. You will find, after a while, that you react less to negative things in your world and when they do occur, you have a buffer of time to adjust your usual automatic response to them. Like any gym, and like any muscle, these emotional muscles take time to build, but this is the first step. You are beginning to tell your brain to spend more time in positive emotion than in negative emotion. Your brain will resist you until neuropositivity has built new neuropathways that are more in charge than the old, negative ones. This is the activity of brain neuroplasticity.

This can sound like a simple denial of negative emotion. We have been taught that we must "air" negative feelings, that they are dangerous if they are internalized and repressed. While it isn't true that we have to air every negative feeling or thought, what is important is acknowledging them for whatever feedback or information they give. There is a difference between ignoring negative feelings and not staying in them longer than necessary and becoming stuck in them. If negative feelings are, in part, mechanisms of feedback, let them tell you what they have to tell you, and then use them as a cue to go to a positive emotion. You can't solve a problem from a negative place, so get to a positive place and then deal with the negative situation.

However, it is important to realize that emotions are more than just a feedback mechanism to tell us that something is good or bad. Emotions are what we live in throughout the day. For many, negative emotion is where they live, along with their mental disorders that surely take up residence in that DownSpiral life style. Negative emotions are, for sure, an alerting system to get us to move. However, we don't have to stay in the negative emotion for it to do its job. Some negative emotion is simply a learned cycle of negativity with an addictive payoff at the end. Most addictions are couched in negative cycles of emotion. Once again, you can have a negative feeling, acknowledge it, but you don't have to live there. Make a choice to live in positive emotions where you can find the solutions to the negative issues. Your creativity, problem solving, and strengths exist in positive emotions in the UpSpiral.

Negative emotion, then, becomes our cue to go to the Emotional Gym and to begin pulsing love, peace, gratitude, joy, or hope. In the face of a problem or negativity, you are exercising a whole other part of your brain as you begin to make this shift. You are moving from the automatic, negative, fear reaction of the brain to another place in the brain that allows you to feel differently and then to behave differently. Your response can become less automatic and more effectively positive because you will be coming from a place in your brain where you can exercise more control over your emotions.

Where do you live in your emotions? Where you live emotionally defines who you are. Even when nothing is wrong or negative, we can live in a negative emotional place just out of habit. We're just used to being there. Think about times when something has not gone well, and you have dwelt on it and made it larger, and just nursed the wound when you could have gotten out of the place much sooner. Notice how easy it is for us to react to a situation with instant negative emotions. We can get to a negative emotion in seconds. Then look back and find some times when you may have nursed that negative emotion and made it last –that's what we call "duration" strength for a negative emotion. And finally, who hasn't taken a negative feeling and blown it up to be much more than it should have been, creating a great deal of drama and no real solutions? Immediacy, duration and intensity, the three measures of positive emotional muscle, are all realities with negative emotions. We already know how to do this very well with negative emotions. What we are learning to do is to have the same elasticity and flexibility and strength with positive emotions that we already have with negative emotions.

But there is a larger significance to these five emotions of love, peace, gratitude, joy, and hope. They are more than emotions. They are States Of Mind. As States Of Mind, they are aspects of the infinite, god, source, higher power, creator, Allah, Buddha, the Christ, whatever you call the spiritual energy that flows through you. These are aspects of that spiritual reality. When you start to feel these feelings on the outside, you are beginning a journey to the inside of you where all of these "states" exist, probably untapped. It is sort of like each one of these states is a balloon and you are breathing air into it. At first it's difficult, but the more you practice, the more you will breathe air into the inner balloons and they will become inner realities, because you are matching on the outside something that exists inside you. Eventually you can feel these realities beaming from the inside of you and moving outward. But they can't until you awaken them and until you realize that they are states already existing within you. As you pulse them on the outside, they will eventually "pulse back." Remember, though, that the first breath of air into a new balloon is the hardest because you have to loosen up the balloon. It's like that on the inside of you. Neuropositivity loosens you up on the deep inside of you.

Negative hits of emotion are stronger than positive ones. This is because negative emotions have usually followed strong negative events and we learn them more deeply and quickly - the impact in the moment is felt more strongly. But- and this is a big "but"- negative feelings have less impact and you feel them for a shorter period of time when you have a reservoir of positive feelings. Negative hits do just that- they "hit" in a way that knocks the emotional air out of us. They are quick or they are sudden, and then they grow. They are the bullies in your emotional playground. Depending upon the degree of the threat which the negative represents, the hit varies, but negative emotion is stronger in its immediacy than is positive feeling because it is an alarm system. But this alarm system goes off too much and it's too loud. Everything is not a tiger or a truck headed in our direction. A negative emotion screams at us, "learn this now, this is very, very important" and we do it. Negative emotion is very linear. However, here is the good news. Positive feeling is nonlinear. That means that the more your reservoir of emotion is filled with the positive, the more it will appear, especially when you need it. You can draw on positive experiences and emotions forever, if you will choose to do it.

If you will make positive feelings a low grade, chronic, ambient background, a sound track of your life, it will take over the negative more quickly and the negative will last less and less time. Think of those times when a negative thought, feeling or reaction was something that hung around all day long until you slept it off. The antidote to the toxin of negative feeling and thoughts that are unwanted, and the "hit" they seem to give us out of nowhere, is to practice positive feelings. Rehearse them, live in them, say them, think them, journal them. Make a list everyday of what you're grateful for. You don't have to produce a big load of positivity here. You're not being asked to be so cheery and bubbly and always so perky that someone would like to stick a cork in your mouth.

On a scale of 1-10, feel love, peace, gratitude, joy, and hope at a 2 or a 3 or a 4 every day. Just a little, just enough to keep your real smile going. This is really what you are doing. You are changing, through the neuroplasticity of your brain, how your brain is wired and establishing the reality of your own neuropositivity. New circuits of learning and being are being built as you do this. You are tipping an inner scale, something like an inner teeter-totter, and instead of going up and down, *you are moving the fulcrum of the teeter-totter so that the emotions with the most weight are positive.*

There is NOTHING in your life that doing this won't affect. When you get to a positive place, you are much more capable of figuring out what the negative feelings are about and what to do with them. You never solve the negatives from a negative place.

So practice and create the positive reservoir that describes where you live inside, because that reservoir, either positive or negative, creates who you are. Make your decision, work these steps, and neuropositivity will rewire your brain until the soundtrack of the life that is yours is one of gratitude, love, peace, joy, and hope.

NeuroPositive Workouts©

Exercise Set #1

1. **Practice *The Emotional Gym* everyday throughout your day.**
   Your UpSpiral Score is where you are on an entirely subjective inner scale from 1 - 100. 100 is feeling good, feeling on top of it, feeling in charge of your life and feeling happy. The cut-off point is 50 and below, and that is identified as your DownSpiral. 50 and below on your inner subjective scale is feeling depression, despair, and oppressed. The bottom is feeling hopeless. Each day, for 90 days, on a calendar, write your UpSpiral Score from 1-100, the UpSpiral score you want to achieve that day. Do not record what your score is at the time when you write it down. Record what you want it to be by increasing it a few points from where you are. It is better to go up a few points a day, like 1, 2, or 3. As you gain momentum, this may increase.

   Then after you have recorded your score, write down something that you want in a word or two. Do this for 90 days.

2. Get the journal/book **Plans to the Universe and the Answers Back** and follow the directions and examples set forth in the book by keeping your own neuropositivity journal for 90 days.

3. Write down 3 things for which you are grateful. It is good to do this in the evening before going to bed. If possible, have your partner do the same and then share what each other has written. That sharing gives each partner vital information.

These three exercises are called **The Basic Three** and they are assigned for all of the 12 Steps.

4. Work with your NPC (**NeuroPositive Coach**) on the *Move Your Mountain* module individually or in a pod. This is an individual choice.

5. Take the **NeuroPositive Mind Test** by going to www.gotoani.com. You will receive your score immediately.

. . . .

The Research Evidence
STEP 1

Fredrickson, Barbara. **Positivity**. New York: Crown, 2009.

Fredrickson, Barbara L., "What Good Are Positive Emotions?, Review of *General Psychology*, Vol.2, No.3, 300-319, 1998

Fredrickson, Barbara L, "The role of Positive Emotions In Positive Psychology, The Broaden-and-Build Theory of Positive Emotions", *American Psychologist*, pp. 218-226. Mar. 2001

Tugade, Michele M., and Barbara L. Fredrickson. "Resilient Individuals Use Positive Emotions to Bounce Back From Negative Emotional Experiences." *Journal of Personality and Social Psychology* 86.2 (2004): 320-33.

Begley, Sharon. **Train Your Mind, Change Your Brain: How a New Science Reveals Our Extraordinary Potential to Transform Ourselves.** New York: Ballantine, 2007.

Step 2

Made the decision to stay in an UpSpiral regardless of events outside of us.

We treat emotions only as if they were responses to some affect. Emotions seem always to have a "why" or a "cause," if only we can locate what that is, because there are many times that we don't know the origin of why we feel like we feel. There are times when we are aware that "this or that" caused the emotions we feel. And very often we are sure that "someone" else caused us to feel like we feel. While we are the cause of our emotions, it is just as true that long existing emotional patterns are hard to control. Memories that are implicit, or prior to our actually remembering, cause deep-seated emotional reactions. However, the answer to managing emotions may be much easier than we expected. Instead of undoing negative emotions and their patterns, we are going to focus here only on building positive emotions. We do not ignore negative emotions, but we just don't choose to live there.

Here we want to reverse the cause and effect of positive emotions. We treat positive emotions as though they are the rewards or the outcomes of living in some sort of way. Something will make us grateful, an event will give us joy, a relationship will give us love, a goal will give us hope, and a pill will give us some peace. Positive emotions are treated as though they are the results of things on the outside, happening to us in a certain kind of way, and when the stars line up, or our problems get solved, or people line up in a certain way, then the result will be our joy or our gratitude. Positive emotions are often results oriented, and we get to have them when something happens on the outside of us that creates that response in us. What underlies all of this is that you have to have a reason to feel positive emotions, and that reason is almost always on the outside of us. So here is the neuropositive flip.

How about this? Feel the feelings of love, peace, gratitude, joy, and hope by choice, for no reason, whenever you want to! There is no reason to rely on outside forces to give you these experiences. You may wait a long time before something comes along and makes you feel joy. Feel joy just because you can, whenever you want to. You can feel all of these feelings instantly, for as long as you want, as intensely as you would like. It just takes some practice and the choice not to live your life directed by outside events.

The response might be that outside events can be very significant and some are very negatively impacting. That's true, some are, but all of them are not. And even for those that are, you will learn that managing your emotional responses and building up a reservoir will make you much more capable of handling outside events.

The key to being able to do this really lies in where you spend the majority of your time - in an UpSpiral or a DownSpiral, or waffling back and forth in between the two. Learning to live in an UpSpiral of positivity greatly enhances your ability to experience positivity, and positive emotions greatly increase the probability that you will play less to outside events as the "cause" of your feelings. In an UpSpiral, there is a much greater probability that you will feel the positive emotions that you choose to feel.

What is an UpSpiral? An UpSpiral is a term that describes ascending and increasing positive emotion that has an energy, and that energy is always increasing. Once you are in the spiral, you can go higher and higher. The top of the spiral is "feeling good." It is simply feeling good. You can go higher in the spiral to states of bliss and ecstasy, but that is not our goal. The UpSpiral is characterized by increasingly better positive emotions that lead to a stable sense of "feeling good." The energy of the UpSpiral is one that increases health, problem-solving ability, life-satisfaction, well-being, attention, creativity, and intuition. It is a place of optimism and hope. It makes it more possible to play to your strengths, which will constitute Step 3. The energy of the spiral pulls you higher in mood and feeling state.

You will feel "on top of it," in control, in charge of your own self, and empowered to be and do the things that make you feel personally significant. The UpSpiral describes increasing positivity being, which includes positive thinking, positive feeling, positive moods, flow, positive planning, visioning and living the well-lived life.

In a DownSpiral just the opposite is true. It is the experience that is cumulative, that things are "on top of me." It is an experience of an increasing sense of oppression. The DownSpiral probably starts with some innocent complaining or negativity, which moves to judging someone, then to blaming someone else, then to thinking about who has crossed you, to anger, then to mulling and nursing this feeling of anger. Your face has dropped, there is no smile, your eyes are probably not focused on the outside world, and there is an internalized sense of heaviness. The DownSpiral is different for everyone, but it expects that things are bad and will get worse. It is focused on problems and not solutions. It is filled with worry, dread, and anxiety. Eventually it leads to depression, flat lining, the sense that nothing has any real meaning, and at the bottom there is a sense of despondency and dread. The DownSpiral is a place of dread and disease. People who live in the DownSpiral more than the UpSpiral have twice the chance of a heart attack or stroke.

If you spend a lot of time "yo-yoing" back and forth between highs and lows, you spend more time in the DownSpiral. One of the reasons may be that you are easily "overwhelmed." It takes only a few things to create the sense of "it's on top of me." People can feel "oppressed" by feeling a little down when they get up, then dropping the toothpaste in the toilet, dropping the soap the third time in the shower, and having to bend over, then spilling the coffee grounds on the counter. But when you find that there is no coffee creamer, that's the last straw - the whole day is down the drain. That is simple oppression from cumulative stress, and everyone has it in one way or another. However, our response to these situations, on the outside of us, does not have to affect us on the inside. The truth is that we are too easily oppressed by things that don't matter, and we have not learned really good recovering skills when things do go wrong, which they will.

Notice how these are all mostly outside events, except getting up feeling a little down. In this case, that was caused by eating too much sugar the night before, so there is even a choice in that as well!

Let's use this rather simple and silly example, which happens to be true, to make some emotional choices that represent being familiar and skilled in using the Emotional Gym. When this person wakes up in the morning feeling a little down, there is the decision that this will just not do. What is the "little down" stuff? No, no way, we aren't going to go there, we aren't giving into that and having it affect our entire day. So there is a decision even before this person gets out of bed to smile very broadly and to pulse each of the emotions 25 times, and to put them forth as the intention of the day saying something like, "This is where I want to live today: I want to live in the emotional states of love, peace, gratitude, joy and hope, and I don't want to give into negative emotions. Brain, cooperate and go there." The smile may be difficult and feel phony, but do you want to feel sad and down all day or be happy? Then smile from ear to ear and pulse joy. But it feels so phony. If you can't feel joy, think it and keep pulsing and get a little joy. Think of something that has given you joy and pull on that memory. You are creating the neuropositive mind by using the neuronal association of facial anatomy, thought, and feeling.

Your toothpaste still falls into the toilet. How much frustration do you want to feel? How upset do want to get over your toothpaste in the toilet? How much drama?

Then just pulse, peace, peace, peace and get on with it. Dropping the soap in the shower can get frustrating. How big a deal do you want to make over this? You want to go to work and tell your colleagues that you're out of sorts over dropping the soap in the shower? "You're going to have to give me a break today guys. I dropped my toothpaste in the toilet and my soap in the shower and I've decided to let it ruin my day, now stay out of my way." And so instead, when you drop the soap, be grateful you can bend over to pick it up, and every time just say and feel a little "gratitude, gratitude, gratitude."

When you get to the coffee grounds, you will already be practiced, and they will bother you less and you will brush them away. And when you find that there isn't any creamer, you can throw up your hands but say, "Oh well, coffee to go," and maybe even feel a little joy that you are not letting things get to you in the same way that you used to. And as you step out your door the air is a little crisper, the sky is bluer, and the morning is good. You have decided to be in an UpSpiral and not settle for cheap negative emotional reactions that rob your joy.

We can always make the choices that keep us in an UpSpiral rather than a DownSpiral. People who cannot make that choice are in therapy, and perhaps medicated, to be able to make that choice better or at least not sink further into a DownSpiral.

We can be better at making the choices that keep us in an UpSpiral. In this step, you make the decision to stay in an UpSpiral regardless of the events outside of you.

Aren't there some events, like grieving a loss, that have to be done in the DownSpiral? The answer is no. Even grief and loss can be experienced in an UpSpiral of positivity, when is it not clouded with guilt. It simply depends on how we choose to view death and how we grieve the death of another. All of the feelings of love, peace, gratitude, joy and hope especially belong to loss. There may well be feelings of sadness, anger and loss, but they don't have to be the only feelings. If the focus is on memories of goodness, there can be gratitude. There can be focus on the things that give us joy.

The longer you remain in an UpSpiral and the more practiced you become, and have the agility and mastery of positive emotional states, the more you realize that all of your life can be lived there by your choice. This is the neuropositive mind. But it takes time and learning and practice.

The more you decide that outside events will not determine whether you are in an UpSpiral or a DownSpiral, the more you will be able to do so.

Every thought you think and every feeling you feel is affecting the structure of your brain. We are becoming what we think and feel. We are always growing neuropathways according to our experience. In learning to live in an UpSpiral, you are changing the structure of the neuropathways in your brain. They will begin to line up differently. As you develop and use new more powerful neuropathways of positivity, the old ones are going to find themselves in a kind of "neuroplastic war." The old neuropathways die a slow death. Literally they are deprived of oxygen and glucose as they cease to be used, and they will fight back to live.

So how do we get your UpSpiral to grow and become stronger? With each of these 12 steps, it will become stronger. Here we begin to quantify your UpSpiral by what is called your UpSpiral Score. The UpSpiral Scale goes from 1 to 100. "1" is despondency and despair and "100" is feeling good, feeling on top of it. Each day you will give yourself a score, in terms of where you are, and in terms of where you want to be. In the UpSpiral group you are reporting back to the group about what your score actually is. 1 - 100 is quite a range but it gives room for a lot of variation. Only you know what your score is. The measure is entirely subjective. But what is the standard, what is the comparative measure? There is none here, remember? We are not interested in the outside context of measurement. We are interested in your subjective judgment of where you are. If you were going to a doctor, you might be asked to assess your pain on scale of 1-10 and you would surely be able to do that. If we can use subjective measures for pain, we can surely use them as measure of our own experience of positivity. After a while, you will get comfortable with your score and you will begin to get a sense of just where you are. You will know when you are higher and lower on this scale.

People start in all places along the scale when they begin. There are scores that start in the 40's and grow, and there are scores that begin in the 60's and grow by one point a week. If you keep track of your score with the intention of your score increasing, it will grow in that direction. The goal of the UpSpiraLife Groups is to get participants into the 90's.

One of the interesting things that happen is that people get upset when their UpSpiral Score falls from a 90 to an 80, which will happen from time to time, and they don't like it at all. They need to be reminded that the 80 they experience today is much better than the 60 they started with when they first came.

How do you get into an UpSpiral and how do you stay there? This brings us back to Pollyanna. This movie was the creation of Walt Disney. It is seen as "superficial." Walt Disney, in designing the aim of his company, insisted that there be a reference to no cynicism in the work they produced or in their attitudes toward producing it. Cynicism is the need to see something negatively or to reduce it and make it less than its significance. In the movie, Pollyanna really only does one thing consistently. She plays a game called "the glad game." Whenever something goes wrong, she insists on finding out what there is to be "glad" about in the particular situation or in life in general. Simplicity is not superficiality. It is brilliance. To make something very complex and reduce it to its most simple elements is difficult. Today science is learning the importance of gratitude and positive emotion through extensive and elaborate research. Pollyanna had it right all along, a long time ago. What is there to be glad about? Or what is there to be grateful about? That is probably the most important UpSpiral issue. What do I have to be grateful about? What are the positive aspects of this situation or this person? What do I appreciate?

These are the questions that grab negativity from descending to cynicism, and get us to think more broadly. Their answers keep us in an UpSpiral.

Another answer to the question about how to stay in an UpSpiral is to use the Emotional Gym. Go back to Step 1 and reread the material about the Emotional Gym and incorporate it into your life until it is second nature. It is one of the primary tools of this program. Just like you would practice the scales to play a concerto, these are the scales of positive emotion that are important to practice everyday.

Learn them, memorize them. Practice putting your emotions through these scales that are the opposite of oppression and projection. They are the neuropositive scales of the positive feelings you play to get to a high UpSpiral. You can play these scales at will. Get better and better at feeling them and you will play them very quickly, very skillfully, very well.

You can get so good at playing these scales of emotion that you can be in a very uncomfortable situation, at the start of an argument, ready to go on stage, faced with conflict, and you can make the choice to run through one of these scales of emotion. Feel the feelings, one right after the other, over and over, just like you were practicing the piano. Make this the "music of your mind."

Once you encounter the concept that there is an UpSpiral and a DownSpiral, and it can be quantified by your own subjective experience, life is never quite the same in terms of how you view it. That is because you now have a way of seeing your experience that you didn't have before. You know whether or not you are in an UpSpiral and you know when you are in a DownSpiral, and are not doing the things you need to do to get out of it and stay out of it. Your choices have been increased by a new way of looking at your own experience. And once you have spent more time in the UpSpiral, you aren't going to want to be anywhere but there again. You will learn what you need to learn to stay there and you will do what you have to do to be in a better-feeling place that is within your grasp. This is an enormous piece of personal empowerment. You always know that the choice about where you want to be in the UpSpiral is yours, not external events. Even though there can be things that drag us down, we know we don't want to stay there.

A word about addiction. All addictions are tied emotionally to a DownSpiral, or they could not exist. They are "neuro-negative." If addictive behavior is a part of your life, you need negativity and the negative cycles of emotion to sustain the addiction. Living in an UpSpiral will tear you loose from your addictions, or at least it will attempt to do so, just because positivity and the UpSpiral do not fit into the negative cycles of addictive emotion. If there is an addiction in your life, you are going to have to let it go or find help in letting it go. This is not a process that treats addictive behavior, although it may greatly help those who have recovered. This is not a recovery program from addiction, and you can't fool yourself that you are in an UpSpiral when positivity may be helping you deny a deeper addiction. The UpSpiral will be harder to sustain until you deal with the addiction and get it out of the way, so that you can see the negative emotional patterns that sustain it.

∏euroPositive Workouts©
Exercise Set #2

1. Do **The Basic Three** exercises from the previous step.

2. Go to the ***www.thepositivemindblog.com*** and write your thoughts to the issue of the week presented there or interact with other participants. You can register with a name the preserves your anonymity if you wish, but we encourage you not to do that unless it is really your choice. Make a comment; share your insights about your experience. You can be sure that someone else will identify with you and learn from you. Or you can ask a question about a concern. This blog is read by people around the world, so you never know who you may be helping by just being and sharing you. Keep your comment in the spirit of the UpSpiraLife group.

3. Make a decision to really get this in place in your life and work privately with your NPC in the ***Move Your Mountain*** module.

The Research Evidence
STEP 2

Fredrickson, Barbara L., and Marcial F. Losada. "Positive Affect and the Complex Dynamics of Human Flourishing." *American Psychologist* 60.7 (2005): 678-86.

Seligman, Martin E.P. **Authentic Happiness: Using the New Positive Psychology to Realize Your Potential for Lasting Fulfillment.** New York: Free, 2002.

Step 3

Dedicated ourselves to knowing, growing, and living our strengths.

It is not possible to stay in an UpSpiral without knowing your strengths and learning to play to them. The first thing that is important to know is that no matter how much you might think that you know what your strengths are, you don't. In tests of group after group, participants were asks to list their weaknesses, which was no problem for them, because we are so aware of what's wrong with us. They were also asked to list their strengths, and even the most astute individuals were able to identify only one or two from a list of 10 of their actual strengths. You will need to take two tests that will introduce you to your strengths, and that information is given at the end of this chapter.

We have long thought that our genes determine our behavior. Today we are learning that this is only partially true. Just because a gene exists doesn't mean that it is activated. We also know that its activation is influenced by a variety of other factors. Each gene has proteins that affect it, and it is the proteins and their diversity that give genes a far greater complexity than we had ever thought before. "Epi" genetics is the field that looks at how environment influences proteins and others factors that eventually determines how genes will express. Some genes that carry disorders may never express because their "switch" to express has not been turned on. Epigenetics suggests a wide interplay of factors between the environment and the biology of the individual. Even identical twins can vary greatly in the expression of their personality.

This process of epigenetic expression is strongly taking place in the first two years of human life, when our major neuropathways are formed and we lose the largest number of brain cells we will likely ever lose. These major neuropathways are our strengths. They have been forming, along with the propensities to use them, since we were born, and especially since we were two years old. These strengths have a long history in us and they "are us." These strengths comprise your real self. Research shows that when you use these strengths you are your happiest. The farther away you are from these strengths, the more disconnected you feel. There is a feeling of not knowing yourself, of not knowing who you are. There is a sense of feeling incomplete, unsure, not in touch with yourself, and not "in sync." It is a feeling of kind of being "out of your own skin."

What is also true is that these strengths all exist on a continuum. On one end of the continuum are your strengths, and on the other end are your weaknesses. It is interesting to consider that your weaknesses are merely a reflection of your strengths that are at the other end of that continuum. So if they are realities within you, which end of the continuum is stronger - strengths or weaknesses? Is it possible to grow only in the direction of your weaknesses, or your strengths, or both? Probably we grow someplace in the middle when we are not sure what our strengths are. The simple answer is this. When we are in an UpSpiral, we play to our strengths, to the best in ourselves. And we do all of this with greater and greater ease, the more time that we spend there.

When we are in a DownSpiral, under stress that usually increases and takes us even more into DownSpiraling, we play to our weaknesses –the other end of our strengths. While strengths can be consistently defined, weaknesses are idiosyncratic and unique to each person. Everyone chooses how to exercise their weaknesses in different ways, as the opposite expression of their strengths. We will have the opportunity to see what that looks like in the example below. Keep in mind that in an UpSpiral, you have a much greater probability of playing to your strengths, and in a Downspiral there is a much greater likelihood of playing to your weaknesses.

Here is a list of one person's strengths:

Strengths	Weaknesses
Creativity, ingenuity, and originality	Rigidity, staid
Perspective (wisdom)	Impulsive Judgment
Spirituality, sense of purpose, faith	Doubt, Worry
Bravery and valor	Fear and Cowardice
Ideation	Comparing, Copying
Relator-Maximizer	Isolating, jealousy
Strategic-Developer	Scattered, aimless
Input	Boredom, resistant
Learner	Narrow, closed

For another person, these weaknesses may be different in character and nature. We all manifest our weaknesses in relation to our strengths in different ways.

Strengths are strengths because they feel very natural, and using them comes very easily. When we use our strengths, it takes very little psychic energy, and we feel like we are just being ourselves. Weaknesses are usually related to angry and negative feelings. Strengths are related to a sense of flow and ease.

Many times, people find themselves in jobs where they are not using their strengths, and they simply hate and want to change jobs. However, the problem may well be that a person doesn't know what their strengths are, and doesn't know how to use a strength for a particular task. Are there very few jobs where you can use your strengths? Problems on a job are often a result of not using your strengths. If you can't use your strengths on a job, then by all means, change jobs. But if you have not consistently applied all of your strengths to a particular job and change your job, you will carry the same lack of use of your strengths to the new position.

The problems we have in most of our lives are related usually to some strength we're not using. That's why they are so frustrating. It is as if these problems are trying to tell us something that we can't understand, or give us a message that can't get through. That message is usually about using some strength we have that we don't even know that we have. And the same situations will continue to appear throughout our lives until the strength that wants to emerge, the real part of us that wants expression, finds its expression as a strength and not as a weakness. Most people who learn to play to their strengths do it accidently, out of following what they love to do and finding the strengths that naturally grow out of that.

Unfortunately, our educational systems do not generally focus on our strengths, but rather the opposite, on recovering from our weaknesses. This has been the shape of much of our education. We spend a great deal of time trying to correct things that we are not good at and never will be, and far less time focusing on what we are good at doing - on our strengths.

Parents were asked in a national poll what they would do with their child if they got an "A" in literature and a "D" in math. By far, the greater majority of parents would hire a tutor to correct the math deficiencies. A small number of parents would have hired a tutor in literature because that is obviously where the giftedness was. Geniuses are produced by growing the things they are already good at doing, where they already show promise, and paying little attention to the other things. Genius is produced by practice and practice and practice of what are the strengths of a person. It takes about 20 years to produce a genius by playing to strengths and by putting no more time than is absolutely necessary on other things.

We have all been the object of attempts to take the focus from what we are good at doing and focusing that attention on a deficit, that in the long run, will change very little. Our weaknesses change very little over a lifetime, but our strengths are infinitely malleable, with no end to how much they can grow. The major neuropathways of strengths are the brain's superhighways of growth when we put our focus on them and grow in that direction.

You will only stay in an UpSpiral of feeling good by using your strengths. Your strengths can take any problem you encounter and give you the skills and answers to work through it, by simply using them. There is nothing you can encounter that your strengths will not be a match for, bringing you to growth and solutions.

However, it is very easy, especially at first, to forget what your strengths are. In a DownSpiral, your strengths don't even seem real, if in fact, you can even remember what they are. It is amazing to see a person in a DownSpiral struggle to even name their strengths. And if they do, it is usually reluctantly and disgustedly, as if somehow their strengths don't work.

We have not been conditioned to look to our strengths, but we have been conditioned to remember our weaknesses. We have learned to make them our focus, because while we are afraid of them, we also use them in what seems like a way to escape from our problems and fears. Oftentimes, this focus on weaknesses creates addictions. Because we can start off feeling negatively and then focus on a weakness, it can become part of a pattern that will take you to some kind of reward, like a drug, drinking, food, or shopping. So there is an investment in the DownSpiral as a way of getting the short-lived addictive reward. Feeling negatively insures the eventual escape, with the drug or the drink, or whatever the escape may be.

You will be directed to the strengths tests here, and when you have your strengths, it will be important for you to memorize them. Also you will want to post them in a few places like the car, the bathroom, the refrigerator, your desk or wherever you will see them and be reminded to "think from" and "behave from" your strengths. Meld them into the daily flow of your life. Your strengths are rich enforcers and builders of your neuropositive mind.

For many, using your strengths will just feel too good - so good that it will seem like you are being frivolous and wasteful, that life should be harder. Life should not be harder. Life should feel exactly like you feel when you are easily and effortlessly using and growing the strengths that are your major neural superhighways. There are even some people who report that they feel guilty when they use their strengths because they were discouraged from doing the things they loved or were good at because it came too easy for them. They were told that they should struggle more. Work didn't seem like work unless they were doing something that was exhausting, using too much psychic energy, and was an attempt to become good at things that were not their strengths.

We have the idea that what we love should be reserved for "rewards," or for time when the real work is finished. We believe in the "no pain, no gain" nonsense that may work in a muscle-building gymnasium, but does not work in the rest of life. Even in the exercise field, the rule of "no pain, no gain" is fast being replaced by steady growth that does not emphasize "pain" as the measure of how hard one is trying. The idea that if the thing you are doing is not filled with struggle and pain, as the measure of really deserving the reward, is an outdated and foolish use of good energy. It is no way to "feeling good," and it is a perfect way to wearing ourselves out and getting tired of whatever the activity may be.

However, it is still difficult to accept the idea that we are best at things we are good at and that we enjoy. Can we really appreciate what we have achieved if we have so enjoyed achieving it along the way? That is the way when you know your strengths and you use them to succeed. You will use less psychic energy, you will get more easily into a "flow," and you will develop more quickly to the point of being exceptional in growing areas that are already your strengths. You will want to do whatever it is that your strengths are lined up to do. That is the "wanting" that creates genius.

The great prodigies are not so different from the rest of us. It takes about 20 years to develop genius in a particular area. If you are recognized for being good at baseball or ice skating or tennis when you are 4 or 5 or 6, and you devote your life to one of these for next 20 years, you will develop the "practiced" skills that will grow because of the practice and a natural "bent." Devote yourself to something for 20 years and see how exceptional you become if you "breathe" it everyday for 20 years with the best teachers and coaches and opportunities, grounded in your strengths, which seem to lead you in that direction. Geniuses are not born. They develop. How many, many geniuses are there out there who have not had the opportunity to develop in a highly directed environment?

You may well be one of them. And by the way, it is never too late to develop genius by pursuing what you love to do, in one aspect or another.

But as powerful as strengths are, it is amazing that they can so easily be forgotten. Even after you have memorized your strengths, you will find that as problems and issues occur, you forget them. Sometimes it is even hard to recall what they are. Why is it so easy to remember our weaknesses and to forget our strengths? One reason is that we have spent a lot of time DownSpiraling and a lot of time in the DownSpiral.

Remember, that when we are negative, we are least likely to play to our strengths. Negativity plays to weaknesses. You will find that the problem areas of your life are most characterized by not playing to a strength. Our problems occur where we are not using our strengths. There is an assessment in Appendix A at the back of this book where you will list how much you are using a strength and how much you are playing to its opposite. When you add up the scores at the end, it is not unusual to find that they are somewhat equal. What that means is that weaknesses are cancelling out strengths and we will feel ourselves in an area of mediocrity. This chart is called the Strengths Portrait Assessment.

There are two measures that are used here to scientifically test strengths. The first test is called the "VIA" which stand for "Values in Action." It is a values-oriented strengths test that was developed by Dr. Martin Seligman and Dr. Christopher Peterson. The test is available at www.authentichappiness.org. You will get results that give you 24 Signature Strengths. These are value-oriented strengths much like those presented earlier in this chapter. They are strengths that you most value and they also represent values in your life that are important. You will feel most whole or integrated, most in "your own skin," when these strengths are at work in your life. You will feel most at odds with yourself when you are not using these strengths.

These strengths were taken from the major religions and philosophies of the world, and they represent those strengths as values that are important to all these systems. You will be amazed at how well these strengths fit you. However, from time to time, someone will not like or agree with their strengths. This means that you have not identified with a strength that is yours, that you need to "make friends" with this strength, to learn about it, and to begin to let it work for you. Your strengths are connected, so as you begin to "pull"on one strength, you will be using all of them to some extent. If you do not like a strength that you have, it is because you don't understand the breadth of the strength and you need to learn more about it. Aspects of the strength that you have considered are yours and they need to be developed. Just because you have a strength does not mean that you have developed and grown the strength, and you may find out that it shows up only as a weakness. An investment in a personal coach is an excellent way to learn and grow your strengths while being held accountable to do so. Your coach and your UpSpiraLife group will see things about your strengths and your interaction with your strengths that you will likely not see. While we can be blind to some parts of our strengths, the usual experience is, "this is the real me." And there comes the sense that you have found the real you. No longer will people say, "I don't know who I am." The more you choose to grow them, the more your strengths will guide you to a deeper and deeper sense of who you really are.

The second resource for strengths has been developed by The Gallup Institute and is the Strengthsfinder test found in the book by Tom Rath called Strengthsfinder 2.0. The book will explain the process and the strengths that are measured. This test is more "talent" oriented, but in a broad, general way. It is frequently used by businesses and organizations to put their employees into the right jobs. However, it is also valuable for individual use. These Gallup Strengths will also have their opposite weaknesses, and what holds for the VIA is also true for this test. These strengths tend to be more immediately applicable than the VIA strengths because they are more specific, and in a certain sense, the VIA strengths have more breadth. It is valuable to combine these strengths with the VIA. You will find that oftentimes one strength will act as a trigger and augment another strength. What you will find that is very strengthening and confidence building is that you have some strength, or combination of strengths, to handle any situation in your life.

These are strengths to use in many ways. But first and foremost strengths are used to stay in the UpSpiral. So long as you stay in an UpSpiral, you will undoubtedly use your strengths. When you start to DownSpiral or are actually in a DownSpiral, you will forget your strengths and you will forget to use them. Your strengths are your guarantee to stay in an UpSpiral of positivity. Nothing will get you down if you engage these strengths.

However, don't assume that you know how to use your strengths. Don't assume that you know what they are. Get some help in learning to understand them and how to employ them. Your strengths are inexhaustible in terms of what you can learn about them. You will need to study and research them, and to appreciate the wide superhighways of ability, achievement and interpersonal skills they provide for you. You have the propensity to allow them to make you a genius in the use of them. Plumb them deeply and let them define who you really are. Remember, the more you use your strengths, the happier you will become.

∏euroPositive Workouts©

Exercise Set #3

1. Do **The Basic Three.**

2. Now that you have been working with The Emotional Gym for a couple of weeks, if you have not already done so, find cues that really work. Evaluate the ones you may have chosen and replace ones that don't work or find some new ones. Noxious or a negative stimulus like a siren make producing a positive emotion more difficult, but they may be more effective. Your pet, your partner's smile, flushing the toilet, a stop sign, a rude person in traffic can all be cues to practice feeling a positive emotion. But the cue has to remind you in a consistent way. If the cue wears off or doesn't work, find one that does.

3. Dedicate each day (except the weekend) of the week to a specific strength. Concentrate on using that particular strength on "Wisdom and Perspective Tuesday" or "Strategic" Wednesday.

4. Work with your NPC individually or in a pod on the **StrengthSmart** module.

5. As your NPC to give you the ***Strengths Portrait Assessment.***

The Research Evidence
STEP 3

Peterson, Christopher, and Martin E.P. Seligman. **Character Strengths and Virtues: a Handbook and Classification.** Washington, DC: American Psychological Association, 2004.

Buckingham, Marcus, and Donald O. Clifton. **Now, Discover Your Strengths.** New York: Free, 2001.

Rath, Tom. **Strengths Finder 2.0.** New York: Gallup, 2007.

Step 4

Found, over time, five personal heroes that would act as guides to the use of our strengths.

Projection onto another person is a defense mechanism in which a person sees in another person what exists within them. It is seeing, on the outside, some negative that exists within the person. It means, according to the saying, that "you spot what you got." Turning around a negative statement made about another person can give the person making it an insight into them.

There is another side of projection that is the more positive side, although it can be exaggerated. It is called "identification." Identification is our ability to see and appreciate the good in others. From identification, we find models and paradigms and even icons of virtues, features and lifestyles that we find admirable and appealing. These models can become "heroes" after which we can model our lives. We all need guides, and while these guides are not people we absolutely copy, they point a way and give us ideas about how to form our own personalities. Wanting to be like someone can be extremely helpful in identity formation at any age. Identity formation doesn't just happen before we are 16 or 18 or 21. It happens all of our lives. We adjust and form our identities on the basis of people who influence us.

Identification can be carried to an extreme, much like most things. A man in his late thirties was so identified with his football team that he was beyond the definition of a fan. He would lock himself in the recreation room of his home and dress up in the uniform of his team, complete with shoes with cleats and a helmet. His family could hear him yell and scream at his team when they scored a victory or had a defeat. He would be depressed for days if his team lost, and would actually avoid contact with people for a time after the loss of an important game. In this case, this man's self-esteem was so low and so attached to his football team that they defined his own worth in terms of how well they did or did not play in a game. When his team won, he walked around with an inflated sense of self-importance, bragging about the victory as if he had played himself. "Fan-atacism" describes over-identification as well as the fanatic. It is rooted in a low concept of the self. Over-identification is not what this step is about. It is about enriching our lives by identifying with people who help us envision and live in a way that helps us experience the well-lived life.

However, it is interesting to note that others do have a great deal of influence on us. Our friends, for example, are very significant and influential in terms of the company we keep. Close friends influence our weight, what we eat, and what we do. If one close friend exercises, we are much more likely to exercise. If a close friend diets and loses weight, we are much more likely to do the same. If your closest friend eats in a healthy way, you are five times as likely to do the same.

We "pick-up," actually identify, with the good and bad habits of close friends. There is a saying that if you hang out in a barbershop, you are likely to get a haircut. So it is with friends, and especially with heroes that we admire or want to emulate.

Whether or not it rubs against our sense of independence, the truth is that we are strongly influenced by the people we spend time with. Our associations strongly affect everything from our choice of food to our choice of religion.

What is true on the outside of us, in terms of physical friends, is also true on the inside of us. We spend time in our heads with people as well. We identify with the famous, the rich, and the infamous, and we carry ideas and notions in our heads about what is right and wrong, about what works and doesn't work, about how we want to be, and about how we should be, based on many of these identifications.

We are able to collect and hold in our brain countless images and pieces of information that we are always trying to make sense of, both in our waking hours and in our sleep and dreams. We are influenced by what we notice, by what captures our attention, and by what we choose or don't necessarily choose to focus upon. Is there anyone who has not gone to a powerful movie and carried the images and messages of the film with them for a long time, maybe even a life time? Things we see, and things we don't realize that we see, influence our judgment, our UpSpiral, our behavior and our choices of what we buy, who we spend time with, and how we feel. Single photographs are able to shape our experience about a single event, to identify that event and to shape our opinion and other's about an entire situation. We are much more influenced than we would like to believe that we are. The decision to live from our internal experience and choices is very difficult. It is made more difficult by an absence of heroes.

We live in an age that has a difficult time with heroes. The media seems to have reduced every hero to such a fallible human being, that most everyone seems to have too much wrong with them to be a hero. We get to look too close, too many times, and too long at most of those who would be heroes. We are thus likely to find their imperfections and weaknesses, which may, in fact, be as glaring as what is positive about them. The death of a hero sometimes helps to forget the weakness and extol the virtues. But heroes have it tough in a time of very "black and white" morality. You must either be all good to be a hero or have enough bad that you can't qualify. That's why politics is difficult. Who has a record clean enough to qualify as a hero? The same is true for a hero in life. Who has enough of an appearance of virtue "or something" as a hero with whom we can identify?

And that is where some adjustment is required in order to have really very workable heroes. Heroes cannot be more than human to work for this step. If they are, you will choose heroes that are on such a pedestal that you couldn't possibly be like them. That's one of the reasons why we have to have perfect heroes- so we don't have to be like them. The trap, though, is that we never measure up to a standard we have set too high for ourselves. Heroes have to be "identifiable." They have to be of the same stuff of life that gives us life. We are going to identify with heroes that can influence us most when they are very human, very real, touchable, tangible heroes that speak to us of something we can be, or of a direction we can take in our lives. They are going to have to be heroes that match our strengths. And that is exactly how you choose a hero. You want a hero that has one of your strengths, regardless of how many weaknesses may lead them in another direction. As long as a person has one of your strengths and embodies it well enough for you identify with that person, you can make that person a hero. People have some strange heroes.

This is the basic question, "does this person you want to have as a hero speak to you?" In some cases, you will find that these heroes, if they are well chosen, literally do speak to you. A hero must be able to create a shift in your thinking when you think of them. You may be in the heat of an argument, and if you think of your hero, doing so can cause a shift in your consciousness. Heroes have to be that powerful, or powerful in that way, not in being perfect specimens of the human race. If we were to put you under an MRI, and if your hero really holds a place in your being, it would be possible to see a shift in the brain when you were thinking of something else and you then shifted to your hero. You would go to a different part of your brain. We want you to have five heroes that get you to go to another part of your brain in any situation. And they will if you choose them well, if these heroes are a match for you.

These heroes are going to become unconscious friends and a source of identification. They are going to be as much a match for you as your physical friends. You "identify" with them. You don't dress like them, you don't talk like them, you don't become them. You "hear" them, you think about them, and you listen for their voice inside your own head, because they will speak to you in your own thinking, depending upon your familiarity with your hero. Heroes build a neuropositive mind.

The right heroes that are a match for your strengths will change your thinking, your feeling, your believing, and your life. Heroes that really matter can be a threat to the ego, because the ego has to move over a bit. While the ego is not a bad thing, it can get in the way if you don't check how you want it to be. Heroes check your ego and reform its nature. You have to be willing to step aside and identify with another person. You have to get a little "loose of" yourself to find a hero that has a strength that is yours in order for the bond of mutuality to form between you and this hero.

Look for heroes that match and emulate your strengths. That's the first rule of finding your very identifiable hero - do they match one of your strengths? Does this hero give you an example of one of your strengths? Can you have an imaginary dialogue with this hero about your strength and a situation in which you are involved? Can you literally have a conversation in your head with this hero? Are they accessible to you with a kind of inner voice?

How is it possible, you may be saying, to have this much of an intensity with a hero? Consider this. There is, in all of our lives, someone that we have detested, talked about, and have given considerable real estate to in our brain. We have been able to imagine what this person said about us, how they talked about us, and maybe even plotted against us. It wasn't that they did much. Rather, it was how they looked, how they stared, how they didn't notice us, or were also whispering to the person next to them. We reasoned that we knew, not so much by fact but by intuition, that this person did not like us, that they were very negative, that they had all kinds of traits that we didn't like, but knew they had. There is someone like this in our lives to whom we have given a great deal of power. We could even hear their voice in our heads.

Then, by some chance, we got to know this person a little better and found out that they weren't so bad after all. In fact, over time we grew to like this person and several others that we started out not liking at all. All of this is projection. If this is the power of projection based on half-truths, innuendoes, and sorely wrong intuition, how much more power is there in positive identification, based on the facts? Identification has more power than projection. Anything you can do with projection, you can do a hundred times better with positive identification.

Consider this. Projection is rooted in something negative in you that gets projected onto the other person. Identification is rooted in something good in you, like your strengths, identified in a positive way in another person. The good you see in another person is a reflection, in part, of some of the same good that exists within you.

So, how to find a hero? Just put it out there that you want to find five heroes that match your strengths. After several rounds of this material, you will find ten heroes to match all ten of your strengths, but start with five, because it will take a while to find them. You have got to get to know each hero better and better and better. It is interesting to note that the more you know your heroes, the more in touch with them that you are on some level of knowing, the less alone you will feel.

Find a hero by looking at people in this life or the next, who appeal to you, and begin to study them. Ask these heroes to begin to reveal themselves to you. They will start to show up. In fact, they will start to show up all over the place after a while. A great place to start is to do a search on your computer and to start reading. A great way to know a hero is to read their biography, especially a good autobiography. Find a movie, find an article, talk to someone who is an expert on this person, or if the person is living, find a way to visit them, regardless of how famous they seem to be, search for a way and be open to all the ways "knowing" them can unfold. Exhaust all of the sources in coming to know your hero until you have a sense of that person and until they begin to be a kind of voice inside of you. You can ask, for example, "What would Benjamin Franklin do in this situation?" And an answer will begin to form, sometimes immediately, sometimes in a while, but it will form. You will get an idea.

You can also sit down with a pen and paper or at a computer and start a dialogue. Be yourself, then take the role of your hero and talk back to yourself and see what unfolds. You will be surprised and amazed!

There are a lot of voices that go on in your brain. It is your brain's job to think and when you don't tell your brain what to think about, it will just pull on anything and think about anything. You know how you can get lost in your thinking and end up in places that you don't want to be at all! Having heroes is a way of directing your brain. In a sense, the more you think about your heroes, ask them questions, refer to them, consider and contemplate what they would do, the more your brain will go in a direction that is corollary to those pursuits. You can train your brain to think on more good things, and certainly one of the most powerful is the good in other people that is a match for your strengths. Your brain is going to project and identify, with or without your permission, so why not gain some personal power and take charge? Anoint your heroes!

NeuroPositive Workouts©

Exercise Set #4

1. *Continue to work* **The Three Basics.**

2. Begin the process of choosing your heroes. Find ones that speak to you in a vibrant way. Start with one or two.

3. Go to **www.thepositivemindblog.com** and share your insights with the world. You can register with a name that preserves your anonymity, if you wish, but we encourage you not to do that unless it is really your choice. Make a comment; share your insights about your experience. You can be sure that someone else will identify with you and learn from you. Or you can ask a question about a concern. The blog is read by people around the world, so you never know who you may be helping by just being and sharing you. Keep your comment in the spirit of the UpSpiraLife group.

4. Choose a partner in your group and give your partner a boost each week through a telephone call, a text, an email or some communication that connects you with your partner in the group.

5. Work with your NPC in personally making the associations you need to make with your heroes in the **Hearing Your Heroes** module. Use the expertise of your NPC to guide you in this process.

The Research Evidence
STEP 4

Seligman, Martin E.P. **Learned Optimism**. New York: A.A. Knopf, 1991.

Maruta, T., R.C. Colligan, M. Malinchoc, and K. P. Offord. "Optimism-Pessimism Assessed in the 1960s and Self-reported Health Status 30 Years Later", Mayo Clinic Proceedings 77.8 (2002): 748-53.

Step 5

Made the decision to know what we wanted personally by remaining, over time, in an UpSpiral and became open to letting a Source greater than ourselves guide us to our knowledge of them.

Have you ever gone to a store with the express purpose of buying something you needed, got home with one or two bags of things, and realized that you forgot what you went for? You may have reasoned that you didn't need a list, but on the way to the store, you weren't particularly thinking about what you were going there to get. You were distracted by the traffic and the sights along the way. You found the store, and dutifully went into your destination without a thought in your mind about what you went for. Maybe you walked in with something gnawing on the back of your mind, but you shopped and got a few things, got distracted by a few others, found a good deal, and knew that you were in a hurry to get back home. Then just before you got into your driveway, you realized that you didn't get what you went for, and you weren't about to turn around and go back and get it.

You aren't alone, if this has happened to you. It's here because it has happened to most people more than one time and usually more than once. It is the way our brain works. We don't necessarily focus on what we intend to want, but more significant than that, we don't always know what we want. In fact, a lot of time we don't know what we really want. We are much better at thinking we know what we want than we are at really knowing our wants and our desires. The whole issue of knowing what we want and getting it begins in this step and continues on in others. One of the answers to this dilemma is to write down what you wanted at the store. But here we take a deeper look at what we write down before we do.

This is a step that will influence not only what we "write down," but it will also influence what we want and desire in the first place.

We notice what we are headed toward, consciously or subjectively. We may not remember what we are headed for because our "subjective" mind also influences, but never rules, our "looking and going." "Subjective" is a word we use here instead of "the unconscious." No one knows what the idea of the unconscious mind is. There is not a dynamic unconscious mind as Freud would have liked us to believe. There is no dynamic interchange of id, ego, superego, and alter ego as he introduced them. That is not the unconscious as we know it today. The unconscious is much more a store house trying to make associations for conscious learning to take place, but it is not an underlying "self" that is truer than our consciousness. It is not a secret life that comes to being in our dreams. It just doesn't work like that. The unconscious, whatever it is, is best treated as all those things we don't have in our conscious mind at one time; it is the storehouse led by our conscious mind. In our dream life it does sorting and learning of what is there and taken in during the day, and does it symbolically, to some degree. So don't get carried away with some power that your unconscious mind has that it doesn't. It is true that we don't carry many things we intake in our conscious mind, and it is true that they influence us in our less than conscious, subjective mind. Don't give up a part of your will by thinking you are determined by your unconscious. You are not. You are much more determined by a neuropositive mind. People get deeply confused, deeply troubled, and profoundly conflicted, of which the subjective is a part, but does not rule. These are all manifestations of what can go wrong with the conscious mind. You will have trouble learning to remember to pick up a loaf of bread if you are always blaming your unconscious mind for what you forget, or don't think clearly and in a focused way about.

So start by giving up these myths of the power of the unconscious mind. It probably is true that we only use 9/10 of our brain, but in a different sense than we usually understand. You are always using all of your brain, all the parts. What we are not fully using are all the inter-neuronal associations and the vast higher and higher realms of learning that come from these broadening and ever-growing associations in our brain interacting with the environment. So if you want to know what you want, and you want to remember it, focus on it and go for it. Get off this idea that your unconscious mind somehow has more power or influence over you than your conscious awareness; it just isn't true. Why would you be so careless as to hand power over to something like your unconscious mind? But since we hand our power over to so many things and so many other people, it is little surprise that we do it to some mysterious dynamic presence that doesn't exist within us. This invention of the unconscious mind is valuable in teaching us that we do not always choose on the basis of what is conscious, thought through and well formed in our minds. For sure this "subjective" brain that collects tons of information is all sorted out, but it is "subjective" and working to make sense of itself. It is not dynamically unconscious and robbing or ruling you of your power to decide and make choices. The subjective affects and influences the will, but it never owns it.

You may be thinking, what about the mentally insane? And while that is not a topic of our work here in living the well-lived life, it bears a mention for those who may still doubt that happiness or the well-lived life can and should be theirs. Even in a case of mental insanity, it is still the conscious mind that is ill. However, it is interesting to note that it is extremely difficult to prove a criminal plea of mental insanity, though possible, because even in those cases, the bottom line is whether or not the person knew what they were doing was wrong. In the vast majority of cases, they do know. That is why a defense of mental insanity so seldom works. Our capacity "to know" and to search ourselves "to know ourselves" is inexhaustible if we will but do it.

But this is appropriate here because we are talking about deep levels of "knowing" in this step. Wanting and remembering what we want, and going after it, is much more significant than we give it play. We treat it something like going to the store for something that we forget. The long-term implications for life are that we can live our entire lives and never really go after or do what we want to do. In fact, we can live our entire lives, never ask, and never really know. That is a staggering realization, but we know people who have done it. Literature and film are full of these lessons.

We have all been given a kind of double message. We have been told that you can have anything you can dream about or that you can imagine, in one way or another, if you are consistent. You can indeed have it all. Then, on the other hand, we have been told not to be such dreamers, to be realistic, to be able to support ourselves and to get practical and to do the things that get us by in life. If you have dreams, you have probably been called a "dreamer" in a negative way. You may have been told to get your head out of the clouds. You may have been told that you are never satisfied with what you have. You may have been taught such a sense of responsibility that you have become somewhat obsessive in your thinking and behavior. Or, on the hand, you may have rebelled and gone to the other extreme. Your dreaming has been shut off by the power you gave others, and you refuse to be responsible for much at all.

If you have dreamed a few times in your life and you think the result has been some kind of mistake or even a disaster, you may have decided that you can't trust what you dream or that what you want deeply just isn't going to be yours. If you have failed at what you dream many times, you may have decided that you are a failure for having had such dreams and being foolish enough to follow them. You were foolish not to have followed them. Whether or not you were foolish doesn't begin to be the issue. The issue is what have you learned. Or if you realized, considered, and were open to the learning, what has it taught you? Many people just close off, not only to what they are dreaming, wanting, and desiring, but they have learned to trust someone else's dreams or someone else's best plan for them, deeply believing that their own "wanting" is flawed.

What about the sacrifices so many people make for other people? Very simple. If sacrificing for another person gives you real joy, then do it. If it helps you lived the well-lived life, then that is your choice. If you do it out of guilt or out of not being in touch with yourself, or by doing for someone else what they needed to do for themselves, you will not help them or you in the long run, no matter how much you dull yourself to your own inner voice. That voice will finally speak, if only in loneliness from the self or in illness or both.

So from habit primarily, based on a thousand different epigenetic factors in our world, we learn not to want, to desire, to dream and to blame it on our unconscious minds or other factors that allow us to escape the real selves that we are with the real desires that we have.

What about the great spiritual ideal to give up desire? If that weighs heavily upon you and you are very convinced of it, you likely don't belong here, at least not right now. Go follow those ideas long enough to make you a little more miserable, and a little more out of touch with yourself, and then come back. Actually, the spiritual disciplines with integrity are trying to do the very same things we are doing here. They are concerned that we give up the desires that are not true to us, that are empty, and that are not our own true journey. There is no sin and you are not less spiritual for seeking to find out what you want. That is the search. If you want to believe someone else's idea about what that is for you, because you think that they are spiritually wiser than you, then by all means follow your guru until you find out that the guru's sandals are clay, just as yours are, and that your life and your search are your own, given one time in the life of this identity of yours that is so precious and absolutely, totally unique to you, if you will let it be. Commonalities with others will help guide you. We can learn much from others, but they must never overtake you in touching your own wants and desires for you in your time and place in creation. No one else is YOU, and if they know better than you, if they know "just what you're feeling," thank them and ask them to pray for you to get the same message they think you should know, then have dinner with someone else.

Just a bit more about the subjective mind. Don't make it dynamic. That means don't give it its own life apart from you. Don't make yourself in any way a victim of your "subjective mind." It does not have more power or influence than your conscious decision making. What you call your "intuition," if you really listen to it, is more likely more truthful and powerful than your subjective mind, even though that intuition is some part of your subjective mind coming through. "Dynamic" simply means that its forces whirl and swirl to make you do things, or to keep you from believing things, or from having faith. It doesn't have that power unless you give it that power. You do not have another "persona" that is your subjective mind inside of you. But what you do have is a powerful source of internal sources and sensations, fed by your senses that is subjective, and to which you can be vulnerable if you put yourself in the wrong position.

What is that wrong position? It is being in a DownSpiral. When we are in a DownSpiral or DownSpiraling, we are susceptible to many voices, and one of the strongest is what seems like our "unconscious." It is actually our subjective mind that is finding an easy way out for anything that is negative by dumping these into your stream of thinking. Just try it. Start thinking about negative things, start feeling sorry for yourself, tell yourself you have failed at many things and will fail at more. Add a few more and then see how easy it is for your subjective mind to feed that DownSpiral. Why is that the case? It's really very simple. When we are in a DownSpiral we do not have the analytical gifts of our strengths. We are instead playing to our weaknesses, and our weaknesses are comprised of the negative material that is part of our subjective mind. It goes like this: in a DownSpiral, you check out the material in your subjective mind that has to do with negativity - disdain, hopelessness, frustration, lack of decision making, and just about anything that makes you feel like everything is on top of you and that you are trapped.

You will never find what you want in a DownSpiral, at the bottom of the barrel, or going down further into it. That may be the case for people who are desperate, who are addicted to a substance, or who are terribly unhappy, but that is not our audience here. They need the original 12 steps that have to do with overcoming addiction of one kind or another. The case could be made here that our addiction is to negativity, and that may be the case, but we don't linger on this idea of addiction in a focus on what leads us to the "well-lived life" and into an UpSpiral. The voices of the DownSpiral are not voices that can be generally trusted because they tell us things that aren't usually really the things that we want, or we think of things that we want in a way that makes them seem out of reach. What you name in a DownSpiral is usually a reaction to not feeling good. It comes from resistance, or tiredness, or exasperation. They are not the ideas that will fulfill you. When you are in DownSpiral, you do not think of things in a realistic way that will make you happy in the long term. And even though there may be exceptions, it is not the rule and it not the easy way to do this. It is not the way that remains firm. So a requirement of this step is to stay in an UpSpiral.

This step is about another decision. It doesn't say to find what you want, to find what you desire, or to get clear about it. This step says "to decide, to make a decision" to stay in the UpSpiral long enough that you can begin to know what you want. "To know what you want" is a key phrase. Many people think they know what they want, set up goals and elaborate plans, only to reach their goals and find out that what they thought they wanted isn't what they wanted at all. Now that's not all bad. Sometimes we have to do that and it's just part of the learning curve. We can always learn from that. But it should not be the rule and shouldn't be the result of serious work on one's goals. The truth is that we can be a lot better at setting our goals, so good that when we get to them, they satisfy our longings. That is what we want here - real goals that satisfy real longings.

That happens first by staying in an UpSpiral for a long enough time that it begins to be possible. The decision to stay in an UpSpiral over time is paramount, because as a spiral, it is a metaphor for a gaining, increasing energy. It builds emotional and mental capital, it builds reserves, and it builds confidence in "you knowing you." The longer you are in an UpSpiral the less time and energy you will spend listening to other people tell you what you should want and do. You just won't be attracting it nearly so much, and when it happens, it will roll off you more and more because it doesn't fit. What does fit, you'll retain because it awakens your inner voice.

When you stay in an UpSpiral over a period of time, one of the key things that happens is that you will use your strengths more. Both intentionally and unintentionally you have to be using your strengths more. And this is the secret. The more you use your strengths, the more you know what you want. It starts to bubble up in you. New desires, new wants, new "knowing" starts to surface. You are open to more, you are looking at more of the world, you are letting more of what enlivens and sensitizes you come into your life. It is the UpSpiral that creates a state of being that makes you receptive to what you want on the outside and more open to what you really want on the inside. Positivity isn't just being happy and it isn't just feeling happy things. These emotions of love, peace, gratitude, joy and hope, you know by now, are states of mind that enlarge our being and they put us in touch with the ground of our being, if we will allow that to happen. In an UpSpiral, you are touching who and what you really are. You know by now that whatever is dark or wrong or "the shadow" is there as a result of being on the other side of positivity. In essence, any darkness pushes us toward the light, sometimes painfully and slowly, but even the direction of the opposite of positivity is toward itself.

The deepest essence of you is love, peace, gratitude, joy and hope. You were made that way and as you exist in these states, you attract to your attention and to your knowing what fits you. Your wanting and your desire will increase, not decrease. What you desire will fulfill you more authentically because you are attracting it from your own state of being in this UpSpiral of positivity in your own way.

Do you remember when being in an UpSpiral seemed questionable? Being there 95% of the time may have, for sure, seemed unrealistic. But now you are more used to it and you know it's possible to at least be in the range of 50 - 100 as your UpSpiral score. Something happens then. The cap we have put on life, the way we have capped our natural desire and diverted it to struggle, illness, and flat lining, begins to lift.

This step is all about a decision. That decision has two parts. One is to stay in an UpSpiral over time, to give it time, to let it grow with patience and some degree of determination to be persistent and consistent. The other part of the decision is to let a "Source" greater than yourself guide you to a knowledge of what you want and desire.

Whatever this Source is, don't get stuck here trying to figure out if it is or isn't. Let this be revealed in whatever way it does with you. Don't get stuck on hearing messages and seeing signs or some kind of "intouchness" that you manufacture to assure yourself that you are growing. If there is a "Source," essence, Universe, higher power, god, whatever, don't worry about it. You will encounter this in the process of letting what you want personally form in you by staying in an UpSpiral. This is very easy and it can't be forced. You will be guided by taking the cap off your desires and listening to your heart, just listening, for now.

These states of love, peace, gratitude, joy and hope that surely dwell at the very core of you are the inroads to what lies beyond you, and that to which we are all connected as one. Find these states within you, exercise them, grow them, let them build, and you will be guided by this Source without any painstaking looking. Just let it be and see what happens to your own experience. This isn't about believing something that you just can't believe or holding on to some spiritual ideas that aren't you or are foreign to you. They will just get in the way. What is spiritual, in essence, is you, and what needs to be revealed will be revealed to you in your way of understanding, easily and gently. This is not a matter of doctrine or religion or of believing in some concept of god that isn't you. If you didn't give it up at adolescence, you aren't going to reclaim it now. If you are in an UpSpiral over time, you have to become open and receptive. That is just the nature of an UpSpiral, and all that's necessary. What needs to be revealed to you will be revealed in love, peace, joy, gratitude and hope. It will be revealed in "feeling good," which is the journey into the UpSpiral.

NeuroPositive Workouts©

Exercise Set #5

1. Continue to build the strength of your Emotional Gym by working on the second dimension of the strength of an emotion: duration. Find a song for each of the five emotions - love, peace, joy, gratitude, and hope. Find a song that helps you create the feeling of joy. Find one that creates the feelings of love. Find a song for each emotion. Then put them together on a device where you can listen to them each day. Throughout the song work on making the emotion the song helps to arouse last throughout the song - that is duration. Duration is making a positive emotion last over a longer period of time. By now you have grown in getting to a positive feeling instantly. Now work on duration with the music you love. Use a head set, blast it on CD in your car or use this as a meditation. If each song is 4 or 5 minutes, you will have a powerful, positive 20 - 25 minute time of meditation.*

2. Continue your **Plans to the Universe** journal and your gratitude exercises.

3. Continue to choose your heroes to match your strengths.

4. Here we begin a very important exercise and it's suggested that you start from here with this exercise which will take the next few weeks. Get some sticky notes and begin to write down on each one, what you want. One "want" to a sticky note and just put them in a pile. Write and write and write and put them in the pile. No matter what it is, write it down and put it in the pile. This is a really essential exercise, so start now.

5. *Another good way to practice "duration" of positive emotion is to get the CD "The Music of The UpSpiral: The Sounds of the Emotional Gym" with original music composed and performed by Douglas Ladnier. Use the first and second tracks as reminders of what you are learning here. Use the last four 2 minute tracks of this CD to feel gratitude, love, peace, joy, and hope. This is a good approach for those who don't do the exercise of finding their own 5 songs.

6. The ***FuturePac*** module is one of the most powerful. Seriously consider working through this step with your NPC. It is strategic and it takes discipline and growth that a private experience can give you. It will skyrocket your growth to focus on your strengths (the real you) privately.

7. Retake ***The NeuroPositive Mind Test*** at www.gotoani.com. Compare these scores with your first ones.

. . . .

The Research Evidence
STEP 5

Reivich, Karen, and Andrew Shatté. **The Resilience Factor: 7 Essential Skills for Overcoming Life's Inevitable Obstacles.** New York: Broadway, 2002.

Schwartz, Jeffrey, and Sharon Begley. **The Mind and the Brain: Neuroplasticity and the Power of Mental Force.** New York: Regan /HarperCollins Publ., 2002.

Step 6

Committed to grow in our belief and practice of a personal VibeCore - that we could have what we wanted in life.

Your VibeCore is a like a magnet of energy you put out that attracts to you what you get in life. It is composed of three parts: knowing what you want multiplied by the solidness of your belief that you will get it multiplied by the openness to allow it to happen however it comes, in whatever package, and at whatever time. Divide that by 3 and you get your VibeCore Score. There will come a time when you won't even have to think of the three different numbers and divide them. You will just have a sense of where your VibeCore is at any given time. It's like a sixth sense of knowing how strong your inner magnet is....or is not. It is an essential part of the neuropositive mind.

Before we get into the actual scores or numbers that involve your VibeCore, let's first talk about the whole idea of a personal vibration. It is not a new idea. You really already know about this if you listen to your "gut" or your intuition, or the sense you have when you walk into a room. It is so much a part of us that we don't even really notice it, but we use it all the time. However, it's possible to be out of touch with this vibration and to be unaware of it as well.

A vibration is your "vibe," it's the vibe you put out to others about who and how you are. And it's the vibe you pick up from others about who and how they are. It is so close to you it's almost like an instinct. It can come as a surprise, though, that we may be better at picking up someone else's vibe more than we are aware of what is our own vibe and what makes it what it is.

But how can it be possible that these three simple things - knowing what you want, believing you will get it, and openness to how it will come, can constitute your vibe? How, you may ask, can it be that simple? It really isn't simple. Profound human issues are behind each one of these three measures of you. But you can be sure that the truth of them is as real as the beat of your heart and the pulse of your own personal rhythms in life. This vibe is you in profound but simple ways. This vibe tells a very great story. Perhaps the most amazing thing is that others can pick it up so easily, at least those who are tuned in to others. Oftentimes we pick up this vibe from others before we are even conscious that we have registered it in our consciousness.

What about a vibration being like a magnet? Does it really have an attracting or "drawing" capacity? Think about it. Does the vibe of another person attract you quickly to them or repel you from them? As you tune into that person, does it draw you more or are you increasingly uncomfortable that there is a lack of compatibility on some level –that you are just not coming from the same place? Or is there the other experience of "like mindedness" or that "this person gets me" or at least could when we are more acquainted?

Think also about how, the longer you are around another person's vibe, that you have learned to be so used to their vibe that you can read them in an instant. We sometimes call it reading their "mood," but this is much more than mood. Mood is an outcome of one's VibeCore.

There is at the core of us this "vibe" thing and it is going to pretty well be described by the three measures we talked about before: wanting, believing, and openess. A vibration attunes itself to what is like itself. A vibration is an energy that permeates the entire universe and interacts with all of the other vibrations of the universe because it is an energy. It might be more exacting to say that we are all made of an energy and we give that energy a particular shape or form or nature that is our vibration.

A tuning fork is an instrument that allows a sensitive and trained ear to hear the correlation between a note that is played and its synchrony to the energy pitch of the tuning fork. We are like that note being played, and our Mind can be like a tuning fork. We can become accustomed to "hearing" if our vibration is resonating with our VibeCore. This is a way of talking about what constitutes the "notes" we play and how they resonate with the rest of the world. The questions are: are we in tune with ourselves? Are we in a state of "mindfulness" about our inner vibrations? Can we hear our own inner VibeCore and "tune" it in to where we want it to be, and to what we want it to be attracting in our world?

The first part of your VibeCore is your "wanting." And there is a scale here to help you. It is from 1 to 100. "100" is knowing precisely what you want with accuracy and "1" is being clueless. There are people today who know what they want, and the clearer they are, the more they are generally getting it. There are also those who are clueless, and you know them because their vibration is very easy to detect. You know them when you meet them, and if you have someone who is clueless in your life, check out what that's telling you about yourself.

Wanting is not an easy thing because we are given so many messages about wanting, and especially about desiring. Religious fundamentalism and narrow understanding of the meaning of "freedom from desire" make this especially difficult.

There is nothing wrong with wanting or desiring. It is essential for healthy attachment in life and we need attachment to be alive. Essentially, those who want us to be free from desire want us to be free from desiring those things that come from what will not really satisfy our wanting. The admonitions to be free of desire are really well-meant intentions to keep us free from things that will take us away from what will really satisfy us and help us discover the real self. However, the truth of the matter is that we want what we want and we desire what we desire, and admonitions from others are generally not helpful. Going after our desires and finding out what we don't want is essential to individually finding out what we do want. Our wanting and desires morph as we have the courage to admit what we want and to pursue it until it gives us information that it does not satisfy and we need to change course. We are made of desire and made for desire, and our creative life force emerges from being honest about it. We create an on-going and unfolding creation of this Universe by allowing our desires to present themselves and our wants to be known to us.

There are for sure desires that do not satisfy us and lead us away from ourselves, but we mostly likely do not really learn that, in a way that shapes our own personal direction, through someone else's experience. Our deeper and deeper "knowing" of our wants and desires comes from our own experience. That is the birthright of our creation –that we have the right to find out for ourselves and not live someone else's experience, unless we make that choice.

Making people suspicious of their wants and desires works to control and manipulate them, but it does not work to free them to find the real self that each one of us is.

We have also been trained, often times, that our wants and wanting are selfish, that we want too much, that we are selfish, even that we are greedy. We are often times told to be satisfied with what we have, that we are never content, always wanting more. Feeling guilt for wanting and desiring is an easy experience for many people. But even in a situation of greed, if it truly is greed, the results of the desire are born forth with the opportunity to learn. What if we don't learn the lessons of wants and desires that don't satisfy? We keep being involved in situations that teach us the same lessons until we learn them in our own hearts. Then our desires and wants morph and change.

It is far more detrimental not to admit our wants and desires, to hide them from ourselves and others where they fester, frustrate, and produce all kinds of problems with our VibeCore. Most of all, we do not pursue what is true to us, we don't feel like we are living in our own skin. We feel separate and apart from ourselves, and problems like anxiety, depression, and flat lining set in, as well as physical problems, expressing these underlying discordances in our VibeCore. It is interesting that oftentimes when we just admit, write down, and talk about what we want, that our wants change and morph –just by being honest about what they are.

Wanting what we want is a matter of an issue called "attachment." Your first job, after you were born, was attachment to the world. We are almost obsessed by "letting go" philosophies and ideas, and for sure there are things we must let go of having and doing. But the great secret of letting go is to define what it is that you really want to attach to. A focus on letting go takes the energy away from defining the next attachment, the next growth, the next piece of progress. Do you have to let go first? No. But you will subtly let go when you even start to think about what you want next, about what is next, about where you are going. Wanting and desire and attachment are more important than letting go. What of loss? Where one door closes, another door opens, always.

The first part of you that will define your VibeCore is how much you know what you want, or how great your intention is to find and know what you want. Give this some thought and see if it isn't true that it doesn't take long to get a sense of whether or not a person knows what they want and to what degree. So on a scale of 1-100 begin to consider how much you know what you want.

One of the greatest reasons why we do not get clear about what we want is that we are afraid that we won't get it. In fact, we have been warned not to want so much what we want because then we won't be disappointed. And we have told ourselves the same false wisdom. Better advice is something like, "It is better to have loved and lost than never to have loved at all." Cowardice is the opposite of all of our signature strengths.

The more that you want what you want, the more likely it is that you will get it. And that brings us to the second dimension of your VibeCore. That dimension is believing. The basic question here is how much do you believe that you are going to get what you want? Anyone who doesn't believe they are going to have what they want is telling you a great deal in their "vibration." From whiny and hostile to angry and cynical, there is always an expression of where our belief in getting what we want is within us. One could say that "believing" in getting what you want is where it all is. And it is true that it is a large part, but only one part of the equation of the VibeCore.

Here is the second scale in our VibeCore Score or equation. It is again a scale of 1-100. In this scale "100" is certitude that you will get what you want and "1" is the cynical, despairing place that it will never happen. You are somewhere on this scale.

Notice the interplay. It is very hard to believe that you will get what you want if you don't know what you want. And it is hard to want what you want if you don't believe you will get it.

Belief is a rather easy and straight-forward matter. As much as we try to make it about the will of god or religion or predestination, it is not about any of that. If you want to increase your belief that you will get what you want, increase your use of your strengths. The more you use your real strengths regularly, the more you will believe you can have what you want. Your strengths are the major neuropathways of your brain, and they are the superhighways of any "spirit" that travels through you to increase your revelation of yourself. You will only learn this is true by doing it, testing it and finding it out for yourself. You believe that you will get what you want when you are consistently using your strengths in your life and playing to them on a regular basis. And you will only do that if you stay in an UpSpiral. In an UpSpiral, you play to your strengths and your strengths increase your believing that you will get what you want. It just works, it's just that way. Little more needs to be said, but much more needs to be done for you to learn how, in your own way, to play to your strengths and use them. That is Step 3.

How much, then, can you see that your belief that you will get what you want will influence the core of your vibration - your VibeCore? Almost immediately we can tell with a person if they believe they will get what they want. They are alive to life, they have a vitality, and they are alert and present in an easy and assured way.

The last dimension of VibeCore is openness. This, too, has a scale in the equation and that scale is from 1-100. Like all of these scales there is a lot of room for subjectivity, for internal determining of the score. You are, after all, the only one that knows where you are and the only one that knows the shades of your own score. A "1" on this scale is having an airtight, absolutely insistent idea, so tight that it squeaks, of what you want and what it must look like and when it must arrive. You have such a tight hold on what, how, when, and who that creation cannot work and you stifle its arrival or you are blind when it comes to you and you miss it. More likely than not, you are in a place or circumstance where what you want cannot possibly be delivered. If it was, you would be blind to how that was happening. A "100" is a complete openness to how what you want can come —in any package, at any time, and under any circumstances. Openness is what takes the "magic" small-time miracle sense of things out of this. Often times, in openness, we will come to realize that we have exactly what we wanted, that it has come so unannounced and so unaware in the seemingly natural events of life that we don't realize we have what we want until some time has passed and we look back and know it has come. Other times are more dramatic and eventful. It is openness that causes us to take our egoistic small time hold off of how the great Universe can produce for us and lets real creativity happen. It is the artist who makes a very large mistake in his work only to find that his work centers around the gift of the mistake that transforms it into the new work of art. You can have anything you want if you will let the Universe deliver it in its own way and time, and if you in the meantime live in gratitude and appreciation of the life that you have. If you spend your time whining and being ornery and despairing because who or what you want has not arrived, you will put yourself in the place mentally or physically where it cannot be delivered, or you are blinded to it when it comes, and you actually refuse what it is that you want.

So there are three scores here. One from knowing what you want; give yourself a score from 1-100. You know what it is! The next is how much you believe you're going to get it. You know that score as well. The last is openness to how it will come and you for sure know how tight your hold is or isn't on this dimension. Add the scores and divide them by three and you have your VibeCore Score. The more complicated you make this, the more you are resisting giving in to its simplicity. There is no reason to force it. Go and live your life as you do for a while longer and see how it works, then return to this when you are ready to be serious about getting what you want.

Eventually you will get so used to taking your VibeCore score that you won't even have to use the three categories. You will know where it is from 1-100. You will just have this inner sense of where it is. And if you get confused and uncertain, take the equation apart and look at each feature. You will find that you have lost a sense of what you want, or that you are not using your strengths, or that you have become tight and stubborn about how what you want has to be delivered. Usually it hasn't happened according to your timetable.

This IS your vibration and you can read yourself like a tuning fork, and so can everyone around you who has any sensitivity to you on the basis of these three measures.

Your VibeCore is the great predictor of the amount of "flow" in your life. It reflects how much you are "one with the music of life."

You do not have to know in a day what you want. You only have to be guided by your own intention to getting there. You do not have to have "certitude" that you will get it, but you do have to be aimed at using your real strengths more and more. Playing to your strengths becomes increasingly your mantra. You will especially need some time to get "open" to the delivery system of the Universe –this kind of openness doesn't happen all at once and it is deceiving when you have achieved it. It is something like showing up for life in a good mood. You are present in an easy way, just enjoying and appreciating. There is nothing about this that is "driven." Everything about it is "inspired" over time by your intention to define these three aspects of your life.

Your completion of the 12 steps over and over again leads you there more and more. In fact, you cannot work these 12 steps and not increase your VibeCore enormously. It just works! The Universe awaits your "aha" to begin delivery in all three dimensions of your VibeCore. Enjoy. It's just much easier that way.

∏euroPositive Workouts©

Exercise Set #6

1. Do **The Basic Three** and add "duration" to The Emotional Gym.

2. Review how you are doing with your strengths and perhaps consider working with your NPC to enhance your progress with them. The "belief" quotient of your VibeCore directly depends upon the degree to which you are using your strengths.

3. Continue to find your heroes.

4. Write your "wants" on your sticky notes.

5. Go to **The Positive Mind Blog** and share and support someone else by sharing your own experience.

6. Give your group partner a boost this week by email, a text, or a call.

7. The **FuturePac** module includes the intricate examination of your VibeCore, essential to what you bring into your life. Work individually or in a pod and laser your focus to this highly significant step.

The Research Evidence
STEP 6

Fredrickson, Barbara L. "Cultivating Positive Emotions to Optimize Health and Well-being." *Prevention & Treatment* 3.1 (2000).

Emoto, Masaru. **The Hidden Messages in Water.** Hillsboro, Or. Beyond Words Pub., 2004.

Step 7

Became increasingly open to the diverse and multiple ways that what we wanted in our lives could come into being and used these steps to build and increase a core positive vibration that became the "flow" of our lives.

Experiences that come to us "out of the blue" with good and great things seem to be very serendipitous. What if they were not so out of the blue as we might think? What if they happen at times when we are in a particular state of personal vibration? Vibration is what is meant in Step 6 by VibeCore. It is our energy field that is a combination of knowing what we want, believing we will get it, and being open to however it will come. Step 7 is an extension of Step 6, and explains how the VibeCore is really a "flow" of our lives. It is "flow" that we get into that is like being "one with the music." It is making the VibeCore of our lives "one with the music" and more and more in our lives "one." This step about "flow" is interestingly enough really about chaos and differentiation. It is about novelty and how much novelty we are able to allow into our lives. The opposite would be how much we choke off life and demand satisfaction from the world around us in ways that become narrower and narrower. The opposite of chaos might be addiction or any other form of extreme narrowing. Differentiation means the ability to allow things to be diverse and different —to be other than us without fear or intimidation of their "otherness" or differentness.

Life is about as interesting as the amount of chaos and differentiation we allow into our world. It is probably obvious that the use of the word "chaos" is intended within its usual context. Chaos here doesn't necessarily mean chaotic in the sense of everything out of order and gone awry, but chaos in terms of the ability to allow and tolerate wider and wider, larger and larger spaces of things that are different and don't seem to make sense, but actually do. Chaos "theory" refers to how random a system can be and how full it can be of different ideas, notions, facets, and particularly of novelty. Chaos here is the potential to allow novelty, newness or differentness. It is the capacity to tolerate and allow "otherness" and diversity in our lives.

Too little chaos or differentiation in a system means that things get boring because the same old, same old keeps showing up. Here's the main theme: the more VibeCore, the greater the "flow" in life, and the greater the "flow," the greater the novelty and differentiation.

Put differently, when you know what you want, believe you're going to get it, and are open to all the ways it can happen, or at least on the way to this, you're beginning to experience "flow" in life. You begin to be cool or easy with a way of life that is one with the music –things seem to be more of a whole. When that happens over time you are going to find that there is more chaos, in terms of novelty and diversity in your life. You will also experience or try to experience greater differentiation. However, allowing chaos (novelty) and differentiation in your life is not always an easy thing. The better you are at your VibeCore, the easier it will be. The more used to a high VibeCore you become, the more you will be capable of increasing novelty and differentiation. The more difficult this is for you, the "tighter" and narrower you are. The whole process aims to open you up.

Let's review this. The more you practice and work on your VibeCore of knowing what you want, believing you will get it, and being open to how it will happen, the more you experience a "flow" in life. You just get into a pace where life is flowing and you are going with it. There are ups and downs but you are, for the most part, in an UpSpiral. Life flows more in the neuropositive mind. What this does is open you to the experience of greater chaos (novelty and newness) and differentiation (seeing thing from a wider and wider and more whole perspective). When this happens your life shifts. It shifts big very quickly or it shifts a little at a time and you find yourself in transition. And transition can feel like very new territory and sometimes like our usual understanding of the word "chaos."

So don't be thrown because you are beginning to change in some particular ways. You are growing and the best way to support this growth is to be increasingly open to all of the diverse ways that what we want can come to us. Often times, this is what seems like "out of the blue."

Sometimes when we begin an experience of personal growth like this one, we do so because we know that our world and the way we are seeing things is incomplete. Often times we know there is more for us and we come searching for this "more." When we get it, it often feels like chaos or at least great novelty. And even more often, the ways we used to see things change radically and we them differently. We are doing greater and fuller differentiation. The brain is growing new neurons and old neuropathways are being challenged as new ones are being built. You are in transition. And if you are not in a transition, you are in a major growth spurt in your life. Where things were once more familiar, they have become less so. It can sometimes seem that you were better off where you were before you started all this. At least you were secure, you say.

However, that security was conditioned by narrowness and a lack of novelty and the push to learn and grow out maneuvered that "same old, same old," and you reached out and started to move toward this growth. Little did you know that what came to you would be some shaking and rumbling in your world as you became happier, more sure of your strengths, and confidently working your VibeCore.

There are times when our world goes "shake, shake, shake" and there is the rumble and tumble of an earthquake of old ideas and old ways of doing things falling aside because they don't work anymore. Things that used to satisfy no longer satisfy. Relationships that used to be fun may now seem a little stale and unfulfilling. Even the food you eat may taste differently.

It is time to let new things into your world. To become increasingly open and diverse to the new things the Universe is giving can seem particularly complex, if not downright puzzling. As you can experience a higher VibeCore and more of the flow of being in a more confident place, the Universe is freer to give to you doorways that don't seem like answers. Novelty and diversity isn't always easy, but it is usually very exciting.

Increased differentiation happens when you begin to see yourself differently, from a place of positivity being. As you do that, you are going to see not only yourself differently but you will also see others differently. Even people you thought you knew will appear with greater difference and diversity. You simply see them differently.

If you stay in an UpSpiral and if you use your strengths, this is exciting and is experienced as new life. From a DownSpiral, this kind of growth looks like you are letting go of your old foundations without the new ones being firmly established. And there is a tendency to want to go back, to revert to old ways of being negative and critical of yourself and others. However, in doing that you just become miserable, and the contrast with the way you are growing with the way you were is just too difficult and you know you have begun a course that you can't change. Once you have experienced an UpSpiral and once you have experienced "feeling good," there is no going back into negativity and mediocrity, at least not for long.

Consider this. The more positivity you experience, the more you are going to be open to novelty (as chaos) and to diversity (as differentiation.) You are going to change your perceptions, your beliefs, and your ideas about yourself and others. In an UpSpiral we are just freer for things to come to us "out of the blue."

It is likely that already some things have come to you "out of this blue." What are they? How have you responded? If they haven't they will because of your increased openness and flow in life.

Some of this novelty may come in the form of just savoring more of life and enjoying the "little" things. Or it may come in being fired from your job or a new and different pathway opening up for you. It may come in a friendship or a romance or it may come in a relationship that ends. But, as you are open, this increased experience of diversity will come.

Increased diversity is the key to greater integration later on. You can't integrate what is not very diverse or novel. There just isn't that much to integrate because life has been pretty boring. Not much differentiation or integration there.

Novelty means just how it sounds - an openness to "newness." Just how open are you to newness, to new thinking, to new ideas, to new ways of doing things, to new people? How well do you tolerate differences as opposed to seeing how everything is really alike? A greater and greater sense of oneness and integration emerges from a greater allowing of differences and novelty. There's just more to work with.

If you are really challenging yourself to honestly facing the quality of your VibeCore and increasing its score, you are challenging yourself to living in a greater diversity of life. If you are really doing the work here, there is a greater and greater sense of life rather than the narrowing sense that comes from being in a DownSpiral. If you are not experiencing life as more and more of a flow, of being more one with the music, go back and work on the previous step. Your VibeCore is not yet where you want it to be because when it is, this encounter with the flow of life is going to mean the experience of novelty, increased differentiation of yourself and others, and it's going to mean a greater openness to what life will bring into being.

Deep within us what is being challenged is how much of a "yes" we are saying to life and how much of a "no." There is a place where we put the skids on life and say, a little less or no more for me! We begin to blame it on many things like aging, illness, stubbornness or regret, whatever the external reason. There seems to be a big "no" to more of the novelty of life. Many think they are just too tired, but those who tire and those who have not opened themselves sufficiently to diversity are those who fear "chaos."

A deeper "yes" to life always happens in positive people, those individuals who are living in some form of positivity being who want to experience more and whose strengths are engaged for the experience. There is a welcome and openness to the diverse and multiple ways that what we want can be delivered.

Matisse and Picasso and many great artists have painted over their canvases time and time again, to begin again, not in the same place, but in the new place that would unfold from their openness to the creative process, as it unfolded in the next painting, and the next and the next. These are artists that never stop painting and we are artists that never stop living the art of life. Painting over one way of knowing life for new ways of knowing life describes this openness to diversity and novelty. What seems to come out of the blue is not so much come "out of the blue" as it is coming from an open life that is always willing to increase three dimensions of the human experience: wanting, believing and openness to how it will all come.

Many today would rather do anything that face novelty or differentiation and the transitions that life demands. They hold on tightly to what they already know and navigate the same waters they have navigated all of their lives. There is little wanting, less believing, and no openness to anything other than their tight and narrow demands to what life must deliver to them. There is less and less a sense of personal meaning and personal significance.

Those who refuse to paint over the canvas and start a new painting at the significant times in their lives give themselves away in precisely this dimension. Their lives lack a sense of meaning and they have a shallow sense of personal significance. A sense of personal significance is not enhanced by "sameness" but rather by novelty and diversity. We do not make meaning by becoming narrower when life requires greater and greater openness and broadness of vision so that differentiating, seeing the differences is unencumbered by prejudice and hardening of the heart and the arteries. Differentiation to the ways that life can deliver its goods creates the greater capacity for vision, for seeing the whole picture, because we are more comfortable and familiar with seemingly chaotic and differentiated parts that have come to make a greater and greater whole. The greater whole is characterized by a greater and greater integration of the brain and the mind which can hold novelty and difference.

We are not growing toward less or toward decline as we get older but to a wider and wider vision of more divergent parts, that for the one who has lived life in a narrowing DownSpiral surely seems like the endurance of real chaos.

This is a lifelong step of growing one's VibeCore and being clear that wanting never stops, knowing that believing always has an object, and that the universe is always delivering its good "out of the blue."

Let's pull on this notion of "differentiation" a little more. Let's look at this step again, now.

"Became increasingly open to the diverse and multiple ways that what we wanted in our lives could come into being and used these steps to build and increase a core positive vibration that became the 'flow' of our lives."

All of this openness to diverse and multiple ways is designed to increase a core positive vibration - the "yes" to life that had to be made at infancy in order to be nurtured is the same "yes," larger and larger, more diverse and multiple, that has to be at the core of us, increasing the desire to experience more and more of life, not less and less.

In an age when depression is at an all time high and on the increase, we have to consider what increases this "yes" to life and "yes" to diversity and the multiple ways that what we want can be found. It isn't being found because, in one way or another, people are not living these steps, particularly this one. It is also not being found, when in the course of a process of discovery, you come to that place where living in an UpSpiral and the steps that follow have brought you to a place where you have to consider the effect of positivity in your life. Indeed, it can make you rethink, re-feel, and redo your whole world, especially if you are spending more time in a DownSpiral than an UpSpiral. Perhaps worse is to yo-yo back and forth.

It will, for sure, introduce chaos and differentiation, perhaps like never before. If you decide that by and large you want to live in an UpSpiral and to develop the strategies that keep you there, you will do whatever it takes to develop that core positive vibration that becomes a flow for you.

A solid VibeCore lived over a period of time creates a flow, but what will you do when what you have asked for comes as novelty or chaos? What will you do when your sense of personal significance gets questioned to its core? How personally significant do you feel in your life? What are you willing to do to sustain a sense of ongoing meaning and personal significance? How will you make your life alive and happy when doing so demands that the canvas be painted over from time to time? We are building and rebuilding the neuropositive mind.

It is an amazing thing to consider that what may come "out of the blue" for us in our claim to "life, liberty, and the pursuit of happiness" is that we have the freedom we have to do so.

The pressure not to go through life's transitions is enormous and complex because life can seem so good and finished and complete in various stages along the way. Even when it is not so good, it can seem better to leave life alone as it is rather than mess with it and make it worse. But life demands not only that you paint over the canvas from time to time, but that you pick an entirely new canvas and begin again. You cannot resist this. You will either go forward and flourish or backward and DownSpiral. The refusal to move through the transitions in life is in reality a refusal to live life itself.

What is encouraging is that the openness to the diverse and multiple answers to our wants and desires does not have to be filled with suffering. If we do not resist, it can be filled with positivity being, filled with creativity, and filled with the ripeness of the journey that cannot wait lest it spoil in fearful lingering.

ΠeuroPositive Workouts©

Exercise Set #7

1. Do **The Basic Three.**

2. Memorize your strengths.

3. Continue to find your heroes.

4. Write your "wants" on your sticky notes.

5. Go to **The Positive Mind Blog** and share and support someone else by sharing your own experience.

6. Give a boost to your partner in some way.

7. **Finding Flow/Staying There** is a module in a special domain of its own. This module is especially for those who have completed the 12 step process at least once. This is an individual or pod experience.

The Research Evidence
STEP 7

Csikszentmihalyi, Mihaly. **Finding Flow: the Psychology of Engagement with Everyday Life.** New York: Basic, 1997.

Schwartz, Jeffrey, and Beverly Beyette. **Brain Lock: Free Yourself from Obsessive-compulsive Behavior : a Four-step Self-treatment Method to Change Your Brain Chemistry.** New York, NY: Regan, 1996.

Step 8

Became increasingly generous and reciprocal with ourselves and our "means" in life.

"Reciprocal" is possible only when we realize what has been given to us and we can bring that realization into a greater and greater exercise of appreciation into our lives. When we do that, being increasingly generous is the natural outcome.

Giving out of our means isn't just about giving from the surplus in our lives, whether that is money, goods, time, or self. Giving from our means is an expression of giving from what sustains us to what has sustained us and enabled us to live fuller lives.

Giving back is essential to getting. Deeper than any karma is a Law of Reciprocity that is about getting back in proportion to what you give. Those who simply "take" never really get the message. In fact, in the world around us, those who simply take eventually are denied what they take, or any sense of satisfaction for which they were taking strictly for their own benefit.

You have surely heard it said that there are takers and givers, or that the world could be divided into those who take and those who give. We have all known takers, and they are usually aware only of their own needs and they usually live with a certain kind of narrowness. They just seem not to get it. At any rate, they seem not to get the whole picture. Takers just seem to be myopic. There seems to be something missing from their apprehension of the world. Perhaps it is not that they don't want to give, or think that they really have so much, as it is that it just doesn't seem to occur to them, not just to give from more than their surplus, but to give from their means.

And here is the rub of this notion of reciprocity. Many think they are reciprocal just by being their narrow selves, and others are too reciprocal for the wrong reason. For sure, there are those who are takers, but it cannot be denied that there are givers who give for the wrong reasons or who give too much in the wrong places. These givers do so to please others or out of obligation or to be liked, perhaps even to be thought generous. These givers are certainly better than the takers for they are, for sure, more in the flow of the Law of Reciprocity –just not in its fullness and in its freedom. They seem to miss the joy.

So we are noticing here two groups. There are those to whom it does not occur to be reciprocal. Then there are those who give but are not reciprocal because their giving does not represent a capacity to give from the "heart" or the desire to do so. There is not real reciprocity. They cannot recognize what they have received and give freely and generously in response from that freedom, but rather from a sense of inner obligation rooted in other motives. They don't truly give back from their means. Both represent blocks to giving and both reflect blocks to wholeness and the flow of reciprocity.

Positivity being will be at odds with both of these tendencies because they do not fit either positivity being or into any group of a person's strengths, because strengths are values laden.

We are all attached to who we are and to what we know in different ways. How we are attached or how we attach is at the heart of this. We are wired for reciprocity very early on, as we are wired for attachment to the world around us. You might say that we are conditioned from the earliest implicit memories (before our recall of memories was actually formed) and from explicit memories that we can recall. All of this "conditioned in" what we attach to and how we do it. It is these patterns of attachment that will affect our reciprocity and, for sure, our means and our surplus.

We will divide the patterns of our attachments into three categories here. There is secure attachment, insecure attachment and avoidant attachment. These categories, in just a few words, describe our patterns of relationships to people and to things. And while everything is not as black and white as these seem, we are looking at trends or probabilities that one of these three attachments styles is predominating, and in some cases, dominating the style of choices and behavior in us - especially how we are or are not reciprocal.

Much of our negativity comes from how these styles work or don't work for us in our everyday lives. And, of course, this is one of the principle reasons why, once we begin to experience positivity, that after a time, negative feelings seem to come from nowhere and may even reappear with greater significance than ever. Positive feelings over time become strongly enough established that they form a reservoir. This reservoir makes it "safer" for negative feelings that are significant to surface. Alfred Einstein told us that problems are never solved from the level at which they were created, and this new level of positivity being allow these significant and important negative feelings and memories to surface in a more secure and whole way. It is not like digging through the memories of anything and everything that comes up in poor counseling and therapy approaches; these negative feelings and memories are much significant. So don't be surprised that after you feel much better and you are feeling good with a high UpSpiral score, that negative issues do emerge. But they can be dealt with in a very positive way as well. This is not digging around to "see what comes up." Over time, it is the negatives that arise in a consistent way and show that they need attention. They are most often related to these styles of attachment in very basic ways.

This is another good place to remind ourselves that we do not deny the negative. We allow it to tell us what it has to teach us, but we listen from a positive, higher ground. A part of that listening is through strengths that have had time to develop. We will learn some very significant ways of dealing with negativity that emerge from styles of attachment as this chapter proceeds.

Secure attachment describes the ability to react and relate to others and the world in ways that are free of anxiety, fear, and discomfort. You have learned that it is secure to attach to others. Love has been consistent and nurturing and adults have not taken advantage or become fearful people. There is no uncertainty that one's needs will be met with a loving and caring response from those who are in charge. Secure attachment tendencies happen in homes where it is secure to attach to individuals who are mature and consistent with their love. We have learned that the world is a loving place.

Insecure attachment comes from an early environment that has been inconsistent in its expressions of love. Trust in the world has been conditioned by inconsistent signals of caring or safety. Adults have had significant problems or issues or have not always been adequate in child-rearing skills. There have been times of fear, anxiety, and uncertainty that have been communicated in a variety of ways that suggest that the world isn't always safe, comfortable, or a desirable place to live. Attachments to people, places, and things are not as "certain" in one way or another and so attaching to those who love and later attaching to those relationships and life itself will be somewhat insecure. This is called insecure attachment.

Avoidant attachments are formed, as the name suggests, when we grow up learning that relationships and the world are not a safe place, and that one has to watch out a good deal of the time. We can become hyper vigilant, always watching and waiting for what might go wrong. Avoiding close relationships becomes a learned response because the world does not seem like an entirely safe place to be, and being loved in a consistent and secure way is not assured. People are less to be trusted, if at all, and there is great hesitancy in getting involved in personal relationships. We will always likely have found or be aware of a way out of any close relationship.

These styles are painted with a very broad brush here. They are not as simple as this but they are suggestive of three styles of relating that are going to affect the basic "reciprocity" in one's world. How much we receive, how much we give of love and of ourselves, will be predisposed by these tendencies within us. We can't trust and love others, we can be unsure of ourselves and others in relationships, and we can be distrustful and hesitant of how we enter into relationships. This is going to affect how we receive and how we give. In short, all of this affects how we are reciprocal.

Can you see how, if you have experienced secure attachments, that you will see and understand how to be reciprocal in different ways that someone who doesn't trust these attachments? Someone who is avoidant in making close attachments may not have as much practice at being good at receiving or giving, because being reciprocal is difficult and not something that has been easily learned. All through our lives, neuropositive being helps us grow in our capacity for secure attachments and more workable, comfortable and loving relationships. Insecure and avoidant attachments come from negative feelings and from DownSpiral living. The DownSpiral narrows us, makes us suspicious and insecure, so it is easy to understand why insecure or avoidant attachments of any kind are the outcome of narrowing and negativity. Secure attachment that is easier and more reciprocal comes from UpSpiral living where positive feelings and being are an outcome of living in this UpSpiral for longer and longer periods of time.

But why is this the case? Over the period of our life time, our task is one of integration of these negatives of the past and present into a greater whole of positivity, understanding and acceptance. That is what the brain is doing as we become more positive. If we are becoming more negative, we can't do this kind of positive integration. In fact, more dis-integration occurs. In a DownSpiral, we become more distrustful, more negative, narrow and we make choices to close ourselves off from the attachments that are full and healthy. Our attachments become more narrow and integration of the negative into a more positive "whole" can't happen. And since this integration or wholeness of our experience is a major task of the maturing adult, when it doesn't happen depression, dis-ease, and a disconnection with one's self, others, and life is the result.

The left side of the brain, called the left hemisphere, is that part of the brain that remembers negative memories, and it does this very well. It remembers them pretty much in order, like a list, and it remembers the details –but particularly the negative details in a very one-sided way –the way the person wants to remember them. The more negative the memory, the more it is cut off from the right side of the brain, called the right hemisphere. This right hemisphere remembers things differently. It remembers things more as a whole and more in the context in which they happened. It remembers with a wider view or a wider perspective; it gets and sees more of the whole picture. In fact, the right side of the brain can store the greater details of a situation and be shut off from the left side of the brain so that the two recollections and ways of seeing the negative thing or the negative memory are cut off from each other. Putting them back together again is called integration. But experiences can be so negative or painful that they can be "jammed" by the left hemisphere in such a way that they never make it to the other side, so to speak.

The whole process we see in getting older that we call "mellowing" or "softening" is probably this process at work in our lives. Over time, we open up and let the right side of the brain take the wider look and include more of the overall picture. We understand things differently. We understand that our fathers or mothers or friends came from situations where their lives were difficult, and we understand that people, including ourselves, do things they wouldn't ordinarily do if they weren't upset or pressured, or just humanly made mistakes once in awhile. People with secure attachments find it generally easier to let go, step back, and let this kind of wider understanding happen. Being reciprocal is easier for them.

The greater the frequency of insecure or avoidant attachments, the harder it is for the most part not to hold on to negative memories, hurts, and experiences. Here is where positivity being is very important. The more we can experience positivity and the UpSpiral and build stronger positive emotions, the more trusting and open we are likely to become; the more neuropositive. We just become more "wired" in that direction. We will let this right side of the brain do its work just as a result of feeling good. When we feel better we let more of the integration happen, even though it can seem negative at first.

Think of it this way. The negative side of the brain keeps track of the negatives in our life and uses them to keep us safe and to warn us from danger - or at least that's what we think we're doing as we get hurt in life and think we are "learning" to be more careful. And to some degree that is the case. The right side of the brain is always wanting to give us a wider, more visionary, and what seems like more spiritual or whole view of the world. When we have enough positivity being, we become more secure in looking at and accepting the negative side of things and bring these things into a wider understanding. It is as if the left side of the brain is writing a biography of your life from a very slanted perspective, as though someone other than the whole and integrated "you" were writing about you. The right side of the brain is autobiographical in the sense that it remembers and tells your story from a wider, broader, more contextual and integrated perspective. Who would you want to write your biography? Someone who knew just the negative part of you as you angrily and selfishly wanted to remember it, or someone who could see the whole of your strengths and goodness, as an autobiography does?

To review, as we grow more of our neuropositive being, we become more secure in looking at and examining our negative memories and hurts that are significant. These are the ones that re-emerge and tell us where we know we have work to do. They are not a list of insignificant gripes and ranting about how life hasn't turned out for us like we wanted. It is not a list of senseless, needless, negative whining and griping about one's self and the world. These are the really significant memories of hurt and disappointment where we have not forgiven ourselves or others or life in general. We work on this integration but we do not get caught in it. We examine the negative feelings and accept them and ourselves, and accept and forgive others, not blankly, but with understanding and the context that the right brain can gives us in the process.

Now we look again at our Eighth Step.

"Became increasingly generous and reciprocal with ourselves and our 'means' in life." We are more generous because the very ground of what it means to us to be reciprocal has changed under our feet. We are more generous, not because we believe we ought to be, but because we have more to be generous with ourselves. We are able to give much more because we have much more - ourselves in greater fullness and integration, our understanding is richer, and our energy is much higher because we are not constrained and bound by patterns of attachment we didn't even know we had.

Our means are seen as much more than our money, although that is a part of it we will not overlook, especially now because our "means" are freed from a selfishness to which we were bound and didn't know it, to a new freedom not just to give our "means" but to have and to own it for ourselves. In other words, we were rich and didn't know it. Now we know it and we can't wait to give it and share from joy and not from obligation.

We are no longer oblivious of the need to give of our means because we are no longer so entirely oblivious of our own need to love and be loved, first with ourselves and then with others. We are not oblivious to the fact that the reason we are often so selfish or self-minded is that we have never valued our own "means." We have not considered how rich we are and how rich our lives can be because we have been so much on the lookout for danger or for whatever is menacing. We can see others and allow them to see us because we are no longer so busy protecting ourselves from dangers we didn't even know we were protecting ourselves from.

We are freer because the angry feelings that would rise up, even when we at our most positive, are either much less or not there at all because neuropositive being has led us to a place where we could be braver at looking at a part of our life that was shut off - from that part of us that can understand and embrace the negatives and the hurts.

From our growth into a neuropositive mind, we have both strengths and means. We are freer now with our means because we have become more able to be reciprocal without discomfort or outright fear. We have new means that are our own richness, and from that knowledge, we share not only what we have, and we certainly share that, but also we share the means of who we are.

This is the Eighth Step: became from our increased life in an UpSpiral more and more able to be generous with our means in such a way that we have set this law of reciprocity in vital motion in real ways in our life.

NeuroPositive Workouts©
Exercise Set #8

1. Do **The Basic Three.**

2. Find 3 ways to be kind and generous.

3. Continue to find your heroes.

4. Write your "wants" on your sticky notes.

5. Go to **The Positive Mind Blog** and share and support someone else by sharing your own experience.

6. Give a boost to your partner in some way.

7. **The Law of Reciprocity** module is for individuals chosen by the NPC for the experience of this module. It is a pod.

- -

The Research Evidence
STEP 8

Bowlby, John. **Attachment**. London: Pimlico, 1997.

Seigel, Daniel, **"The Neurobiology of We"**, audio book, Mind Your Brain, Inc., Sounds True, 2008.

Seigel, Daniel, **The Mindful Brain**, W.W. Norton, New York, New York, 2007.

Step 9

Formulated five malleable five-year goals and three action steps every four months to move toward these aspirations

Wanting what we want and owning that we do can be a difficult thing to do. There is a hesitancy to wanting what we want because we have beliefs that we are being selfish and self-centered. Denying ourselves what we want seems to have some special virtue. The guilt of "having" can cause us to be less than honest about what we are wanting. Living with less can seem to be more "spiritual." There is the idea that if we live with less, the goods of the world will somehow magically become a more equitable distribution of good. And so we hang back for a while, denying ourselves, before we impulsively and compulsively give ourselves what we've been depriving ourselves of having.

The simple truth is that you're playing less than, you're having less than, you're holding back from being and having the fullness of who you are, and what you want helps no one. Your acting like you don't want lovely things serves no one. Your being "less than" for the sake of some misbegotten notion of modesty and humility keeps you from entering into the wholeness of the person that you have been created to be. It also keeps you from contributing to a consumer economy which is, by far, the greatest means by which you are likely contribute to the good of the world.

Healthy patterns of attachment mean an ability or capacity to want what we want and to be able to attach to it with appreciation, full of enjoyment and a sense of ownership that is proud and grateful. Attachment also applies to job and professions, to friends, associates, and to relationships. Attachment is a mark of mental health. Healthy patterns of attachment are developed from childhood, and even when they are weak and not so healthy, they can grow and develop by being honest about our wanting. Ambivalent patterns of attachment cause low self-esteem because we are never fully able to attach, to own, to be a part of, to have and to hold nearly and dearly those people and things that are significant aspects of our wanting.

Avoidant wanting will express itself in the voices that fail to appreciate their own capacity to have. Avoidant wanting not only does not know what to want, but would rather not want or have goals. These are the people who prefer to allow their lives to unfold without goal-setting. And they will get just what they want, "unfolding" here and there with little or no direction or purpose. Not only is this not the way life works, it not the way the attracting brain works. Avoidant personalities are reclusive from relationships and isolate from others. Being in touch with their "wanting" means being in touch with others, with the ways and the systems that fulfilled wants come to us. Avoidant wanting is reclusive in nature and the person does not unfold and develop.

So we are back to healthy attachment and to laying claim to what it is that you want. It is a process of owning your wanting, from the smallest of things to the largest, that will start to define 5 five year malleable goals. Sometimes, what we think we want changes when we begin to get clear about the smallest and the largest desires. Other times, you will find that when several wants have been looked at together, that the desire changes and they become much less important just by the process of admitting them and getting them written out in front of you in the special way that we will do that.

In this step you will be fashioning 5 malleable five years goals. The key word is malleable. If you are a year into a goal and it becomes obvious to you that you need to change the goal and go in another direction, the goal has served its purpose. Goals are only important if they will deliver, upon accomplishing them, the satisfaction you believed was in them. There are two things that help to establish solid goals. The first is practicing your strengths from being in an UpSpiral. Goals emerge from doing so. The next is to write down all of your wants. And that is what you will begin to do here. Get several pads of post-it notes and write down absolutely everything you want, one each on a post-it. Just pile them up in a scrapbook and don't worry about sorting them yet.

Over the period of a few weeks, write down everything on a post-it note. Write down everything from the ice cream you like to the car you want. Leave nothing out of these notes.

Make notes for all of the following categories and then you will combine these categories into 5 or 6 when you get to the sorting phase. In sorting, you will put post-it notes that are alike on the pages of a scrapbook and you will be able to move the notes around. As you move them around, they begin to take on a life of their own and they will begin to talk back to you. As you work with them, in the sorting process, 5 or 6 goals will emerge for you.

These are categories for you to consider.

Financial

Spiritual

Physical

Friends

Family

Intimacy

Home and Environment

Play and Fun

Education/New Learning

Adventure (*even if you think you're too old for it, you're not, so put it down*)

Growth

The Completely New and Novel

New Learning

Breaking taboos

Let's consider goals a bit more. Goals are mechanisms of attachment to life. They seek to create a fuller, more satisfying life and their very nature is to believe that the goal is possible to reach. So goals are healthy indicators of attachment to life, especially when they are pursued with intention. The difficulty with attachment shows itself in a lack of hope, in fear, in the dread of being disappointed and let down. This disappointment-oriented thinking results in flat-lining and in depression. It is a deeply rooted pessimism. Goals are expressions of positive expectation and of hopefulness. Goals expect to be met. To grasp the goals means to grasp the hopefulness that keeps the believing going that the goal will be met.

The first part of the VibeCore is "wanting." The greater the wanting the higher the first part of this score will be. Goals are also outcomes of a high UpSpiral. The more intact your goals are, the higher your UpSpiral. And, likewise, the higher your UpSpiral, the more creative and the more completely are your goals an expression of the repertoire of your strengths and abilities.

Goals are like engines of energy and productivity that create a synergy that will bring into sharper and sharper awareness what the vision is for your life. Your brain has its greatest synchrony and economy of energy when you're clear. Your brain knows better what to seek out and what to be receptive to in its sorting process. The brain knows better what is being "hunted" and what the focus of attention ought to be. With clear goals, the brain can use the limited amount of psychic energy it has each day, using that energy most wisely. Clear goals help create a neuropositive mind.

So, you will be writing down everything that you think of that you want. Get everything out on your post-it notes. When you have piles of them, it is time to sort.

In sorting them, you put things that seem alike on the pages of your scrapbook. As you place them, see what themes begin to emerge, and they will emerge. The "wantings" you have placed will start to talk back to you and you will want to move your post-it notes around in various configurations. As they speak to you, start to draft your first goal from your first group of notes. Maybe the category was "work and profession." Where do you want to be in 5 years? What is the goal that emerges out of everything you have listed?

On another day, and at another time, do the same thing with "play and fun." Where do you want to be with play and fun in 5 years? Your first goals may be drafts and you may want to take time to think about them and to share what you have written with others.

These intentions, as you alter them, will manifest. We create what we imagine and see for ourselves, and you are creating your roadmap. You will likely find just how much of a roadmap this is when you have finished your 5 goals. If these 5 goals really reflect what you want and who you are, you are going to have a sense of knowing where you are going. It is the step on the way to a vision, and for many people it is awesome and a spiritually enveloping experience. But first the five year goals have to be in place.

After you have your goals in place, you will write down 3 action steps, pretty easy ones, that you could take in the next 3 months. These are not steps that you struggle with. They are very obvious. We call them "the next indicated step" or the next right step. You are not struggling with a big "how" here, but rather with just 3 steps that you can easily do for each goal in the next 3 months. It can be nothing more than a telephone call, a meeting, reading a book —something that moves you in the direction of your goal.

Now consider this. You do 3 steps for each goal, every 3 months. That works out to be 12 steps in one year. That also means that in 5 years, you will be taking 60 steps toward your goal. Each step will open a new door. Does it look like you could accomplish a 5 year goal in 60 steps? What is even more likely is that you will probably accomplish most of your goals in less than 5 years!

Goals take us back to strengths. It is our strengths from which the deeper ideas and notions of our goals have emerged. Likewise, as well, it will be our strengths that will work to actualize these goals and make them come true. Not only do they provide a life direction, but they also provide a workout for one's strengths. Remember, the more you use your strengths the happier you are. Goals are a sure fire way of using strengths. We will not accomplish these goals without using our strengths to do so.

A good way of assessing how you are using your strengths is called the Strengths/Weaknesses Assessment. It is at the end of this chapter. Write down all 10 of your strengths, 5 from the VIA and 5 from Strengthsfinder. Do this in the right hand column. To the left of each strength, write down what the opposite or weakness of that strength is for you. The opposites are very idiosyncratic because it marks what we're doing when we are in a negative place and not using our strengths. In an UpSpiral, we play to our strengths. In a DownSpiral, we play to the opposite of our strengths in some way.

After you have listed your score on a scale of 1-10 (the total score of both sides will be a 10) for all items on both sides, add them and find the total for your strengths and the total for your weaknesses. This score is very telling. When we feel confused and divided; so will our score. When we are hopeless and feeling down, it will be reflected in a score for our weaknesses that is much higher than the score for our strengths. When we are using our strengths and that number is high, we will have a high UpSpiral score and be feeling good and productive because we are playing to our strengths.

Goals are steps to finding who you really are and for them to work, they must be your own. The experience of moving through a goal and experiencing its results must be your own. What you need to learn by accomplishing a particular goal may not be another person's learning. You may learn that the fulfillment of a goal is just "not all that," and that is an extremely important lesson in learning what is to be valued and what is not. It is the way you learn to set new goals that have a different nature.

Goals are major neuropathways in the brain. It is not so much that we only use 9/10 of our brain, but rather that the associations of neurons have enormous potential. Goals are this association taking place in the brain as we work on major projects in our lives that expand our neuropathways on every level. These 5 goals are leading toward your particular stand in the world and your legacy, which we call your vision. When these 5 goals are in place, your Mind will go there.

ΠeuroPositive Workouts©

Exercise Set #9

1. Do **The Basic Three.**

2. Find 3 ways to be kind and generous.

3. From the sticky notes you have accumulated, begin to formulate your five malleable 5 years goals.

4. Go to **The Positive Mind Blog** and share and support someone else by sharing your own experience.

5. Give a boost to your partner in some way.

6. This step is an especially good place to work individually or as a pod of 3 or 4 with your NPC group leader in formulating, strong flexible goals and the three action steps that accompany each of the goals.

7. The **Goals Before You Die** module is designed for an intense probe of the match of your goals to who you are emerging to be. This is an in-depth look at goals that satisfy and an examination of whether or not your goals really reflect who you are and what you want with the scrutiny and attention of your NPC.

The Research Evidence
STEP 9

Klauser, Henriette Anne. **Write It Down, Make It Happen: Knowing What You Want-- and Getting It!** New York: Scribner, 2000.

Latham, G.P. **Work Motivation: History, Theory, Research and Practice,** Thousand Oaks, CA: Sage, 2006.

Locke, E.A., & Latham, G.P. "Goal Setting Theory: Theory Building by Induction", in K.G. Smith & M.A. Mitt (Eds.), **Great Minds in Management: The process of theory development.** New York: Oxford, 2005.

Step 10

Allowed these goals to lead to the emergence and development of a vision for our lives.

A vision emerges from the deep structures of reasoning that exist within all of us. It is far more than "purpose" and much more still than being "purpose-driven." A vision is not "driven." It unfolds in the truest form of creativity. It doesn't feel creative at all. It just feels like the beginning of something that goes on to the next thing and the next, inventing itself in the process of its discovering. To everyone else, a vision looks creative and inspired, but as most artists will tell you, creation is a process in which the doors open as you successively knock on them. This vision starts in the earliest stages of reasoning and flowers in a later stage. A true vision blossoms from and is inspired by the stage of reasoning in which you find yourself in life. When it finally emerges, you realize that its essence has been with you for a very long time, waiting to express itself.

A vision doesn't just pop up as a moment's inspiration, even though it might seem to. You have been readied for a long time to bring it into being when your reasoning and believing could handle it. Visions start with specificity. Many people don't believe that. They like the idea of a vision being something like popcorn - put a kernel under a little heat and it just pops. When that does happen, much else has gone before.

A vision is a result of some kind of discipline or strong intentional life. Visions emerge very well from goals. Setting goals is like setting up the brain to let the vision emerge. Goals that are well formed, hopefully like the ones you did in the Step 9, are the precursors to getting your brain to take the vision "leap." If you have been diligent with your goals and you really fleshed out your wanting so that you have five strong goals that really represent you, your vision is close, if in fact you don't already know what it is. If you don't, keep working your goals until they are very clear and precise. This is sometimes difficult because between the stages of reasoning are transitions. It is difficult, in a transition, to get goals in place that lead to a vision.

Visions emerge from "stage solid" people and not often from those in transition. Clear goals help move transitions along. If you had difficulty being clear and precise with your goals, just keep working on them, changing them and adding to them. The way you reason in a transition isn't always going to be clear. It will be one way one day and another way another day - frustrating but a necessary process.

Let's look more closely at the stages or structures of reasoning. Each stage contains a meaning-making system or schemata. It is the way one reasons that holds the world together and makes sense of life. Everybody has this meaning-making system, and it's very hard to budge because people tend to have an airtight hold on what they believe at this deep level. For example, when people believed the world was flat and that heaven was above, it was very difficult to change their minds. Those that tried were often tried for heresy.

Each stage of reason also has its "sense of personal significance." The meaning in a stage provides for each person a sense of being personally significant or at least what one is supposed to do to achieve this sense of personal significance. People work all of their lives to become "personally significant" according to the confines of their meaning-making system, only to find out that it no longer works. What provided a sense of significance no longer works. It no longer gives meaning because they are moving on, via a life transition, to another way of looking at things.

There is one other feature of structures of reasoning that's significant. It's called mutuality. Each successive stage has a clearer differentiation of self and other. What that means is the capacity to more clearly see the differences between self and other. As structures of reasoning grow, the ability to see others more clearly for who they are, rather than through our own projections onto them, marks a kind of maturation and growth that is called mutuality. Mutuality means that you are growing and expanding your ability to see others as "other" and to be more cognizant of different people and more capable of tolerating diversity and novelty.

So then, a structure of reasoning contains 3 variables. The first is a meaning making system, the second is a sense of personal significance, and the third is an increasingly differentiated sense of self and other called maturing mutuality. Oh yes, one more important element. Each stage has its own expression of vision, more or less clearly expressed in one way or another.

Let's peer in on some folks in various stages and transitions. They may or may not be clear about the vision for their lives. These cases appear as solidly in a stage of development of reasoning called "stage solid" or transitional, which is the shift period of movement from one stage to another.

There are two stages before the first one we will examine here. They are childhood and adolescence. We start here with a stage of meaning-making called Relationships. The meaning-making system in this stage is all about relationships in one way or another. They are the central concern and the measuring stick for most things. Meaning in the world is constituted by having or not having a relationship with another person, a group or a community. "Belonging" to someone or to a group outside of one's self is all important. What is good is what is good for the relationship, what is bad is what is negative for the relationship. Personal significance is measured in terms of being in a relationship. Consequently, if one is not in a relationship, there is a relentless search to find one and a sense of incompleteness and inferiority for not having a relationship.

One of the biggest problems in this stage is the third element of stages which we earlier called "self-other differentiation." In this stage the relationship is largely constituted by projection. The "other" is a large mix of the projections of what one wants the other person or group to be. So there is a great deal of let down when the "other" doesn't meet the image of what the other expects. The "other" is largely constituted by the unmet needs of the self to be in a relationship. The "other" is seen as truthful, trustworthy, faithful, authentic, attentive and that may be the way it all starts. But very quickly the veneer wears off and there are disappointments, disillusionment, disgust, outrage, and arguments, because one's "other" isn't measuring up to expectations. A great deal of time is spent being what the other needs. This might be called holding another person "hostage" to meeting one's own unmet and unsatisfied needs.

The vision in this stage is what constitutes much popular music: love songs about wanting to be in love, falling in love, or searing rejection of the break-up of this all important relationship. Visions here are based on perfect and ideal relationships, in one way or another. But they are not always relationships of a pair falling in love. They can also be relationships in communities, such as religious communities, belonging to a political movement, or belonging to a particular kind of organization like a cult or church.

This vision is usually so ideal and immature that it crumbles like a divorce, usually with as much disillusionment and anger. Cults and political movements with too lofty goals or an unusual interest in sin or condemnation coupled with human leaders usually don't last without great disillusionment, as one's vision or dream is grossly disappointed and must die a usually painful death because relationships have been so all-involving.

Because this is so, the immaturity of this Relationship stage experiences what cracks this stage from being stage-solid to entering into transition and growth. At least that is the normal progress of development. Usually something finally happens that kicks the person into the transition to the next stage of development, but that is not always the case. People can hold on to a stage of development because of fear of growth. We wonder why people go through the same thing over and over again, repeating the same pattern with the same unrealistic hopes, full of projection, and setting themselves up for rejection. The reason is the refusal to transition into the next stage of growth. This resistance keeps people in a DownSpiral and, over time, makes them ill in one way or another. In this case, a vision turns into unrealistic demands and expectations that never get met with any more than the person's own disappointment and eventual despair. This is a vision of meaning that needs to grow.

The growth is marked by a transition from Relationship to Self which is usually not easy, although it can be. Detachment would earlier not be a solution because everyone has to go through this stage called Relationships, especially if you are in a monastery. You cannot grow into a larger vision of unity or wholeness without experiencing what you have to experience. However, detachment is appropriate at a certain point and that point is in the first third of this transition. Detach from relationships that are not appropriate, attach to the those that are, and go through the complicated sifting of the two. Actually, we really know at this point, but it is difficult to let go of unproductive and unhealthy relationships because the "what" we must attach to is not clearly visible.

Rachel was in a relationship with the same man for 11 years. It was comfortable but they weren't going anywhere. Her boyfriend was as comfortable spending time away from her as time with her. But he was the center of her world because she was not her own center. Rachel's life was lived almost solely in relationship to her boyfriend. It's just the way things were. For Rachel, coming out of this relationship was like coming out into the fog. She didn't want to be alone, but she no longer wanted to be with anyone in a relationship. She couldn't go backwards and she didn't know how to go forward. At least that's how it seemed.

Rachel was on her way to being a "self" in her own right. And the next stage is the Self stage. But it takes a transition to be a "self." The transition was characterized by a breakdown in her meaning-making system. Nothing made sense. She didn't know where she was going or what she was going to do and she felt lost. As she needlessly compared herself to others, it seemed like everyone had a purpose or a direction, while she had no sense of personal significance. She could not make meaning of her life and any kind of vision seemed out of sight. In this transition, the real issue is what Rachel would "attach" to that would lead her to meaning. The issue was not nearly so much of letting go of relationships as it was finding where to put her "attachment" motivation for life.

The same was the case for Lenny who belongs to a street gang. Fierce and ferocious for his friends, he was a weakling in defending his deeper self. Lenny would risk his life for his fellow gang members while he projected the belief that they would do the same for him. They would not and did not after a street brawl where he was wounded seriously and his friends left him to fend for himself. The vision of the strength of the brotherhood of a street gang was so disillusioning that Lenny spent a long time wandering while he attempted to find where his attachment motivations could find a place. The gang had constituted his only meaning, his only sense of personal significance, and was the place of immature and misguided loyalties that were projections of what he wanted and needed in his life.

We have all been part of relationships that strung us out or failed our test of loyalty and shook us to our roots. Perhaps the experience has not been so dramatic for everyone, but it has been there at some level, because to grow, we have to experience this stage to mature into the next one.

Becoming a self is for sure a more mature stage of development in reasoning. Through the transition from relationships, the self has formed attachments that have unfolded into others in the journey toward becoming this new, more clearly defined and self-certain person. Some manner of productiveness and purpose has unfolded. There is an increased sense of right and wrong that also expresses in a more definite sense of black and white. Things are this way or that way. The law is the law and a deeper, while by no means complete, sense of principle has developed. One can become a knee-jerk conservative saving the country from spending or a knee-jerk liberal embracing the next cause that will insure greater democracy.

Larry is a high school coach completely dedicated to his work but also maintaining some sense of balance as a father. He is a solid citizen, a good worker, and an idealist who hates to lose. Those that know this best are the young men he coaches with hard and fast rules about homework, sleep time, and even dating and girls. He has a winning team most of the time, and agonizes that he has let his boys down whenever there is a loss. Everyone will tell you that Larry is very hard on himself. He also is something of a hero and is often recognized for his accomplishments, which are everything to him. Ask his wife; she knows she is second place to the row of trophies on the mantle, but she is also a solid stage "self" and supports the example her husband sets for the community and for their children. Larry's meaning-making system is constituted by being productive, accomplished and successful. His personal sense of significance is winning games and his vision is a state high school athletic championship.

LuAnn is a liberated woman in the market place of finance. She has worked hard to get where she is. She lets you know what her political views are long before you ask. She also lets you know that she is a woman who has worked hard to get where she is and that knows no one has done her any favors. Clipped and purposeful, she always gets the job done; in fact, she's always ahead of you. She works long and hard to stay that way. Her meaning making system is being productive, successful, and on top of everything. She is bright and competent and she is purpose-driven. Her vision, which is for her well thought out, is a certain monetary number for retirement and the ability to live well in the last third of her life. Her personal sense of significance is derived from being right and being on top.

Transition will come to both Larry and LuAnn in very different ways. Larry will lose his wife to cancer and LuAnn's company will be purchased by another company, not keen on keeping her and succeeding in letting her go in the reorganization.

Both are pushed into the transition that is the most difficult of all - an existential transition - which means that their sense of meaning-making is wholly questioned, really crushed. It is their "dark night" as surely as it came to Mother Teresa and all of the other saints. It is not that their vision is lost. It is more that it no longer has any meaning or purpose. Being "purpose driven" is a self-stage issue. It is far better to be vision-inspired.

This fog is thicker than ever before for both of these people. But as they question the meaning and purpose of their lives, both will find quite different solutions - one very spiritual and the other doing much the same thing in a different setting with altogether different motives and outcomes. But they both will experience a sense of this transition as the bottom dropping out. Nothing makes sense and little matters. Depression is a daily friend that will only be met by walking through it, albeit with a doctor's help in one case. In this transition everything that gives a sense of personal significance is deflated, and all that has given meaning is questioned and even dismissed as irrelevant. Most people in this stage have to go without any sense of purpose or meaning, while pretending for others that everything is fine or at least workable.

It is possible to hold on to this "self" stage sense of meaning and to pretend. But the result is flat lining, bitterness, stroke, heart attack, or some other serious mental or physical price. However, while it is difficult, is also very possible to see this time, often described as a mid-life crisis, as a time of change and renewal and an exciting, new beginning as folks move into a much more sophisticated and mature structure of reasoning and vision that is more clearly themselves than ever before.

A word needs to be said about the importance of each of these stages. You have to go through them. You can't detach from them and move ahead in a phony pretend way of being. It just won't work. If you are stage solid in your relationships, that's where you are, live it out until it's time for a change because it will come. If you are stage solid in your "self"stage, live it out and enjoy it. Change and transition will come, and because you know it will you can welcome it. All along the way you can have a healthy vision for each stage. Live it out fully and you will grow and mature more easily, and your transitions will be faster and easier. The post-it notes and goal setting of the previous step are tailored to enhance being stage-solid or transitional, but they will move you along your way. Don't underestimate the importance of these five goals you have set in the last step. The sooner you name what you want and get clear, the sooner you make goals and get clear, the sooner you will move forward with greater clarity.

As the crisis of self-stage transition moves forward, a whole new world emerges that is highly idiosyncratic. For each person it is different and unique because it is closer to the real self of the person. The next stage is Self/Other, and it is a mature stage of differentiating self and others. It is an increased time of mutuality which means that you more and more clearly see other people for how they are different. You are more easily able to differentiate from others and to tolerate diversity and novelty. Because that is so, you also have a clearer view of yourself. It is not that you have been wrong before; it is that you have grown on top of previous stages. You are smarter and wiser and more filled with gratitude.

In the Self/Other stage of meaning-making, the all-or-nothing, black and white judgments are disappearing and there are more and more grey areas, but also a deeper sense of enduring principles. Meaning-making may be more complex or it may be radically simple, but it is very personal and much less influenced by the externals. You know what you want and are much less influenced by distractions. Your sense of personal significance comes from a vision of what it is that grants you satisfaction and peace. This vision is not purpose driven. It is inspired by clear goals that are usually simpler than those that have emerged previously.

Vision emerges from goals, and these goals change whether in stages or transitions. The clearer you can be about what you want, even if it changes a million times, and the less you leave to stumbling along with chance, the more fulfilled you are likely to become - your brain likes it better that way and cooperates much more.

The bottom line is simply this. You are made to know a sense of personal significance that emerges from the way you make meaning in your life, all of your life. There is always vision for you if you will cooperate with life and not give up living it fully, high in the UpSpiral. A sense of personal significance is a strong manifestation of a neuropositive mind.

ΠeuroPositive Workouts©
Exercise Set #10

1. Do **The Basic Three**.

2. Find 3 ways to be kind and generous.

3. See if your goals begin to suggest a vision for you. If not, review your goals with your NPC.

4. Go to **The Positive Mind Blog** and share and support someone else by sharing your own experience.

5. Give a boost to your partner in some way.

6. Reread this step alone, review what is significant for you and spend time meditating on your vision for your life.

7. The **Vision for Personal Significance** module explores more individually your relationship to your Vision, your meaning making system and your sense of personal significance. This is an individual or pod experience.

. . . .

The Research Evidence
STEP 10

Kohlberg, Lawrence. **The Psychology of Moral Development: the Nature and Validity of Moral Stages.** San Francisco: Harper & Row, 1984.

Fowler, James W. **Stages of Faith: the Psychology of Human Development and the Quest for Meaning.** San Francisco: Harper & Row, 1981.

Step 11

Allowed this vision to navigate us and to attract to us others whom we allowed to be guides and sources of wisdom, who became the experience of MasteRevelation for us.

As you increasingly know what you want, you will attract to you people who can do a variety of important things for you. They will provide sources of information, clues and hints for the journey, connections, personal support, and some will believe in what you're doing. Your vibration is different when you have a very alive, very intact vision for yourself and the world. These people, and it is not always people, will point a direction and they will show up both when you expect them and when you don't. Their messages may not always be crystal clear and may take some interpretation and some time before they unfold. Sometimes it can be a fortune cookie. Keep the ones that seem to fit and disregard the rest, but remain open.

MasteRevelation springs forth with the knowledge of a greater and higher connectedness to things. It is like plugging into a vast network that you didn't know existed. Sometimes this network is buzzing and busy and other times it's quiet and seemingly inactive. But rest assured, once you have plugged into "the network," what you need will come to you in one way or another.

MasteRevelation is very simply those times when something happens that causes you to know there is a force, something beyond yourself, which you are a part of that is lining up the contacts and the happenings that awaken revelation. You know that there is a revealing that is significant. You just know that you're plugged into something greater than yourself of which you are intrinsically and essentially a part. What experiences like this have you already had?

Vince went to a group meeting and someone mentioned a book and a single author that proved, upon reading it, a major source of transformation and future direction.

Elizabeth met a business man on a flight who gave her his card. He was in international commerce. When she had a crisis in import/export issues for her company, she couldn't remember his name but remembered something unique about his card. She found it in a box where it had been tossed with many others. Elizabeth called him "out of the blue," told him her dilemma, and he immediately gave her the name and number of a man in Customs and international import and export who solved her problem and was a guide for her with any issues in Customs. One call, after fretful days and nights of trying to solve a problem, and one memory of a brief conversation, brought to mind this fellow she had met on the plane and the shape of his business card. That's MasteRevelation.

Margaret's husband died and the boss she had never really cared much for saw that she needed to be challenged and busy and opened the door for that to happen. She has a wonderfully expanded career from someone she didn't really even like.

It is very interesting to notice how many times people that we don't like or care for come through for us in a pinch, or offer help we would never have expected.

How many times have you disliked a person and later on they became a friend or even a spouse? They make movies about this. Some call them coincidences, but those that do have probably fallen away from this group by now. It's hard to get this far in these steps and think that all of these kinds of things are coincidences, when they are so perfectly orchestrated and choreographed. That's not to say that they can't seem awkward, difficult, and even embarrassing, but when you raise a certain curtain of skepticism and doubt and look behind them all, you begin to realize how much your vision connected to a reality larger than yourself has been "inactively" at work.

These experiences of MasteRevelation can happen so smoothly and seem so natural that it seems to be "just what is" - just very natural. The philosopher Thomas Aquinas once said that grace builds upon nature. Call it grace or whatever you will, but it's very slick and uncanny as to blend so beautifully with what is "natural" that it's just the way things unfold. It doesn't have to be troubling or come at the last hour, but sometimes it does. This is not about a god that has a predestined plan. It has nothing to do with predestination or divine plans. This is about your plans, goals and vision in which you have infinite freedom to engage, so long as it is for the good. And engagement is the key word here, because it is engagement that is something of the "god" here. To be engaged in a vision of life that builds your life and the lives of others - by that very fact, you are plugged into something like a grid or another part of the matrix of living that allows your good to unfold.

Amy had a great deal of difficulty with where to go to college. She got an unsolicited flyer in the mail, followed through, and ended up at the college of her choice. What a coincidence! Easy, natural, and "just there."

Albert was a noisy, hard to get along with, brilliant man who went through three graduate schools before he found his ideal place at the fourth. It was the only place that would take him, given his record. He would never have gone there in the first place, but he ended up there as the last place, loved it and became extremely successful in what he did. No so easy, not so natural, but quite a series of events for him to end up where he could have started, had he not been so completely in his own way. There is something to that - this "being in your own way," that a vision helps enormously but not completely, for you are always living and being through the lens of your humanity in both its strengths and their opposites.

Is there a key factor in MasterRevelation? The answer is yes and that factor is harmony. Coming from a harmonious place seems to enhance attracting people, especially in terms of MasteRevelation. They seem to show up more easily when harmony exists in one's world. If you are in conflict and putting the world around you in conflict, then you will have more difficulty listening and hearing MasteRevelation when it shows up. A harmonious person more easily allows others, both people and ideas, into their lives. Harmony is not just a matter of getting along with people. It more about getting along with one's self. Harmony is a signal that your VibeCore, your Step 7, is working for you.

Having 5 - 6 five year goals and an intact, viable vision does a great deal to create inner harmony. It just quiets you down, and the experience inwardly is one of greater peace and harmony. If it isn't, then review your goals, your wants and desires and see if they are coming from the person you are being.

The right hemisphere of your brain is the largest single part of your brain and its function is to get the whole picture and to perform the integrating function of the brain. It puts everything together in a more holistic sense. It provides for the wider, larger, wiser view and perspective of life. It works to create a greater harmony. Its function also provides for a better use and conservation of psychic energy. While the brain's potential is untapped, psychic energy is limited to a certain allotment each day. You only have so much of it and getting the bigger picture is one way that you can conserve energy. So harmony is extremely important.

What are the things that exercise and more greatly utilize the right hemisphere? Certainly having a vision is one of them, because you are working in the domain of the larger, greater picture. You are telling the brain how to organize and around what it is to organize. This is the right hemisphere at work. There are other activities that increase the use of the right hemisphere. The slow down of problem-solving thought processes of the left hemisphere is one of them. Both hemispheres are intricately connected and there is a not a strict division of hemispheric function. However, the left hemisphere is much more engaged in the daily business of keeping your life organized and moving throughout the day.

Meditation, contemplation, and thoughtful practices engage the right hemisphere.

A lack of stress engages the right hemisphere and allows it more psychic space to work. Within your brain there is the erogotrophic or work and stress center of the brain and there is the trophotropic (trophic means light) center of the brain. Less stress and more relaxation and savoring of a coffee, an object of beauty, a person, are the kinds of activities that help to slow down the left hemisphere and to engage the right in a greater sense of inner harmony.

Negative memories are stored and managed by the left hemisphere of the brain if they have not been worked through and integrated by the right hemisphere. The left hemisphere, not particularly concerned with harmony, remembers every detail of a negative event within the context in which it happens. It remembers both the memory and what slants and configures that particular memory, which means it may not be an accurate memory because it is the perception of the memory that is held in the left hemisphere.

Traumatic memories and negative memories that influence present day activities affect the lack of harmony and functioning of a person. It is the right hemisphere that performs this integration at the right time. During times of quiet, dreams, and reflection, the right hemisphere creates a larger understanding and mold for this memory and integrates it with the rest of life. Talking through negative memories in accurate and helpful settings that are integrated provides this function. However, reliving these negative memories, for the sake of just telling them, does not help, and in fact, is harmful because it rehearses the negativity again and even adds new and untrue dimensions to the negative memory.

At the right time, negative memories will surface in the right ways, and with the right techniques of managing negativity, they may be integrated by the right hemisphere in the overall larger picture with understanding and forgiveness. Negative harmful emotions that create on-going stress will be diffused. Positive emotion and positivity being don't repress negative memories or deny them. They actually are the ones that need attention to float to the top and then to be addressed from a more positive place. You don't have to go digging for negative memories, you don't have to unearth them in countless hours of analysis. They will emerge over time lived in the UpSpiral or they will be healed in your dreams, your work, and your life, and the positive process of your life moves forward. All this time, the right hemisphere will be performing its "wisdom" function of helping us see and look at many things differently, and maturation will create deepening levels of harmony. You do not have to chase your shadow side or your bad side or your past lives, if you believe you ever had them. What is necessary will be handled by the massive right hemisphere, but it will be handled best and most effectively by a life of ***positivity being*** that is led by a fuller and fuller vision which you form for your life as your UpSpiral, within your own sense of ever-increasing freedom.

If you focus on the negative, on the negatives in your past, and if that isn't enough, if you have to stir up imagined trouble from your past lives, you will surely have more and more negatives to resolve. But if your focus is on your vision, a positive vision backed by goals that are carefully formed and malleable, your vision will heal your past like an animal that sheds a skin. So go ahead and vision - and shed the skins of the past. As you do shed these skins that need no further examination than getting on with your life, it is the unfolding future, living life in an UpSpiral, using your strengths, that will create the harmony that will surely attract the many aspects of your MasteRevelation to you. It just happens.

Looking closer at the brain we find that the frontal lobes (called frontal lobes because they are just behind your forehead) perform what is called the "executive functions" of the brain. Millions of years in formation, balancing the reptilian brain of survival and fight/flight responses, are these lobes of great power and significance to the unfolding of our consciousness. In the back of the median portion of these frontal lobes are things called mirror neurons. They are truly amazing and fascinating. Their function? They enable you to recognize and experience the world of another person in terms of the meaning of what they are saying, and particularly the feelings or the nuances of the other person's experience. In other words, these are the neurons which help us understand how a person is feeling from their perspective and from their unique "feel" and take on the world. It is the way we "sync-up" and get in harmony with the experience of another person. Some people use them a lot; other people use them, well, not so much. You have to be a receptive listener, capable of "getting" or comprehending the experience of the other. Many people don't care about another's experience and some are too busy always telling their own story or how everybody else's story should go or how it should end. You know who they are, don't you? These tiny, tiny mirror neurons are part of what is essential in the ever maturing self-other process of differentiation discussed in Step 10. As you become more mature, more tolerant of the "other," more capable of experiencing, allowing novelty and diversity, these mirror neurons are more and more at work. They help to create this deeper and deeper sense of harmony as they are allowed to mature and grow into the fullness of a person whose UpSpiral experience is secure enough to get out of themselves and into the really different experience of another. So be very careful the next time you quickly say, "Oh, I know just how you feel." Everybody believes their experiencing is unique and usually this comment doesn't provide a sense of understanding for the other person. Don't say it because it's not true, and most people don't like to hear it. If we have to say anything at all, we say, "I may have had a similar experience, does this sound something like yours?" or something like it that creates a sense of identification, rather than experience for the other person of trying to share their life with a "know-it-all."

Use your mirror neurons to identify and attune yourself with others. As others feel comprehended and understood by you, they seek to understand what you're about and what you're doing. Whether or not you believe in auras, your attunement to your own feelings and state of being in your UpSpiral and your Emotional Scale is perceived by others and particularly by people who are drawn to you and to your vision. See who you meet, see who begins a conversation with you waiting in a line, observe those times when you went to something that didn't seem at all promising and you made a contact "out of the blue." Your capacity to attune yourself to the experience of others will give off signals that will bring to you people who are parts of your larger MasteRevelation.

There is a lot of talk and concern about negative core beliefs, about going back into one's past and healing them, changing them, picking at them. People who are concerned about this, even professionals, usually don't have a full enough repertoire at their command to know what else to do to accomplish what they call problem-solving.

You may have some negative core beliefs and they may also be deep-seated. It will do no good to dig them out, pull them out, uproot them, hypnotize them or anything else that doesn't allow them to emerge, if even that is necessary. Negative beliefs will emerge in a positive UpSpiral. They will emerge naturally, if they need to, and they will emerge at a time when you are in a place, so different from them, that you can actually look at them, examine them, and change them because they just don't fit anymore.

It is true that when we approach the negative and take it on in a definitive way, anxiety and stress drop, simply from not avoiding and resisting them. However, that is the case for present and conscious negativity that we are trying to avoid. It is not the case with negative beliefs that are comfortably buried by a particular shape and expression of the ego that works for a while. If you get higher in your UpSpiral and as you live there for a while, what you need to work on, especially in terms of negative core beliefs, will come to you easily and much less painfully. A neuropositive mind handles negative information and memories more effectively and efficiently. And what you do in your examination of these beliefs will get much more than a temporary fix. The results will be lasting.

A part of the great power of vision is that it changes negative core beliefs just because they don't fit anymore. They aren't workable and so we change our minds and move in different and far more satisfying directions.

A vision doesn't have to have a purpose or a meaning, in terms of a black and white explanation of the good and the purpose of anything. The purpose of a vision is joy. What you do for joy will always give back in its own time and its own way to those who are able to receive. A vision has purpose because it makes you a channel of love, peace, gratitude, joy, and hope.

ΠeuroPositive Workouts©
Exercise Set #11

1. Begin to develop the "intensify" phase of the Emotional Gym. You can do this with **The Emotional Smile** exercise. When you awaken each morning, smile as widely as you can. You don't have to feel like smiling, you just smile as widely as you smile. Pulse each of the emotions of **The Emotional Gym** 25x, intensifying the feelings as you practice each emotion. Remember to smile broadly while you do the exercise. Smiling broadly wakes up neuropathways in the brain that are happy and positive and you begin to create your mood for the day.

2. Do the other two exercises of **The Basic 3** and follow the usual regimen of assignments to this point.

3. Make a list of 3 people you can invite into your **MasteRevelation** experience by talking with them and getting their advice.

4. The **MasteRevelation** module is about networking and more than networking. It is about building alliances, partnerships, finding and letting the people find you who carry out your vision. It is also about what you have to "stop doing" for revelation to work. Talk with your NPC. This can be a pod or an individual experience.

The Research Evidence
STEP 11

Gladwell, Malcolm. **The Tipping Point: How Little Things Can Make a Big Difference.** Boston: Little, Brown, 2000.

Csikszentmihalyi, Mihaly. *Creativity: Flow and the Psychology of Discovery and Invention.* New York: HarperCollinsPublishers, 1996.

Rath, Tom. **Vital Friends: the People You Can't Afford to Live Without.** New York, NY: Gallup, 2006.

Step 12

Shared this program and these steps with those who, demonstrated by their lives and interest, showed a readiness to hear them.

Here you are, if you have worked each of these steps through at least once, in a whole new place with an entirely expanded consciousness. Here, on this side of the process, how do you and your world look? It is uniquely, idiosyncratically a different change for everyone, but there are some common strains of experience.

You know that you see things differently. You know, because you can recognize and manage being in an UpSpiral or a DownSpiral, that your life has new power that seems so natural, like it's always been there. You're aware, if you have worked these Steps, that sustaining an UpSpiral has become a part of just the way you are, the way you do things. It just "is" to the point that it is hard to believe that there was never a time when you differentiated between being in an UpSpiral or a DownSpiral. Those DownSpiral times that just seemed to be a part of life that came and went on their own power are now a myth. You know that's not true and that you control, within a wide sphere, where you are and how long you stay there. By now, you are so extremely discontent with yourself when you aren't in a higher UpSpiral that you want more and quickly to be able to get there. But the more times you work these steps, the deeper and more quickly that happens.

At this point, it may even be a little hard to believe that everyone doesn't just "get" living in an UpSpiral. It seems to be such good common sense, even though we know better than that. Isn't it incredible that at this point, all of your life has been spent at least somewhere in the

UpSpiral and little or none in the DownSpiral? We wish it for everyone, we want it for those we love, and we're even willing to do what it takes to help others to have the experience, or rather their experience, of what this journey is like.

Wanting to give it away is a natural experience. Wanting to influence others to the journey is in our blood. We just want to give away good things and share them with others.

It becomes harder and harder to understand why others want to hold onto negativity to the extent that for many has become an addiction. The old ego that wants to re-emerge has a tight hold on keeping itself alive. It will create an addictive grip on those who will be satisfied with yo-yoing within some up and down space of the Spiral of life. But this almost, and not so almost, addictive negative hold of the old ego isn't an easy thing to have the courage to move beyond. Sometimes you feel that you've just come so far, it's hard to remember what it was like to know yourself in a limited, narrow way that no longer worked - but you did it anyway because you didn't know a new, better way and couldn't risk following it. To those who have not taken the journey, positivity being can seem such a shallow way to change. And that is the power of the old ego. Are there any worse or more belittling accusations in our world than having to have the answers and to "know," only to be told that we are superficial, unrealistic, limited in our experience of pain and suffering, and that we just don't know what it's like?

The caterpillar and the butterfly are such good models to remember here. When a caterpillar spins its cocoon of isolation, maybe it is even thinking, if it thinks in its own way, that it is safe. How in the world does a caterpillar become a butterfly inside that cocoon, when they are so entirely different? If you cut open a caterpillar just before it spins its cocoon, there is no evidence of a butterfly whatsoever. But this is even more compelling. In the process of the transformation, the caterpillar has killer cells that attempt to kill the new emerging growth in its process to protect itself. How much like human growth! It is as though the old ego has killer cells to protect itself against the new emerging ego and its fuller expression of the real self. But you know, if you will remember how much easier it was to be your own isolated caterpillar. How incredulous did it seem to you when you heard that you could become a butterfly of unique beauty, while you were still a caterpillar wanting to isolate in your safe world of what was known and comfortable? These claims that you have experienced and shown to be true seemed so impossible, formidable, incredible and even ridiculous. You were not about to be another Pollyanna, as it seemed that was what this was all about.

But here you are, a butterfly wanting to tell all the caterpillars in your life that they don't have to crawl - that they can fly. And as you have discovered, not everyone is willing to hear it, try it, or wants to bother. There are a lot of old caterpillars in the world who made the decision to remain just as they are and crawl on the bellies of their discontent and negativity. Humans have this thing called free will and choice about whether or not they will spin the chrysalis of change, enlightment and expanded consciousness, or remain in a world reporting the bad news of those who feed and sustain the old ego by soaking it up.

Before we step further into this desire to share and include others and the responsibility we have for doing so, let's consider a little more what we have experienced to this point in building a neuropositive brain and mind.

After we were convinced, from our success at it, that there really was something to this business of remaining in and sustaining an UpSpiral, the ability to differentiate between UpSpiral living and DownSpiral living gradually became clearer and clearer. In some cases we changed friends and surroundings, and we certainly became clearer about what we watched, listened to, and engaged in. We became much more selective about what we wanted to feed the brain. Our brain food came under scrutiny. We moved from things that were unnecessarily negative, melancholy, and victim-supporting, to the things that feed a positive mind with new images, ideas, experiences, and even music. Just naturally, we began to move away from things that were not UpSpiral things for the Mind and the brain. We had long suspected that they were not doing us much good but we were convinced that we had to stay "informed" until we realized that the news just wasn't informing us. It was conditioning us to believe that it represented our world. Do you remember your first reaction to someone's suggestion, early on in this process, to turn off the television or other predominant forms of external entertainment for 90 days so you could assess their effect and what you really wanted? Many of you didn't even think you could do it. We have never heard anyone say that they missed it, once they had begun. Positivity being is ready to fill a vacuum of emptiness or loneliness.

After thirty days of marking on a calendar what you wanted your UpSpiral Score to be and also writing down something you wanted on that calendar, you saw results. The results were very real and they belonged to you.

With the beginning capacity to lean toward, and even move more actively, by using the Emotional Gym and others exercises toward the UpSpiral, it was time to find out what your strengths were. The superhighways of values and abilities became so strengthening that you found out that it was true that you had the strengths at your finger tips, strengths that were uniquely yours to stay in an UpSpiral, by using them. It was incredible, do you recall, to learn that the more you used your very own set of strengths you had been growing all of your life, the happier you would be. The fact that there was a direct link between using your strengths and becoming happier took some time to learn because it was so simple. How could this have been overlooked in our education? It was so obvious. But now we know that what we do not know and comprehend isn't obvious until we learn it, especially when it's so simple. It is difficult to apprehend the truly simple when the old ego that is fighting for its life to stay alive is working to keep the brain from apprehending new truth. Sometimes it takes a while, it takes repetition and example from others, but most of all the ongoing flow of life will bring the situations that demand a new apprehension of truth. And still the old ego will fight a dirty fight to stay in control of a consciousness that no longer serves us.

Being tested for real strengths and realizing that they are who we are has been an explosive experience for many. Others have known all the time but paid little or no attention because these strengths weren't valued. Many of us were even criticized when we used the very strengths that were who we really are, so we put them away and even hid them or pretended that we were something different. It was hard to escape the impact of our strengths when they resulted from a scientific test and were in front of us on paper. But what a gift they were! Learning that all of our strengths had opposites called character defects or weaknesses, that these realities were the opposite ends of the same stick, was sobering. Almost as sobering was realizing that when we were DownSpiraling, we had conditioned ourselves to use the opposite of our strengths, rather than our strengths themselves. It was also surprising for many of us when we learned that our addictions grew out of spending too much time in this territory of our DownSpiraling weaknesses.

Depending upon how many times you have been through these steps, that may still be happening, but eventually it stops because knowing and growing strengths more and more deeply makes our weaknesses become irrelevant to our lives.

It was an easy step to take strengths into a discovery of the phenomenon of "flow." The repeated and continual use of strengths walks us easily into this concept of life that we can be "one with the music," in flow with the things we love, with the power to make lesser tasks flow activities as well. "Just this" has been a complete surprise that our meditation could be the very living of our lives, and we still discover that on deeper and more expansive levels. Turning everything into "flow" seemed so impossible, but the longer we do it, the more we expect it to happen and the more we create it in aspect after aspect of our lives.

For many of us who had difficulty with focus and attention and all of the mind emptying exercises, it was a relief to find that this focus that elevated us to joy and gratitude and oneness could be found in the experience of flow as meditation, and became so much easier for us than we ever thought it could be. The detachment exercises which had been so much and so confusing became so much easier when we found that the best way to detach from distractions was to focus on the attraction of the flow experience. We learned to let go to it, we did "just this," we forgot the ego, and immersed ourselves in what we love - and away we went as hours flew by in what seemed to be short spaces of time. We have learned to keep the ego out of this by not evaluating or comparing what we are doing, focusing on "just this" and loving doing it. We get so good at this that we can even apply it to things that we thought were going to be much more difficult.

Flow is an experience that deepens us and plugs us into our longings and desires. The more time we spend in our strengths, the more we become aware of what we want. Some of these things have been small things, some of them material things, and many other things, just things we had to get out of our system so we could move onto other things. All of these desires and longings and wants that were unleashed expressed themselves in five goals that we have already accomplished, made great progress in doing, or realized, after a time, that we didn't want them but that they pointed to something else that was even more important.

Some of us balked at the idea of having goals because we thought it meant that we couldn't be the free spirits that we fashioned ourselves to believe that we were. We wanted things to "just unfold" and realized that they had been unfolding all over the place, and that we had been all over the place keeping up with them without either a sense of direction or a sense of knowing who we really were. These goals have not limited us, but have given direction to what will always unfold - the pathways to what we want.

What was perhaps more surprising that anything in this process was that our goals, when they really reflected who we were being and becoming, gave rise to a vision for our lives. How we would give who we are to the world and leave our own unique legacies, with great freedom, led us from being purpose driven to vision inspired.

The particulars of the vision may have changed, but there was always the guiding North Star when we aimed our sights at finding out what it was.

MasteRevelation has seemed to come out of the blue. We now know the people who show up and the experiences that happen that guide our course give us answers, connections, and just simply network us to our oneness in this universe of ours. We could all make lists of the "coincidences" and surprises along the way that revealed our path and provided what we needed, if not before, then just when we needed it. New life, new friends, new significant connections, little and very big shifts in consciousness, have been the way of MasteRevelation which has just happened as an outgrowth of having a vision.

All of this is ours and we want to share it because we know this truth very deeply. You cannot keep what you do not give away. In the end, we know that we really learn what we teach and share. And so here we are at the doorway of this step with the recollections of what we have experienced, knowing we must give it away. Sometimes it's hard to realize what we have and what we've been through in this process because it has happened gradually and as a seemingly natural part of our lives. It is easy to take for granted and it is easy to forget where we were when we started, or that we ever really were there. It sometimes seems impossible to grasp. That's just the way growth is.

But we pause here to know and touch the belief that our deepest desire is to give and share this. We know that not everyone is ready, that many are not even open - or so they seem. We would like to believe that we have attracted those who need to hear this to us by our own nature. And that is actually the truth. It is also true that you never know if what you say or do will be acted upon by another. You may never know. But you can trust that the people who are around you and the folks that you have the capacity to influence will hear and make choices. You already know that those you least likely expected to be interested are also now those going through these 12 Steps, and they will love you forever for having been their way in the door.

Perhaps the greatest danger is complacency, because the process of learning here, after a time, seems so normal and so much a part of our lives that we forget to talk about it and share it. It just is! But others do not have it, and without a prophet, the people don't hear. You are that prophet. The word prophet does not mean to tell the future. It comes from the Greek word which means "to bear forth or to bring forth, to proclaim." A prophet proclaims the truth and you, yes, you, are a prophet.

It seems so simple to say that positivity being, an UpSpiral, strengths, flow, goals, a vision, and the revelation that brings them all to us is the sheer magic of the Universe. Who can believe it? Those who are hungry, those who don't know what they want, those who are caught up in negativity as a way of life, those who are lonely, those who have no peace. And on and on...

Everyone's experience with this process you now have within you will be different, but everyone deserves the right to know what an UpSpiral and their strengths can do in their life. The pursuit of happiness was written into the founding documents of this country because their authors knew it was absolutely essential to freedom.

Proclaim freedom in your way. But set in your sights the folks you want to reach, and be forever open to those you thought you never would. Use every opportunity to share your experience. Create opportunities to share your experience. It surely is true that the more you give this away, the more will come to you in return and belong to you. Your consciousness will deepen as you see those you have influenced respond in their way.

You have learned that there is a new story about your life. You have stopped telling the old story of being a victim. Your new story is so full of authenticity and vitality that only you can tell it, even when you think no one is really listening. They are listening, even while they may be trying to get away from you. You may be the start of their journey or one more voice along the way, or you may be even more of a guide for them along the way.

There have been enough solutions, well-meaning as they are, that are only band aids to feeling flat-lined, purposeless, and lost in what seems meaningless. People most want to experience a sense of personal significance, a sense of importance, and a sense of Oneness. Those who need it are hard-pressed to believe they will find it in another 12 step program, especially one that aims toward an UpSpiral. The homelessness problem is an external sign of a larger interior epidemic. It is not essentially one of no external place to stay and call home. It is not finding a home within one's self. Keep inviting the "homeless" into the warmth of your own UpSpiral home, until they find a similar home within themselves.

∏euroPositive Workouts©
Exercise Set #12

1. Make a list of the people with whom you will share these steps.

2. Do **The Basic Three**.

3. Use the regimen that you have developed throughout the program.

4. Work these steps again from the beginning and deepen each one.

5. Blog.

6. Give your partner a boost.

7. **The Reflections** module is for gaining the broad, integrative view of what your journey through the steps had produced for you thus far and what the next journey through them needs to accomplish in you. This is an individual module.

8. Take the Post Test of **The NeuroPositive Mind Test** at www.gotoani.com.

- -

The Research Evidence
STEP 12

Csikszentmihalyi, Mihaly. **Flow: the Psychology of Optimal Experience.** New York: Harper & Row, 1990.

Wagner, Rodd, and Gale Muller. **Power of 2: How to Make the Most of Your Partnerships at Work and in Life.** New York: Gallup, 2009.

12 NEW STEPS FOR A NEW MILLENNIUM
The UpSpiraLife Group

PART II

The 12 Ways & Means

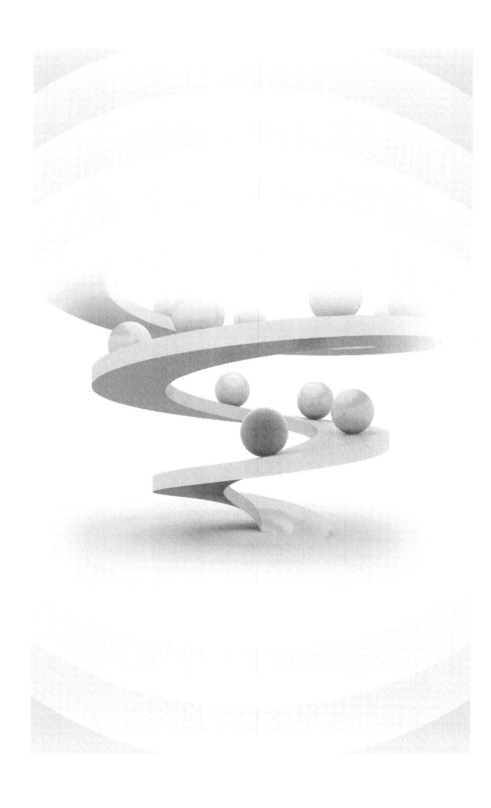

The 12 Ways and Means
The Culture of the Group

The "ways and means" form the culture of the group. They are the ways we do things, the means by which we do them. A "way" is a path to be followed, a direction to be taken on the journey. The "means" are the tools to make the journey. They are the basic ways that the UpSpiraLife process works. Groups will differ from place to place, but these guidelines are essential to maintaining and guiding each group. Groups should be similar enough so that someone who is going to more than one meeting or several meetings in a short period or someone from a group in another place can recognize the meeting, slide into the comfortable shoes of familiarity with the process and the culture and know they are in an UpSpiraLife Group. This is the way it works. The Ways and Means are tested and proven tried and true.

The Ways & Means

1

Heart-To-Heart Identification

The core and soul of the UpSpiraLife group meeting is "heart to heart" identification. "Positive Identification" is the signature feature of the cohesion of the group. It is the central way learning happens. When people identify with each other, it creates oneness and instant learning.

The basis of the UpSpiraLife group is "heart-to-heart" identification. This identification reduces resistance by "being heard," for the purpose of moving higher in the UpSpiral. "Heart-to-heart" means the attempt to listen, hear, and to get some feeling for what the other person is saying. This is more than polite listening and nodding your head, although that's a part of it. You are getting the larger picture of what another person is saying, identifying with something in your own experience. Empathy is probably the word used to most to express this intention, but this is a little more and different than simple empathy. Empathy is the capacity to feel what another person is feeling. Heart-to-heart identification is more like, "I hear where you're coming from and I understand." Here you are also listening to the content of what someone is saying so that you can "get it and be there with them in their experience." This is the capacity that creates great friendships and even romance.

To do this we have to have some degree of attunement with ourselves. We have to have some level of "in touch-ness" with our own inner experience. Attunement means that we are in touch with what we think and feel. This is what the UpSpiraLife group process helps us to do. It is an ideal we aim for. But doing this also enables us to be more in touch with ourselves. You will find that when everyone in the group shares at some level of this attunement with self and others, that oneness begins to develop and grow stronger in the group.

What we are actually doing is using the mirror neurons that are behind the forebrain. These mirror neurons are expressly for the purpose of being able to identify with the experience of another in such a way that they can feel understood, and thus you have the experience of understanding. People who only talk and never listen, and really hear, have not developed the capacity of the mirror neurons. Ever increasing mutuality is a sign of maturation. It is this maturation that gets derailed in selfishness, addiction and mental illness. The individual is less and less able to accurately see and understand the experience of another, and actual regression in development can take place. Ever increasing mutuality means the ability to more and more accurately read and know what another person is experiencing. It is an increasing ability to get out of your own experience and to get into the experience of another. But it also means that you are able to be more and more in attunement with yourself and able to be more transparent to others. You are more easily seen and heard by those you wish to understand you because you are clearer and clearer with what you are feeling and being. Your mirror is less cloudy and cleaner and at the same time. You are better able to see through the cloudiness of the mirror of another person. A clear indicator of maturation is this ability to take in, to accurately apprehend, and then mirror back to the other person an increasingly accurate sense of what they said and where they're coming from. A good technique, when you are trying to give the gift of understanding to another person, is to simply ask, "Did I get it? Did I get where you're coming from?"

There is another part of your brain that helps this process as well, and it is the right hemisphere behind the right forebrain. This large area of the brain, its most massive computer in a sense, has the function of getting the whole picture. Most of the time our left hemisphere is just getting us through the day. While it is a stretch to claim that the left hemisphere is in charge of daily problem solving, and that the right hemisphere is more of the "whole picture," it is still basically true. The brain works as a whole and a high differentiation of left and right hemisphere functioning is not altogether correct. But it is largely the case that the left hemisphere is more given to daily problem solving and that the right hemisphere, behind the right forebrain, is doing the larger work of perception and integration. The step back from the left hemisphere to the right hemisphere is one of tuning in, slowing down, opening the heart, so to speak. You have the strengths to do this essential piece of UpSpiral growth into neuropositivity being.

It is the foundation of true support. People most want the experience of being understood. It helps us all make sense out of our lives. So listen and hear. How receptive to hearing others are you? How open is your heart? If your answer to this is, "not very," as it is more your desire, it will open you more and help you into the UpSpiral. Not everyone begins at the same place, so be gentle with yourself if you have difficulty with this. However, don't be so gentle that you don't challenge yourself to grow.

But how will the other person know that you hear them? How do you know when someone really hears you? You know, you just know. "Being there" and hearing communicates our presence which is different than just showing up and hanging out.

This is a capacity that grows with practice and comes over time. If you find difficulty, just be patient. A great starter is eye contact. Look at the person who is looking at you, rather than at your watch, your book, the door, another person, or someone's great shoes. And, please, don't look at the ceiling!

Wrap your mind with your emotions and take in the experience of the other person. As much as you can, feel what they are feeling, understand what they are saying, and positively identify with the positive experience they are sharing.

Our deepest need is to be understood, to be connected to others by feeling like they get us and we get them. In fact, this is oftentimes the beginning of romance and significant friendships. Feeling understood and feeling like you are in touch with another person releases the oxytocin hormone. It is the feel good, feel loving, caring and connected hormone in us that connects a mother and father to a newborn and also connects us to one another.

Where in your world are you understood? Where in your world are the positives in you understood and appreciated? It is important that our negative experiences be understood by someone who knows us. Negative identification is important, but it is not the purpose of the UpSpiraLife group. Positive identification often does not happen with anyone in our lives, even those to whom we are closest. Positive identification is the purpose of the UpSpiraLife group. There is enormous power in positive identification. It is this enormous power that you will discover when you experience it in an UpSpiraLife group, especially on a weekly basis.

In summary, it is possible that identification with another person can occur just in listening and being able to mirror back their words. Even that level of "parroting" can be effective in letting another person know they are heard. Having what we said parroted back to us is better than not being heard at all. At least we know that we are being heard, even if there is a sense of not being received. It is far better and much more effective to mirror back what someone is saying with understanding and a felt connection with their experience. It is an amazing thing when it actually happens to us in communicating with another person. The mirroring back is best done with deep listening, paying attention, a receptive look, like a smile or a nodding head. People know when we are hearing and receiving them, and we know when we are heard in an understanding and compassionate way. This is empathy, but with a little more attached to it.

The Ways & Means

2

Adhere to the Format

All groups must adhere to the prescribed format of the UpSpiral Life Group as set forth by the Applied Neuroscience Institute. Do not change or vary the parts of the format of the group. They are there and in this order for a purpose. So, adhere to the format.

The leader's share at the beginning of the meeting is the leader's own identification with the material that is read. The leader starts the sharing with "I" statements and their own personal experience with the material being read. The documents for all UpSpiral groups are in this book, beginning on page 5. See page 13 for the format. So, adhere to the format.

Can this process grow tiresome and old? Yes, but the solution is not to try and make things more entertaining by adding new activities. You cannot invent enough new ones. The central aim of the group will become diffuse, and members will stop attending. Yes, it can grow old if three things happen.

1. The process is as alive as the "heart-to-heart" sharing of individuals and the "heart-to-heart" hearing of the members.

2. A lack of a flow of new membership into the group. As people learn and pass on what they experience, especially to new members, the group grows.

3. The three reinforcements of the group process are not utilized.

They are called MPB. That stands for meetings, partners, and the blog. Each of these is discussed in other portions of the Ways and Means. In short, everyone is most reinforced in their participation by attending a meeting, making a contribution to the UpSpiraLife Group national blog, and by having to connect with (email, text, phone) their group partner to share briefly each week about their journey in the UpSpiral. Reinforcement and mutual support are key.

Do these things regularly and well and you will see your groups grow and flower. There are, however, many things that can be done outside the one hour session of the UpSpiraLife group. Other groups have had workshops only on strengths, or flow or vision, and others have developed pods of two or three members who work on their goals together. So, adhere to the format.

Activities outside of the regular meetings for fun or learning are strongly encouraged. But the format of the group is something like "sacrosanct" (and that doesn't mean that anything can't change over time), but there has to be continuity from one group to the next. The process needs to feel as comfortable as slipping into an old pair of slippers. An UpSpiraLife group should be an UpSpiraLife group, wherever it's happening, and going there should be comfortable and should enable easy participation in a familiar process. Within the format, though, you will find that each group has its own distinct personality, focus and manner, and that there is great variety and novelty in all of the groups. In fact, it is having the solid core of the format that allows for a starting place for diversity, creativity, and novelty. So, adhere to the format.

Questions about adherence to the format and its use can always be directed to the national office.

The Ways & Means

3

Share How It Works Not How You Don't

What will help everyone is if you share from your heart and from your gut. Nix the "teachy-teachy," "let me teach you from my experience" talk. Tell your story to tell your story for your own self-expression. The Universe will know exactly who needs it, why and where to take it. Most of the time, you may never know. Share the negative, share your struggle. But focus on solution-finding.

We begin with the Preamble each time because it reminds us that this is not a problem-oriented group or a discussion group. It is a particular process for growing the well-lived UpSpiral life and growing the UpSpiral of your positive mind.

You will introduce your share in the Group by stating your first name, along with your UpSpiral Score.

The purpose of your share in the UpSpiraLife group is to increase the UpSpiral of the entire group by demonstrating how you have used positivity and the tools of **Growing The Positive Mind** in your life. <u>**Your share is characterized by specific examples of times you have used your positive mind and spirit and increased the positivity and UpSpiral in your life.**</u> You can bring a challenge you might be currently facing or have already dealt with, but always by using the tools of the UpSpiral in the unique way that you apply them in your own life. The challenge is not the focus of your share, but rather the tools of the

UpSpiraLife group that you have used to deal with the challenge. At all times, you are encouraged to share in a focused, purposeful, and concise manner.

If you have questions or comments about the process or design of the group, they belong in the "meeting after the meeting." They are not part of the regular format of the UpSpiraLife Group.

A small portion of your share might consist of what seems negative or problematic, but only as a means of talking about how your positive mind is dealing with an issue or problem. Neither the focus nor the bulk of your share is ever on the problem or the issue. This is not a problem-oriented, issue-sharing, "fix-it" group, except in the ways the positive mind and the tools of the program provide that solution. This group is not a discussion of how your week has gone or a general reporting in - it is specifically focused on growing the positive mind. How are you making it work? This kind of share from group members will emerge as an overall "roadmap" that will lift and increase the positive consciousness of everyone in the group who has dedicated themselves to growing a positive mind. There are many, many tools. How are you using them in the events of your life?

You are sharing how it works, that is, how what you are learning and the always deepening levels of positivity are enlarging and engaging you in a happier, more satisfying, and more productive life. The UpSpiraLife group is not a place where you come to "dump" what is not working. "Dumping" is talking only about what is negative without offering the solution you are working on, or how you are attempting to use the tools to meet the challenge. The purpose of the group is not to fix or solve your dilemma.

Simply put, you are growing your UpSpiral positive mind and you are sharing the good things that are coming from doing that. You are not sharing your struggles, or blocks, or resistance, or lapses in not doing so unless you can show the group the positive turn or benefit you are making from engaging your UpSpiral positivity to deal with them. There is nothing wrong with sharing what is negative, what doesn't feel good, and what has caused a DownSpiral, so long as you share what tools you are using to grow the neuropositive mind. Don't dwell on the negative. Dwell on the solution.

If you haven't been working your positive mind, if you haven't done the homework or haven't engaged the tools you are learning, then it is best to just listen and be lifted by the shares of the other members in the group. Sometimes, the best way to get back into an UpSpiral is to be a part of the group and just to listen.

If you have questions or comments about the process or design of the group, they belong in the "meeting after the meeting." They are not part of the regular format of the UpSpiraLife Group.

The Ways & Means

4

"I" is the Pronoun of the Group

"I" is the pronoun of the group. "You" is rarely ever used because you are talking about "I," your own experience, your own insight, and your own application of growth in positivity. "We should" and "you should" and "I have a suggestion" is off-base language and is not permitted at any time. The only "shoulds" and "suggestions" are for one's self, never for another group member.

"I" is the pronoun of the group. "You" is rarely ever used because you are talking about "I," your own experience, your own insight, and your own application of growth in positivity. "We should" and "you should" and "I have a suggestion" is off-base language and is not permitted at any time. Suggestions are for one's self and not for other group members. This is a guideline worth repeating because it is so essential.

When in the world do you have an experience of being able to talk about yourself, if just for a few minutes, especially in a positive sense? Not often. People don't seem to want to hear what is good and positive about us, but that is not the case in this group. The richer and the more "textured" you give your "I" statements, the more it will help the group.

What you are reaching for in your "I" statements is not a superficial, off the top of your head kind of thing. You are really reaching inside yourself and you are describing your "I am-ness." You are not just talking about what you think, but you are also talking about what you are experiencing.

Talk from the gut about your challenges in using a neuropositive mind, and be broad in your description of what you did and how it worked for you. Paint a picture of your experience that it is easy for members of your group to identify with and to experience along with you regarding what's going on in your world.

You want to make it easy for group members to identify with what you're saying by not being superficial. Reach for words, phrases, even colors, that describe your experience. Don't be surprised if your group leader asks you for clarification and to say even more about what you are experiencing. You are the artist and you're painting the picture of what's going on with you so well that your group members can identify with you. **Don't make people guess at what's going on with you.**

Use the "I" and talk about what you are experiencing and feeling. While it is a difficult thing to do, you are not telling your story by giving a long, drawn out account of what's happening with you. Share as little of the story as possible and as much about what you are experiencing and feeling as you can. Especially share, in great detail, how you used neuropositive strategies to deal with what you're sharing.

A good rule of thumb is to be short on story-telling and longer on the experiential/feeling/gut level reactions you have had or are having. How are you bringing the negative into the light of the positive? Sometimes this is very difficult and you just can't do it, but you can share the attempt.

We very seldom get to hear people share strategies for how they remain positive and how they stay in an UpSpiral. That is what this group is for. So when you share that, do it with texture, color and fiber. And if this is difficult for you when you start, know that over time, you will get better at making an UpSpiraLife group share.

The great temptation is to get into "story." We tend to want to share our stories, blow by blow, not missing a detail. If you like to do this, there are groups that specialize in story telling. Join one. But you are not learning to be a storyteller here, as valuable and wonderful as that skill might be. You are learning to be a positive UpSpiral person who can live an UpSpiral life. Your "story" can actually get in the way of your description of how you use the tools of positivity, and the latter is the focus of this group. Learn to give just enough information to frame what you have to say about the positivity work you are doing, and dwell on what being in an UpSpiral does for you, how it feels, and what it creates and brings into your life.

This is a group where you get to do something that you don't get to do for very long anywhere else, and that is talk about the positive things, the good things, and how you are bringing them into your life. Not only do you get to talk about your UpSpiraLife growth, but you also have people who are going to listen to you and identify with what you say. Usually people don't let us talk very long about what is positive in our lives before they indicate some kind of disinterest. Here you get to share the good and have what you share received by others who actually want to hear it.

It is an incredible journey to find the positive "I" and to speak from it. Take the journey and find your gratitude, love, peace, joy, and hope, and share it with others so they can experience your "I" with you.

The Ways & Means

5

Bring A Listening Heart

Bring the gift of what your "I" has to share with your own personal "voice." And then bring its companion, a listening heart. Open your heart and listen; really hear what people are saying or trying to say but can't. Be the ears that make everyone in the group "feel" and have the experience of being "heard," without comment, suggestion or evaluation. Just being able to talk with your own voice and be heard is a great, great gift.

"Lock on" is a term used when a fighter jet has locked into position a target that is being pursued, in such a way that when the missile is fired, it will automatically be guided to and find its target. There are neurons in the brain called "mirror neurons" that do this kind of "locking on." They track another person's conversation and behavior and they "lock on" or identify with them. We want to use the mirror neurons in the brain to do this "locking on," only for much more constructive purposes than missile warfare. "Lock on" means you are in a tracking mode, that you are tracking the conversation of another person, so much so that you are zeroing in on what they are experiencing. Learning to "track" a person means to closely follow what they're saying, "to track them." Doing so gives people the great gift of being really heard. We want most to be understood. And that is the gift you give to others every time you come to an UpSpiraLife group meeting. You give each other the gift of being understood. The particular and very special gift is that of being positively understood, and there is great, great power in that.

The basis of the UpSpiraLife group is "heart-to-heart" identification that reduces resistance by being heard, for the purpose of moving higher in the UpSpiral. "Heart-to-heart" means the attempt to listen, "hear," and to get some feeling for what the other person is saying. This is more than polite listening and nodding your head, although that's a part of it. You are getting the larger picture of what another person is saying, identifying with something in your own experience. Empathy is probably the word used to most to express this intention, but this is a little more than and different from empathy. Empathy is the capacity to feel what another person is feeling. Heart-to-heart identification is more like, "I hear where you're coming from and I understand." Here you are also listening to the content of what someone is saying so that you can "get it" and "be there with them" in their experience. This is the capacity that creates great friendships.

Not only does it create great friendships, but it is also healing. Positive identification heals the negativity within us and over time heals negative memories and the sense of a negative past. This doesn't happen right away. Positivity engages the right hemisphere of the brain which is charged with "getting the bigger picture." When we get the bigger picture, and we do this for extended periods of time, negativity is more healed in us. Neuropositivity undoes the residues of negativity. It "oils" us to move on with our lives and renews our hope and trust. We have a greater tendency to let go of negativity that does not serve us.

Listen, listen so deeply that you are like a missile "locking on" to the sharing of another person, so that they experience being heard and being understood.

The Ways & Means

6

No Cross-Talk

Cross-talk, advice, and suggestion-making are stopped mid-sentence. Just put up your hand, palm outward, and say "hold on" or "use the I." You will find your own ways of stopping cross-talk, but you must stop it from the beginning.

Cross-talk, advice, and suggestion-making are stopped mid-sentence. The leader of the group will interrupt you and stop you mid-sentence if you cross-talk or give advice to another group member. It's just not allowed.

You are not allowed to be critical, negative, or to question what another group member is sharing. Your group leader is well-equipped to handle situations that occur in the group.

Why is this so important? You can't cross-talk and be listening to another person at the same time. And your sole job, while someone else is sharing, is to listen and to identify with where they're coming from. What if you don't agree or what if you don't like what's being said? Still try to identify with where that person is coming from. It's not your job to fix or change anything in the group. Sometimes, people just need to get out what they're saying. Many times, we don't realize how incorrect or off-base something we are saying is until we have said it. The important thing is to love them anyway. Think of the number of times you have said things that you have regretted or wish that you hadn't said. Think of the number of times that you have said something and then said to yourself, "what was I thinking, how could I have said that?" And then consider how often people just nodded, accepted you for who you are, and were kind enough to let you be off-base, believing enough in you or in the unfolding circumstances in life to know that you would probably change your mind or see things differently.

Cross-talk aborts the flow of the group, and it diminishes the important sense of "oneness" in the group that is occurring and deepening. The group leader is not going to correct everything someone in a group says that may not be on target. The leader knows when to correct and change the process and when to let things pass. Try caring about someone even when they are saying something with which you do not agree. Regard it as just where they are at that moment.

And there is one other important dynamic. When someone in a group bothers us, irritates us, or gets under our skin, and we want to react outwardly with some of what we are feeling inwardly, we are really reacting to something on some level that exists within ourselves. What "you spot, you got," in one way or another. When you are bothered by someone else, by what they say or how they behave, your behavior is rooted in their display of something that exists on some level in you that you have not accepted, admitted, or brought to the light of your acceptance and self-love. People only really bother us when they are mirrors for something that exists within us. Try this. Write down what the other person "should" do or "should" say, and then substitute your own name and see how or where it fits, because on some level it will. If this persists as a problem, talk with a NPC who will help guide you to what and why you're reacting as you are.

When you cross-talk, the person you are really talking to is yourself.

What about giving advice, especially when you have such a really good suggestion? You may have really good insights and good suggestions, but this group is not the place to make them, so don't do it. And don't corner the person after the meeting. Let it go. NO advice, NO cross-talk, NO suggestions about how other people should live their lives. Trust that what that other person needs, they will find on their journey and not on yours.

The Ways & Means

7

Save Your Questions

The definition of a weed is a plant that is growing in the wrong place. A rose bush could be a weed in a corn field. So it with questions; no matter how good they might be, they can choke out and divert the intention of the meeting. Questions are not a part of the format and they need to be asked at another time other than the meeting.

We are always encouraged to asked questions in most places. The UpSpiraLife group is not one of them. You may have a burning question about the process or about something someone has said. You may have questions about the leader's share at the beginning of the meeting. Save your questions. It is highly likely that in the process of the group they will be answered, as the group mind unfolds during a meeting.

But if that isn't the case, save the question to ask the leader after the meeting or give the leader a call at a later time in the week and get your question answered.

Questions have a tendency to turn the group into a discussion group, and to take the group in directions that are not intended in the format.

When you begin, you will have lots of questions. That is why we suggest that you read the two primary books of the UpSpiral Life Group, **Growing the Positive Mind** and this 12 step book. You are also encouraged to watch the videos and to read the material on the ANI website at www.gotoani.com (under the 'UpSpiral Groups" Tab) before you begin attending the group. In some groups, this is a requirement. We do not encourage "drop-ins" at meetings so people can observe the process and decide whether or not they want to be a part of the group. It is highly recommended that people have some kind of preparation before attending a meeting, but we leave the decision of what this should be up to each individual group leader.

Some substantive preparation of some kind is required.

Just a word about process here. Once the group begins, the "group mind" takes over. That is to say, the shared consciousness of the group begins to operate as "one mind," and that is when the magic happens. There is something in every group meeting that is pertinent or relevant to every person there. There is always something to learn and to take home if the **Ways and Means** and guidelines of the group are being followed. If that is not the case for you, you might want to speak with the leader, and if you are not satisfied with that conversation, discontinue your participation in the group for a time and see if this experience is the one for you. If you have more questions than personal experience of positivity to share, then consider the timing and, perhaps read more about the group from the resources suggested and give yourself some time. You might also want to benefit from individual coaching before you continue with the group.

But one more time, "the group mind" is a magical and enchanting process as it works among people who are invested in this "sanctuary of positivity" and why it exists. Creation speaks through the process. Listen and let it work, and contribute from your heart. All of your questions will be answered over time.

The Ways & Means

8

Subtle Cross-Talk

Subtle cross-talk is sharing something that is your experience, not because you need to share it, but because you think someone else will be helped to hear your experience. You have no idea that may be true. You are in the group to say what you need to say about you from your own experience, not to be an aid to anyone else's learning.

Just about the time you thought that quite enough has already been said about this topic, here is some more - because this is such an important area for the establishment and deepening of trust in a group. Subtle cross-talk is coming up with a story or an instance that happened to you, telling it as though you were sharing it as your very own share, but actually with having the motive of making a point. It gets your point of advice across in a disguised manner as though it were your piece of learning.

The problem is that it is not a legitimate share. In the group, your work is to share where your UpSpiral is and how you have stayed there from your experience and from your heart. It is solely about you, all about you, and not about anyone else except you.

People who need to do this would rather be right than be happy. They would rather make their point than stick to their own business. People who need to give advice and need to be right rather than happy are probably not ready to be a member of an UpSpiraLife group. They need to work through personal issues in another setting.

What is the need to be right really anchored in? Why do we need to be right? It is essentially an issue of self-esteem - more essentially, it is an issue of control. People who need to be right need to be in control. The need to be in control is really a security issue. Insecure people need to be in control because they believe that they should be. Under the surface of the control issue is a belief that if one is not in control, one is "less than," diminished, and not significant. A lifetime can be built on the need to be right or in control rather than being happy.

The Ways & Means

9

Other Resources

Other resources are wonderful in other places, but not in the UpSpiraLife group. Outside resources may be directly relatable and reinforcing, but so that each group leader does not have to be put in a position of judging, keep it simple by using only ANI resources in the UpSpiraLife group meeting.

In a world where there are so many wonderful resources, it is very difficult to say that these resources, no matter how good they may be and no matter how appropriate they may be to teach and make a point, are not allowed in the UpSpiraLife group. Only materials that are ANI materials are used and referenced in the group.

Believe it or not, no one really wants to hear your book report on the latest meaningful thing you just read. It is not in the spirit of the UpSpiraLife group share. It might be good conversation before or after the group, but not during the group. If you want to share a good book or resource with someone in the group, call them or send them an email, but don't use the group meeting to do it.

A book or another resource may say perfectly what you want to say, but your share is what you have to say, not another source you are using to try and say it for you. Even the greatest resource that perfectly supports the UpSpiraLife process is not shared in the group. While this may be up building for everyone, what is most up building is the personal "heart to heart" share that can only come from you.

This also helps us from having material that is inappropriate introduced into the group. If the material or reference doesn't come from ANI, leave it out.

Also, while there are other wonderful group experiences and churches and lectures and films, don't recommend them in the group. What one person thinks is wonderful may be offensive and not helpful to another. This allows the group leader of not having to be in the position of approving of some announcements and sharing of resources while not approving of others. It reduces conflict and it keeps us centered on the purpose of the UpSpiraLife group as it is stated in the **Preamble**.

Don't bring cookies to sell, tickets to hawk, or information on great causes to the group. Leave it all at home and bring yourself to the sanctuary of the UpSpiraLife group, trusting that group members will find all that they need to fulfill their lives in other places and in others ways. Don't bring quotes from other places, clever sayings, or the latest and ripest pertinent news. **You** are the news and your growing being of neuropositivity is what we want to hear from your heart and your heart alone.

The Ways & Means

10

Anonymity

Anonymity may seem desirable but it is not guaranteed. People will want to share the good you share with others. If you wish to have a guarantee of anonymity for something you share, it might be best not shared at the group level unless that degree of discretion is developed and practiced by your group. Information that requires anonymity should be shared individually with the group leader.

Anonymity in an UpSpiraLife group is not guaranteed. While we would like to appeal to people's good judgment about what to share and not to share outside of the group, there are always people who do not have good judgment. They may be newcomers who are just getting started, they may be visiting the group, or people may simply be well-meaning and want to share something they have heard that they think will help someone else.

It is certainly true that intimate and personal things will be shared in UpSpiraLife groups, and while we would hope that members would exercise discretion, there is no oath or promise of anonymity here. If you are sharing what is good and positive in your group, there may be little reason to want it to be guarded, especially since others may well benefit from it. Deep, dark secrets are not the subjects that are generally shared here, unless there is the positive solution to go along with them.

We would caution people who expect anonymity to lower their

expectations that this will not be the case, in a guaranteed or absolute way. Someone who hears that what they have shared in a group was shared outside the group should not be offended, or they should not have shared their "secret" in the group to begin with. The expectation of anonymity is simply not realistic and to presume that a group of people would not share their experience in a group is unrealistic, especially if the experience has been meaningful. We are sharing to open this experience of neuropositive being with the world.

However, we also encourage discretion and wisdom. Some things will be shared in a group that could hopefully remain in the group, but to promise that creates more problems than it solves by having an oath of anonymity that people, in the innocence of wanting to share good things, might tell another.

Be wise and caring with information in your group and let love be your guide. A good guideline, if you want to share something someone has said, is to ask them if you have their permission.

The Ways & Means

11

Respect The Process

Some of what is said won't "hit" or "connect" until people are three days away from the group. Never assume people are getting exactly what they need to get in the way they need to hear it or at the moment they hear it. The power is in "the process." The one mind of the group will order the group in perfect synchrony and establish group harmony. There is rarely a need to judge the effectiveness of a group session. Let go.

It is easy to judge a particular meeting as good or bad, or better or worse. It is best not to bother. If the **Ways and Means** that are set forth here are followed, the need to judge the effectiveness of a meeting will be a moot point.

"Some of what is said won't hit or connect until people are three days away from the group. Never assume people are getting exactly what they need to get in the way they need to hear it or at the moment they hear it. The power is in the process." Believe in the process. It works best when you don't do a post-mortem or debriefing of the quality of every meeting. Leave it alone and let it stand with the intention that has gone into it. "The One Mind of the group will order the group in perfect synchrony and establish group harmony. There is never a need to judge effectiveness." You will never know, in so many ways, how the group has been effective. But if you will leave it alone and just do the work, the feedback will come back in the most surprising and amazing ways. Trust the process. Adhere to the **Ways and Means**. And leave it alone.

After the meeting, gossip that is negative and judgmentally evaluative is an exercise in ignorance. That sounds harsh, but in the truest sense of what "ignorance" means (not knowing) - that is the case here. No one knows the effectiveness of a meeting and no one knows what the One Mind of the group expressed in the process is doing.

Certainly you can share about what you have learned and about what was significant, but it is not in the spirit of the group to gossip, in the name of evaluation. Follow the Ways and Means and the group will do its work, sometimes explosively and powerfully and at other times quietly and under the cover of individual consciousness. Let it work and trust that it will, and it will work.

The Ways & Means

12

Let The Leader Lead

Group leadership is not an easy task. The social brain must process a billion bits of information over the course of a single meeting. Leadership can be exhilarating but it can also be exhausting. Be good to your leader and let them use the skills they have spent a good deal of time developing in order to fill this function.

Being a good follower is not very much respected. However, if there were not followers, there could not be leaders. No place is that more true than in an UpSpiraLife group. Your leader is well-trained. Follow. Followership, for all of its negative connotations, is a mark of maturity. Be a good follower; work at it, and you will help your group mature. Mature people can exercise "followership" as a part of generativity. Generativity is a term that applies to an experience that unfolds, grows, and fulfills its purposes. Use the leader of your group to talk over what you don't understand, where you have difficulty, and what puzzles or perplexes you.

If your group leader does things that you don't understand or with which you don't agree, don't "pair" to gain power. Pairing is talking to someone else to get them on your side so you feel more right. Go to the leader before you "pair." Talk to the leader about your concerns and be honest. Give your group leader the benefit of the doubt. They are juggling many issues in a group of which you may not be aware.

If, however, you go to your group leader and you don't feel heard or you disagree, then find someone else in the group (pairing) who agrees with you, and both of you or three of you go and talk to the leader. But do talk to the leader. Don't gossip and cause unrest within the group. Be honest and get whatever it is out in the open. If this causes situations that cannot be resolved, you can write to the national office for advice about your concerns, but don't write until you have followed these directions and expressed your concerns to your group leaders.

Likewise, tell your group leader what you appreciate, what is good, what you're getting from the group. In this way, you are probably reinforcing what you want in your group the most.

Your group leader is highly trained in the UpSpiral group process. Use them for individual consultations, pods to grow even more in your experience of neuropositivity, and give them ideas of how they can help you.

12 NEW STEPS FOR A NEW MILLENNIUM
The UpSpiralLife Group

PART III

The *12* Promises

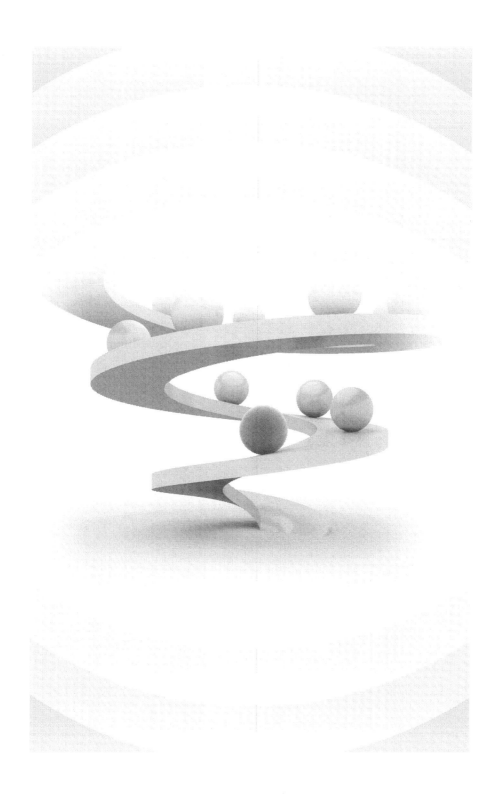

Promise

1

You can feel the positive emotions that you choose to feel if you lean your consciousness consistently and gently over time in that positive direction.

Your consciousness is your Mind telling your brain what you want it to do. However, oftentimes the Mind is not as good an employer as it might be and the brain has a lot of time to wander. If you were to add up the amount of time your brain has to wander from thought to thought and emotion to emotion, what would do you think you might find? Some time would be taken with events that we might consider negative and others might be taken with events we consider positive, but a large amount of the time would be spent on the brain just going from thing to thing to thing. The brain has a lot of time to think up thoughts (which is its job) and a lot of time to go from feeling to feeling to feeling, unsupervised a lot of the time.

If you decide to tell your brain to go to positive feelings and to feel them, just a little, gently, over time, you will feel the emotions you choose more regularly and consistently and you will grow in an UpSpiral. It's as simple as that. Positive emotions, positive moods, and a positive consciousness take time and it takes intent that builds upon itself overtime.

You are constructing new neuropathways composed of new neurons and cells that can reconstruct the nature of your brain, your perception and your consciousness.

Every cell in your body "hears." Not only do your cells "hear" music at the same level of your audible hearing, but your cells also hear what you are feeling and thinking. Every thought, every feeling is heard by your cells through sound waves and sensory transmissions that are audible to the sensory mechanisms of each of your cells. Stop and consider this for a minute. Every minute of everyday, you are telling your cells how to feel. How do you think that affects their health?

So what your cells assimilate and what they expel, and how they function in healthy or unhealthy ways is fundamentally and radically affected by their environment of sensory information. That information comes from your choices about how you feel and how you think. ***Positive emotion is the most powerful anti-toxin.***

Make the choices for love, peace, gratitude and joy throughout the day. Maybe everything isn't going like you planned or expected, maybe there is a downer or two, but you can still feel these emotions on some level of 1-10 from just a little to more and more. Can't feel them at all, you say? Then think them. You don't have to deny negative feelings, but you also don't have to stay in them, live in them, or obsess over them. Let negative feelings be a signal to find something to be grateful for and start to pulse a little bit of a thought and feeling of joy.

You move in the direction that you intend to go - into an UpSpiral or into a DownSpiral. And your cells are listening to the choice you make. What effect do you suppose this choice to feel toward the "good" has on the health of your always "listening" and sensory receptive cells, to each and every one of them?

How much conscious control do we have over emotions and feelings and consequent mood? The figures vary, but there is one interesting observation in all the research. The more consideration we give to states of mind and happiness, the more control over emotions than we would ever have thought. Research tells us that we have 40% control over our emotional state and about 50% is genetic.

You have 40% of your own will that is working with 50% of a genetic predisposition. Of the 50% genetic predisposition all of that is not "sour" or negative. No one was born with a totally "sour" disposition, although there are some people who are trying to win the title. At least 20%, and the very least, of your 50% of genetic predisposition is positive or toward the positive range of emotion. If you take that 20% and your own 40% of choice, that's 60% and that's enough to keep you in the upward elevation of mood and emotion all of the time, pretty much regardless of what your genetic nature might be. Even with genetics, it is not a sure thing that these inclinations lead to the subtle on/off switches of the genes being thrown in one direction or another. Being in an UpSpiral or a DownSpiral is largely a matter of learning and choice and with the exercise of choice learning can be undone and new neuroplasticity can change the brain.

However you cut it, there is an amazing space of choice in emotion. Most negative emotional patterns are learned. There are some, in a small percentage, that are inherited, but most are learned. And even in inherited, chemical mood issues, there is still a larger range of choice than we believe, that aids in healing and balance.

Here is what is important to know. You can learn and develop a pattern that is like a default setting of the emotions of gratitude, love, peace, and joy. The amount of time your mind just wanders is the amount of time you can choose toward a positive emotion. Consistent positive emotion at a low grade, like a 1 or 2 or 3 on a scale of 1-10 is more effective in maintaining happiness than one big event of happiness once a month.

The best way to manage mood and to elevate mood is consistent practice of positive emotion over time. Consistent means daily. Tip the scales of your life strongly in the direction of positive emotion and you will feel better and be healthier.

It just takes remembering and practice, and those are the hardest things. But you can tip the scale in the direction of positive feelings. You know that there are those, who by their own choice have tipped their scale in the direction of the negative. Just do it in the other direction.

If you start to lean in the direction of neuropositive growth in your brain and consciousness, your mind will get more and more used to directing your brain in that direction. As the lean begins, it will become greater and greater and the place where your brain and being feels most at home will be in "feeling good" and positive.

Promise

2

Positive emotions will increase for you on three dimensions. You will be able to get to them rapidly, you will be able to make them last in duration, and you will be able to increase their intensity.

Take one of 5 emotions and make each day of the week associate with an emotion. Monday is peace, Tuesday is love, Wednesday is gratitude, Thursday is joy and Friday is hope. Then choose to feel those emotions all day long. You will be astounded at what you can create in your brain. You will be even more astounded when you realize that you have the power to give a positive emotion the duration you choose, and that you can intensify that emotion by your choice and your practice. The next time you feel joy, the promise here is that you can feel twice that amount of joy, if you will allow yourself to learn to go there.

The Dharmsala Monks are able to lower or raise their body temperatures by 15 or more degrees, "on-call" as a result of meditating. Think about the power of raising or dropping your own body temperature 15 degrees in the heat or the cold. It would be quite an energy savings over a year.

This is a startling example of our ability to direct and intensify "energy." Another is in the area of radiation. Small beads of gold are used to surround a cancer and then radiation energy is directed at the area of the cancer and the gold beads better catch and direct the signal of radiation that works on the cancer. This is a great example of the direction of energy that can't been seen. Consider the implications of increasing the intensity of an emotion, on call, by your own choice, because you can with practice.

If we would increase the intensity of our feeling of love 15 degrees and direct it and measure its impact on a particular target "person" or target "situation" what we might find. Pick a target for the intensity of your love. You are learning that you can make an emotion last (duration) and intensify it or increase its emotional "muscle." Take aim at your target of love and give that emotion some duration over time and then intensify it and stay directed at your target. Send "love" treatments in a particular direction. Send love to someone or some situation as surely as if it were a wave of radiation.

As we consider intensifying an emotion, it is significant to consider that love is an energy and gamma wave measurement is the first way into measuring the power of that love. We have an infinite capacity to heal ourselves and others by learning to direct love as a source of energy and healing. The best news about it is that the more you send it, the more you have it. Find your target of love, aim your energy, and let the love go.

We are only beginning to understand the implications of what we can do with positive emotion. But we know this, as surely as you can go to a negative emotion instantly and be "wounded," and as long as you stay there nursing your wound, and as much as you can intensify the wound over time, so can you do that with positive emotion. We can get to a positive emotion in an instant, we can stay there as long as we choose, and we can intensify it. Admit it, you do it with negatives, this is the promise that you can do it with positive emotions.

Promise

3

You can stay in the UpSpiral 100% of the time and by being there raise both your happiness and emotional set-points and "feel good" most of the time.

It can seem, after you have done this work for a while, that is just almost too obvious. But if you didn't think about it before, if it just never occurred to you, it is a revolutionary awareness. You can live in the UpSpiral 100% of the time.

Consider this. Where do you spend your mind and to what does your brain retreat? In an UpSpiral or a DownSpiral? Our most precious resource is the psychic energy we have in a 24 hour period to do what we do with our mind and brain. The Mind is the larger master of how the brain thinks, feels, perceives, and does it work. The Mind directs the brain............or it does not. Mindlessness is a lack of consciousness about where we are spending our psychic energy. It's like writing checks without ever looking at the balance in the account.

Mindlessness is what advertisers depend upon. Mindlessness is what people who don't want us to think depend upon. The Mind just wanders from this to that. Think a negative or angry thought and see where the brain goes when you send it mindlessly down that road. Mindlessness just gets the errands of the day done.

There is a principle in psychology called the Zeigarnik effect that states that we have a 9:2 in our tendency to notice, to lean, and to remember in a negative direction. It's considered an evolutionary tendency.

If you could quantify the time your brain spends on the positive and the negative, focused on what is beautiful or whining about what you don't have yet, what is right in your world, what's wrong, where would you come out?

What would be your ratio of the good in your world, as compared to the negative that draws you in like a fly caught in a web? What is your ratio of positive to negative thinking?

Here is what the significant research of Losada and Fredrikson shows us. To flourish, you need an average of 3 positives to every negative, in whatever way you want to weight them. We need a ratio of 3:1, positive to negative events, on the average, to flourish. For some folks, we need 5:1, others may only need 2:1. These are thoughts, conversations, and events.

Mindlessness is the enemy of flourishing in your life. Flourishing takes mindfulness of the world within you and the world around you. Mindfulness is being awake to yourself, it is attention, it is savoring, it is aliveness. It is what it takes to stay in an UpSpiral. It is not just going along negatively reacting to the weather, to politics, or putting your focus on what is wrong or negative. It is your focus on the solution that comes from being in an UpSpiral and using your strengths. Mindfulness is your disciplined focus on where the popcorn is popping and not the kernels that didn't.

What Is An UpSpiral? It is living at a higher quality of life by managing the ups and downs of life more effectively. It is creating a mood predisposition and it is State of Mind Management (SOMM). It is living more up than down by using the power of your choice and learning the ways to do it.

An UpSpiral Score goes from 1 - 100. 100 is simply "feeling good," feeling optimistic, and feeling generally "on top of it." 51 - 100 is an UpSpiral and 50 and below is the DownSpiral. The bottom of the DownSpiral is despondency and despair. It is characterized by pessimism and negative mood, anger, resentment, and feeling "oppressed". Life narrows in the DownSpiral.

PEOPLE WHO SPEND MORE TIME IN THE DOWNSPIRAL THAN THE UPSPIRAL HAVE TWICE THE CHANCE OF A HEART ATTACK OR STROKE.

Most people live far lower in the UpSpiral than they need to be, and most people yo-yo between being somewhere in the UpSpiral and somewhere in the DownSpiral. We have come to believe that this up-and-down is a normal part of life, when, in fact, it is just learned behavior. We have far more choice and ability to remain in an UpSpiral that we usually know or believe.

Is it possible to be very high in an UpSpiral all of the time? Is it possible to always be in the 90's on this scale? Two answers. First, our research for the last eight years shows us that people can live in an UpSpiral in the upper 90's most all of the time, once they learn how to do it. Second, it is also fair to say that we can live somewhere in the UpSpiral all of the time; that DownSpiral experiencing isn't really necessary. We may not always be in the 90's but we can always be above 51. Despair and the narrowing of depression aren't necessary. It doesn't have to be.

We live by this myth that there are ups and downs in life and that they are largely created by external events. The truth is that, for the most part, there are external events to which we respond and our response to these events determines where we are in the Spiral, not the event itself. Either you are a victim of a difficulty or you are stripping a problem of everything it has to teach you and becoming stronger and wiser. Or you are learning to let one door close so another can open.

100% is the promise. 100% of your time in an UpSpiral. Sometimes that may only be at a 55 or a 60, but it's not in a DownSpiral of 40. You're learning the skills of the UpSpiral, you can learn them so well never to be in a DownSpiral. The oppression of the DownSpiral is a choice that is learned over a lifetime, but it can be unlearned and our time does not have to be spent there.

Promise

4

Negative feelings, over-reacting, and the sense of the fear of oppression will decrease. Unnecessary anger and anxious over-reactivity will eventually be replaced by expecting and seeing the best in others and in outside events.

There may be an end of the emotional scale that is something like a 911 emergency, but they are very few. If we are honest with ourselves, most negatives in our lives don't need to hijack us into a DownSpiral, if any. Most of our negatives are best served by getting to a higher place, to a better place where we are experiencing positive emotion and can do our problem-solving from the place of being plugged into our real strengths where we can do our best problem solving.

Negatives are seldom emergencies and most of the time they do not deserve all of the attention we give them in the first place. The range of our negatives is likely, already, much less, than we might think. Our negatives probably aren't as negative as we make them, and as we add to our positive reservoir they are going to seem like they are less and less and they will last less and less time.

There can be an elegant process of emotional sobriety at work here. When you feel negatively or when you are DownSpiraling, go to the Emotional Gym and start pulsing the positive emotional state that is easiest for you to get to: love, peace, gratitude, joy or hope. Pulse it, feel it, chant it, until you feel some of it. Then it can occur to you to go to your strengths, rather than their opposites, and use your strengths to begin to develop a strategy, if it's only to back-off and do the problem-solving at a later time.

Our sober moments are in an UpSpiral and our strengths can best be used there. There is this saying that goes something like "preaching to the choir." However, that would never be necessary "if only the choir would do what they have learned to do."

So it is with building the positive reservoir that desensitizes negative experiences.

If there are few negatives that are 911 emergencies, one might ask just where negatives fall in the overall experience of a day or a week. Many are sometimes not good, but they are also not terribly bad or even bad; they exist somewhere in an "in - between."

The "in - between" is not a reference to your physical body. It's a reference to the swing and sway of your everyday moods or states of mind. The top is feeling very good and that is at 100. The bottom is feeling oppressed, overwhelmed and despairing and that is zero. The mid-point is 50. The in - between, where, where most people are, is 35-70. So, on a scale of 1-100, where are you? I've stopped addressing people that are below 35, the therapists can work with them. If you are, in part of your life, in this "in - between" state, yo-yoing up and down and back and forth or just fixed at a 60, then consider moving that mid-range to over 70 - to the feel-good range.

This in-between state is where many folks live thinking that it's just them, just their life as it is, but we guarantee that you can live at a higher point on this scale and experience feeling good more and more and more often. We even guarantee that you can get to feeling very good 95% of the time. Living there decreases the amount of time you will experience negative feelings, the intensity and their duration.

It takes a long time, but the results are immediate sounds very contradictory, but it's actually true. You will sometimes see immediate results and other times you have to be patient with results that come over time. It just takes practice and it takes practice in those times of our day when the mind wanders, lots of that time.

Consider the amount of time in each day that your mind just wanders. Consider the amount of time you spend worrying about this or that. The amount of time your brain spends wandering is a part of the time we want you to claim back for "feeling good." You don't need extra time in your day to "feel good," you just have to decide to use some of the time in your day when you're thinking about something negative or something bothersome or just wandering over a dozen things that hit you, just one after the other. Take that time and say and feel gratitude, love, peace, joy, or hope. Say it over and over and over and feel a little bit of it. We are repetitive in teaching this exercise. Remember you have to build the positive reservoir for the negative reacting to grow less and less.

We are repetitive in hoping that you will follow this simple direction.

In meditation, if you do it, you focus on one thing. This is moving meditation and focuses you on feeling positive feelings. We have gone through a lifetime not giving much thought to the fact that we can "feel good" by choice over time. It doesn't happen in a month or two or six or a year. It happens over a process of 3 to 5 years, but it will also begin to happen almost immediately. You have spent all of your life letting your mind wander. In the future, the great science and learning will be channeling the energy of the mind toward positivity as a means of prevention of disease and disorder. We are way ahead of what is coming, way out on the cutting edge. You do not have to wait to "feel good," you can create the ambient soundtrack in your life that is positive, that will lead you to better and better moods for longer and longer period of times. If this weren't so simple, it would be easier to do.

Simply, but with patience, immediately and over time, your negative feelings will be less, you will be less negatively reactive and you will expect the best in life and in others.

It takes a long time, but the results are immediate.

Promise

5

By knowing and using your strengths everyday, you will become happier, more content, and increase your sense of personal autonomy and competence.

Strengths are also called virtues and values because of their fundamental importance. They are your ways of "being" who you really are. These superhighways of neuropathways are unique to you and they are the only ones that you can travel and be who you really are. Your values, as your strengths, are who you are. Get off the highway and some voice within you, first of all your feelings, will start to give you messages that you need to change your direction, make a turn, take the next exit and go back - just as surely as the GPS system for a car won't give up until you're on the right track.

The greater your alignment, your consistency and your focus is on your strengths, the more in alignment with your Real Self you are going to feel. You will feel more in sync, more in control, more in harmony, more like you are "in your own skin." It is when we play to our weaknesses that we begin to feel "out of sync," disconnected, out of alignment, anxious, frustrated, and in a state of discord.

The more you use your strengths, that are also your basic values and virtues, the happier you will be.

Restless, listless, out-of-sync, unsettled and out of your own skin; these are the word that describe us when we are not playing to our strengths. They are the things we experience when we are playing to our weaknesses.

When you know your strengths (because they have been scientifically tested) it's easier to play to your strengths so long as you stay in an UpSpiral. In a DownSpiral or when we are down spiraling, we will not play to our strengths, but rather to their opposites, which are our weaknesses or our character defects. The opposites of our strengths are wonderful things because they warn us by feeling restless, listless, out-of-sync, unsettled, bored, irritable, and frustrated. The more we play to our weaknesses the worse these things get.

You know your strengths by taking the tests that we give that tell you. However, your weaknesses that are the opposite of your strengths are uniquely yours. Only you really know what they are. Take a piece of paper and list your strengths, then list what is the opposite of that strength for you. How does the weakness side of the strengths show up for you? What is your unique way of doing the opposite of your strength?

A good exercise is to make a list of your strengths and score how much you're using each one from 1 - 10. Then on the opposite side of the paper to the left of your strengths, list your weaknesses (what is for you the opposite of your strengths.) Then score how much you are playing to your weaknesses from 1 - 10. Then add up your final score for each. If they match each other, your weaknesses are cancelling out strengths and the pleasure you get from using them. If the score is higher for your weaknesses, you are in a DownSpiral.

Get the score for your strengths much higher than your score for weaknesses.

The alternative is to continue in the DownSpiral of not using your strengths. It is amazing that we think so little about using our strengths when we are DownSpiraling. They are just not in our focus. That's because the DownSpiral is characterized most by narrowing, but it starts by questioning and doubting yourself. Go down a negative path with a particular negative thought and it's very much like going from a "1" or a "2" to a "10."

From doubting just a little, in a few short minutes, you doubt where you live, where you work, who you love, and why you're doing anything you're doing. That's a bit of an exaggeration but you can identify. Then there comes the sense that things are beginning to get on top of you–that there is just too much to deal with. That is followed by the sense that you can't make sense out of things - they just don't seem to fit together in one way or another.

The DownSpiral shuts you off from your repertoire of strengths, options and abilities, it shuts you off from faith, it shuts you off from doing the very things that keep you in an UpSpiral and gets you to question whether they work or not. When, in fact, if you were doing the things that worked to stay in an UpSpiral, you wouldn't be in a DownSpiral.

Sound familiar? It happens to everybody in this journey. That's why we practice using our strengths everyday. Writing a "Daily Plan" of how to use your strengths and journal in **Plans to the Universe** is a sure way to stay on track.

Promise

6

You will come to know that every negative event is an experience that can take you to your strengths, providing, over time and with practice, solace and solutions that are empowering and that build personal confidence.

There are oftentimes negatives in your face. What is their wisdom?

"Ships sail out, and ships sail west,
By the very same breezes that blow:
It's the set of the sails,
And not the gales,
That determine where they go."

The wind in your face, that is for sure a negative, can cause you to despair of going further or the negative can be the gift that it can be: reassess using your strengths and the always present Source beneath them and the Universe gives up its secrets for a change in direction and then what blew in your face becomes the energy that fills your sails.

Take a quick test of when negative is normal.

Negativity is a warning and an indicator that leads us in another direction. We are not intended to stay in negativity, but it is a normal part of life as an indicator.

Some say that good feels good and bad feels bad and it's as simple as that. It's not. If you are out of touch with your feelings and intellectualize or over-think things, your feelings may not be as good an indicator as you might think.

There is also a kind of negative thinking called emotional reasoning. Emotional reasoning means that what you feel isn't necessarily the truth about a situation and can be based on faulty judgment and thought patterns.

Answer these five questions and see where you rank:

1. I talk about other people; it tends to fill my conversations. *Yes No*

2. When I get into a conversation and can't think of anything else to say it's easy for me to turn to something that's wrong or "off." *Yes No*

3. When I talk about myself, it's usually in negative terms; I don't spend much time giving myself a lot of credit.   *Yes No*

4. When another person starts to go down a negative track, I usually go along; I don't stop and tell them I don't want to go there. *Yes No*

5. When I take tests like this I usually give myself higher scores than I deserve so I can look good to myself.   *Yes No*

How do you think you did? If you scored two or more "yes" answers, you are too negative, yes, too negative. You are negative in a way that holds down your UpSpiral from generating all the good things that can come to your life.

We are all going to have negative times and slumps when we are obviously not operating with all of our cylinders of energy and positivity firing. They are called our BRAC cycle. Our BRAC cycle happens about every 12 hours and at one end we are at our highest and best and at the other end we are at our lowest. Why does it happen? It is a natural flow of energy.

Why is that we can have a down day or a down "several days?" When you all get finished asking the wrong question, which is "why", and come up with a thousand different answers, it doesn't matter. It just happens. The question is how do we use it? Use the time gently and be as encouraging to yourself as you would be with your best friend.

Treat yourself as nicely and as lovingly as a friend who was having a slump. Would you beat up on them and ask them a thousand questions until you got to the very "bottom" of their souls? Of course not. Tell yourself about how good you are when all your cylinders are firing. Tell yourself what it feels like when you're not in a slump, tell yourself that you know you will bounce back, not only back but that you are very resilient, and that you will be feeling even better and that you will be higher and higher in your UpSpiral.

BRAC is an acronym for our daily biological clock of our highest high and our lowest low within a 24 hour period. But regardless, this is not an excuse to feel worse, think worse, and expect something worse at the lowest point of your day. Use your skills and tools and manage this cycle more effectively.

Slumps just are and if there is a reason for them, the reason will "show up" when you feel better and it will come to you. It will just come to you if you leave it alone. In one way or another it will come to you. The more you nag at it and dissect it and talk about, the more you create it. The best answers to your problems come when you aren't thinking about them or the answers surprise you when they come through someone else or a movie or a book, or just a knowing. Stop beating your slump and yourself to death and practice the principles that we teach here. You become the emotions you choose to live in. Lean, just gently, peacefully lean toward the positive, if you can only do it a little.

Every negative is a gift or solution in disguise.

Promise

7

**Your VibeCore is at the heart of you and can grow.
As it increases, you will, over time, get more of what you
want.**

Your "vibe" is your magnet. Every one has a vibration that is an expression of where they're basically "coming from." We read people's "vibe" so naturally that we don't even realize that we're doing it - and they read ours. We are drawn to some people and repelled by others.

Our vibration also tunes us into the world like a magnet and determines what we attract into our lives by the nature of where we put our focus and by how strongly we put our focus in that place.

Try this for what constitutes your "vibe." It is knowing what you want, believing you're going to get it, and being open to all the ways that it can come in its time frame and not necessarily yours. The "package" may look different than you expect and may come when you aren't expecting it.

The stronger you are in knowing what you want, believing you will get it, and being open to how it will arrive, the stronger your "vibe" will be. It will affect the nature and strength of your focus which acts as a magnet.

If you are wishy-washy about what you want, don't really believe you will get it, and rigid about how it has to come, your "vibe" will be conflicted and weak and so will your "personal magnet of focus."

Notice that none of this is about the "how." The "how" shows up wonderfully when these other pieces are in place.

What this is all about is your "VibeCore." So you have this "vibe" that you transmit as surely as a frequency or signal and it's rooted in what has brought you what you have in your life.

It is not your positive thinking or your negative thinking that so much attracts what you want or don't want; it is your neuropositivity being or your negativity being. It is the very nature of your reasoning.

Today's cults of positive thinking dangerously deny the reality of the "vibe" of "positivity being" by pretending to be positive while carrying out an agenda of confusion, illusion, and pretense that is one more cover for a need for approval, power, and personal significance. And while preaching abundance, they are always short on funds. While they mean well they have not navigated the waters of transition into "positivity being" and the "oneness" that is inherently there.

It is the structure of your reasoning and your "meaning-making" system that attracts into your world what you're getting and not getting. That reasoning emerges from positivity being, negativity being, or a sloppy, transitional mix of the two. While they help start the movement toward transition, this is much more profound than positive thinking and affirmations.

Your "vibe" sets up your consciousness of the world and exists as the way you see yourself in the mirror and then becomes the world you bring to life.

Your VibeCore is what you want, how much you believe you're going to get it and how open you are to however it may come. If you're very tight about how what you want has to come, then your reasoning will squeeze what you get until it takes forever or never comes at all.

Your VibeCore emerges from your "meaning-making" structure that isn't usually conscious until you get very clear about what you want, which will change or radically sharpen, the clearer you get. Getting really clear about what you want starts to alter and change your structure of reasoning. Until you do, your VibeCore brings all kinds of things into your life, it is the structure of your being and it is a "vibe" sending out the signal that is bringing you back what you get.

NeuroPositivity is not just positive thinking. It is what it means to begin to alter the nature of your mind and to be able to live in an UpSpiral of growing consciousness that brings back the "oneness" you begin to see in the mirror.

However, at the core of it all, at the core of "vibe" is knowing what you want.

Everything starts with knowing what you want. We have all been given messages about wanting too much, about the greed of our wanting, about how holy it is not to want. In life we often get the message that you will get what you need but not necessarily what you want. Or someone may have told you, "All you do is want, want, want; you're never satisfied with what you have." That's right, while we are deeply grateful everyday for everything we have, we are never satisfied in the sense of being finished with our wants and desires.

Many people were told to save their money for a rainy day and, for sure, that rainy day always came to take what they had saved.

We have to get clear about what we are wanting because the Mind and the brain are always creating whatever that wanting might be. If the wanting is on a subjective level, we are creating it. The Mind as a creative force is unimaginable. Scientists have tried to recreate models of the power of the right hemisphere of the brain and have simply given up. There is no way to quantify its power to produce, to store, to calculate, to create.

If you want to get out of this life, if you've decided that you're tired of it and that your life is basically over, there is an illness that will cooperate and help you do that. If you're lying to yourself about the level of your happiness and you're really just treading water and you'd like to escape that, you're a perfect vibration for some dramatic thing, usually an accident or an illness to change all that. We powerfully create our worlds through the strength of our VibeCore. As your VibeCore grows you will increasingly get more and more of what you want.

Promise

8

***You will live your life in a flow,
more and more one with the music of life.***

Anything in life can be a flow experience. Just go back and remind yourself of the steps for creating flow and you know that anything can be a flow activity, if you can get to "oneness" with it, forget yourself and get to that point where you are one with the music of whatever you're doing.

Ever been asked to be the greeter at the door of social event and you don't consider yourself too much of a greeter? Here's a great chance for flow. The event is in the evening and you know that you will be bored with this long string of people, most of whom you are probably assured that you don't even know. Worst of all you have to gr-e-e-e-t and smile and act, not only like you're glad to be there but are happy to see all these people. You may not see yourself as a greeter, you're not good at cocktail parties or small talk, but probably you're filling in for a friend if you got stuck with this job; that's the dangerous DownSpiral story I told myself.

Because of what you've learned here, you know this is an excellent opportunity to turn something you don't want to do into a flow activity. As you greet people, you will find that your story changes. Forget your ego evaluating you and observing you with your fake smile on, and let that change to a genuine pleasure at seeing folks, which it will, and then there are humorous exchanges, hugs, and chit-chat that you will wish could have lasted longer and were over before you knew it. There just weren't enough guests to greet and the evening flew by. Now you know that any experience can be a flow activity. When you can make anything a flow activity, you have surely found those things in your life that are your really true "autotelic" flow activities. These are the easy ones, but you have learned that you don't have to limit the experience of flow to these.

But what is the nature of this change –just getting out of one's self? Too simple. Within us, at your choice to use them right on the spot, are skills and abilities and caring and love that were so easy to tap with just a decision to do so. It is what we call that place of flow and zone and can become a learned choice.

I shake your hand, I kiss your cheek, I hug you, and I am me in this Oneness we share because I can make the choice to get out myself and focus on on "just this, just you, just you, just you" and the line is so much shorter than it looked.

What is amazing is that "flow" is like a drug or a medication. We are concerned about the affects of drugs and medications, particularly psychotropic or psychological drugs. What we don't realize is that social interaction, the way we think, what we talk about and the social context around us affect us, particularly the brain, as much, if not more than drugs, in the long-term.

Your thoughts affect the development of neuropathways in the brain. Negative and anxious conversations about "bad" things and people affect the amygdala of the brain which is a center of fear, negativity and anxiety. The more you focus on the negative, the more extensive and tightly bound are the neuropathways that are connected to the negative memories that are held by the left hemisphere. As you greet people and as you forget the "ego" of the left hemisphere's daily problem-solving is very much like a drug creating a shift in the brain.

Your conversation, even in a receiving line, is as potent in creating "side effects" as drugs and medication. Negative beliefs and pessimism create long-term patterns of negativity and stress.

The words we use, the conversations we have, and the images and programs we take in have the power to create a DownSpiral of negativity that releases cortisol, a major stress hormone, adrenaline, thyroxin (long-term adrenalin), and ACTH, the body's basic stress response.

Don't like to take medication? Don't want to use drugs? Then make "flow" the medication you use. As it shifts you from your left hemisphere dominance to the larger picture of the right hemisphere, that sense of being one with the music, that subtle shift turns the "feel good" chemicals and gives you distance, perspective and it adds to the neuropositive reservoir.

The more you are in flow and the more you experience being "one with the music," the more you build it into your life, you are building your reservoir of psychological capital and you are also building a "buffer zone" of positivity. This buffer zone protects against what is negative and creates a resistance to disease and a greater immunology to what seems negative in life. It will take longer for things to affect you in a negative way. Negatives will have a shorter life. You will be less reactive and you'll experience less stress. We are always moving the "lean" of the brain toward a positive state of feeling. Focus on what is positive; your brain "runs" better.

Make positive feelings the ambient sound track of your life is another way of talking about being "one with the music" of life. "Just this" learned as a skill in even the most boring of tasks, can turn just about anything into an opportunity to practice focus and to forget and escape the evaluative ego.

Promise

9

Your goals and action steps, expressed over time in writing, will give you a sense of direction in life.

I used to love to play baseball because next to hitting a home run, stealing bases was the most fun. Walking to the next base, because a team mate struck out got me ahead a little, but it was not fun at all, really. I remember that we turned the street in the neighborhood into a baseball field and *played into the twilight*. What a great preparation for learning about how to do goals in life. The games we play give us a developing sense of direction by having clear rules. Life is not always like that

I wouldn't play the game if I didn't imagine the home run. What are the home-runs today? We need to know. What if we strike-out - a lot? There are a lot of times at bat and a lot of innings. I never quit until the game is over. I knew the next swing would be a home-run, or I'd get on base and steal to the next.

I remember that I was never discontent or driven to get to the next base, I was just excited at the thrill of it.

Can you be on your own "first base," whatever it is and not be discontent or driven, but rather be in the thrill of what will get you on to second base? Often it's the risk of going out on a limb.

That's the skill of real goal-development. As fast as we can do it, discontent begs to become imagination. How fast can you turn discontent into imagination and vision and not let it become drivenness? Are you even really playing in the game of your life or have you turned it into "flat land" or dampened its intensity for some false sense of stale peace?

In the same way I can turn a game into discontent and drivenness because I don't think I'm winning, can I do the same with life? How often have you been on third base and didn't know it? How often was that the next hitter that would have brought us home someone or something we never expected? Play the game, know your goals, and play well into the twilight until the light is gone.

As we play into the twilight of our lives, fully alive, an inevitable theme in having goals that are malleable and that change over time is this theme than runs between "holding on" and "letting go."

We have an idea of ourselves as having too many attachments with the need for a great deal of "letting go." I suppose the quick argument is that we are attached to the wrong things. All of this can greatly complicate a sense of direction in life, but it need not, if we don't buy into it. I like my stuff. I like it a lot. And I really like finding more of the stuff that I really like. I am a collector and I appreciate beauty and excellence. I even like looking at the mosaic of the toothpaste on the shelf in my store with its enormous variety, color, and choice. I am also told that I probably have too many choices for my own good. I am told that having too many choices can distort my direction in life.

So what am I going to do in a "let go" world full of too many choices? I'll tell you. I am going to attach. I am going to find what I want and love and I am going to attach. I am going to go toward, think toward, believe toward and move toward attachment to what I want. How do I know? Because it feels good. What if it doesn't feel good after a while? Then I let go and then I move on to attach some more.

Life and its transitions are not essentially about letting go; they are about choice and attachment. It is the fear of attachment that drives us to hold on more tightly to what we need to move away from. It is this that will destroy our sense of direction from having goals, more than anything else. When we know what we want to attach to, letting go is much easier. When we focus on what we want or even kind of want, letting go is slicker.

The only thing that is more difficult that "letting go" is not "letting some god" do it for us, by knowing what you want. If there is a god, he, she, HP, or whatever isn't telling you what it is, but rather letting you extravagantly choose. If there should be fewer kinds of toothpaste and televisions to choose from, should there be fewer kinds of flowers, clouds or sunsets? I even have the freedom to choose to pay more attention to the flowers than the toothpaste. Variety of choice need not limit a sense of direction.

Attachment. It makes many shudder. We want no more attachments, no more entanglements, and no more things (or people) to wonder about. But we get through major life transitions when we grow toward, when we have the courage to attach, to connect, to move forward, and to define new wantings and unclaimed desires.

And while we consider the whole issue of attachment and a sense of direction, here's another. Can I have it all? Can you want the "whole" of experience without the feeling that you have to scale back? Can you want it all and still have a sense of emerging direction?

I was recently asked this question by a young, ambitious, dedicated and devoted business entrepreneur. What would you say? Would you tell her, yes, if she worked very hard, burned the candle at both ends and was success-driven? We all know that those are not the directions that insure "having it all."

I told her yes. I know that you can have it all if you know that you do have it all today. Setting goals and having a sense of the direction they provide never tears us from any sense of gratitude for what we have right now in this day.

If you can, today, look around you, proclaim that you have it all and live in that sense of abundance and gratitude, more will come. If, however, you are discontent, striving from a sense of lack, and driven because you will be happier than you can be today, any sense of real authentic direction will be taken from you and be replaced by drivenness and blinded ambition.

"Having it all" is a state of mind of gratitude. The secret is to live in such gratitude and appreciation of today and its richness that you are open to even greater things. If you live in a sense of lack and discontent and "if only," you will bring more of that into your life.

Gratitude is a word that is used so much that it's hard to grasp its significance. Every positive emotional state - love, peace, joy, and hope and all others rest in gratitude. Gratitude is a deep knowing of one's own goodness and richness of life. As soon as we take it in, loving life as it is, it opens its treasures even more abundantly.

Having it "all" is a matter of perception. And the sense that you have it all causes even greater desire and wanting that will become goals that give direction both for self and others.

Promise

10

Your goals, malleable and given written expression over time, will lead to an inspired vision.

Roving street gangs in our cities concern us. Gangs form around poverty and powerlessness as a form of support, especially among young people. Negative support and hate seems better than no support at all. And that is exactly true, in fact. The idea of roving gangs creating havoc and violence and gaining power from their numbers is something we abhor. To increase their sense of size and power, oversized jeans, big thick belts, metal pierced flared nostrils, facial tattoos, t-shirts and jackets sizes larger than the person exaggerate and give an impression of working very, very hard on dominating and creating respect from fear. And the death toll of young people on the streets just keeps rising.

We just don't like the idea of roving gangs on our streets.

We don't like them at all.

Add to that loud, in-your-face rap music, vulgarity and pornographic lyrics and we fear what in the world can come next.

The gangs on our streets are a perfect metaphor for what happens when we have no goals that are leading to no vision. We hate the gangs and we hate the negativity that roves and raves in our minds when we feel lost and aimless.

There are times when getting lost in a gang might seem appealing to us as some form of protection and power, however misplaced.

What a perfect image they are for what goes on in our own heads.

The lyrics and power-driven pagan drum beats are a perfect image for own self-talk at ourselves when we have no real goals and no emerging vision. When our own "lostness" gangs up on us and puts on clothes larger than we are, when its rhythmic beat is a drum that keeps beating in our heads, we wreak a greater violence on our own sense of self than roving gangs of kids could ever do. If anyone else beat up on us like we do, we would want them shot. But this is what we do when we have no goals and no sense of an overlying vision. It plugs us right into our deepest sense of shame. And much of the time we don't even know it is shame we are feeling.

Street gangs mirror on the outside the lack of vision and direction on the inside of us.

When having no vision gangs up on us what that tattoos on the brain is a greater violence than anything roving our streets. Our culture has created on the streets, the negative gangs of meaningless, no direction, and lack of vision in our heads. We fear the slums because they are too much of a mirror for us of our own lack of direction, meaning and vision and the shame we feel because we are just as lost.

There are gangs of negative thoughts that "rove" the streets of our brains, sometimes with great, great freedom. Sometimes, we haven't done a thing to stop them.

There is another gang in town, another gang on the streets of our brains and it is the louder and louder sweet pulsing beat of:

Malleable goals given expression in thought-out written down statements of what we want and where we want to be in five years start an emerging inner life. These statements we call goals are also the inklings, if they are true and really represent our deepest wants and desires, of an awakening vision in us.

The inner pulsing of goals and emerging vision grows in size when it increasingly takes over the streets of our brains and returns freedom to one's self-image, along with a sense of hope and anticipation of something to live for.

There is a war in the streets of our cities and there is a war in our brains; let's heal the streets of our cities by healing the emptiness and purposelessness and powerlessness roving in our own minds.

Can you imagine a world where everyone belonged to an UpSpiraLife Group and worked together on increasing their UpSpiral Score? Who then were challenged to go use their strengths (which they knew) and to listen to their heroes give them solutions? When we capture our thoughts and turn them to goals and emerging vision, there will be no gangs in our heads or on our streets. So within, so without.

As your goals are written and become clear, you are like a laser grow light for your emerging vision and also for these goals themselves. Write them down, stare down your collection of post-it notes and make them speak to you of what your goals are and a special light comes. Dare yourself that direction will not escape you.

There are special lights that you can use to enhance the growth of plants called "grow lights" - they have special rays that enhance photosynthesis in plant life.

You, as a member of an UpSpiraLife group are a "laser grow light," especially if you have gotten as far as really working this step. The laser part is your ability to find and hone in on what is good and great, and by your "Zeno" dense attention focused upon it, you enable it to grow. You enable conversations about what is good in your life inside your own head and outside to others. There is no time for gossip. There is not time for listening to wandering conversations about things that don't work.

Consistently over time as you bring your laser focus to your goals, using your UpSpiral, your strengths and your capacity to be in the flow of your own life, you allow people to encounter someone who has a life, a plan, a set of goals that are leading to a vision, and a "sense of direction." What do you suppose is the effect of being around someone who has a sense of direction? What do you think that does for your friends, your kids, or your lover?

You are going to find yourself in deep quality conversations about what is good where another person wants to know more about you. See who is attracted to you and listen to the questions they ask. You may not like their response, especially if they are threatened by your sense of direction, but you know you are living in a way that people want to know more about you. It starts with what is called this "art of the quality conversation," focused on the good and allowing the other person the time and the space to talk about it, over and over until what is good eclipses the weaknesses that used to preoccupy their attention.

This special grow light you have inside of you is apprehended by those who want a sense of direction and by those who are afraid of it. Try living without their approval and their appreciation and try living in the light of your own reality for thirty days and see how much fun you can have and how fast you grow. The power of goals and this grow light inside of you is that you will actually care less about what other people think without realizing that you are. What if this inner grow light causes your goals to change quickly? What if you find that a goal you set isn't the right one? Use that information to sharpen the laser focus of the grow light and morph to a goal that makes your heart beat faster or at least easier. Goals are not necessarily for accomplishment; they are pathways to an emerging vision - they are just friends along the way to get you to where you really, really, really want to be. The clearer you become the more the grow light increases the growth.

It is just the opposite of raving, roving inner emptiness and endless mind chatter about how worthless your life is. The inner gangs of roving thoughts have ceased their power; the baggy clothes of self-inflation and the gold chains of false self-importance are gone and the clothes of your life fit you like your skin, because you are living in your own skin.

You are a Zeno Laser Grow Light with written goals inspiring an emerging vision.

Promise

11

You will find and define the vision of passion for your life.

We are discovering that it is a "vision" of one's life that will most heal the negative core beliefs of the past. It is also a wider vision of the future that will grease the passage through a transition. Negative core beliefs and transitions cause us to go into a DownSpiral and to "clutch" at "what is," making ourselves the victims of this or that trauma or change. This focus on "what is" closes us off to a whole other dimension of experience and that is one of receptivity. How much time do we spend being open to what the Universe will deliver to us? What would it be like to spend a day engaged in just seeing what we notice when we are looking for what the Universe delivers? Can there be any surprises for us or any nuances in our everyday life when we are so caught in reacting to "what is" and mindlessly going through the motions thinking we always have to respond?

Actually, the brain is simply attempting to conserve glucose (the fuel of the brain) in order to maintain a constant level of synchronicity. The ego and the brain are conspirators in keeping things the way they are in responding to things, even when they are different, as though they were "like" things. When our lives step outside of looking at "what is" that is a very new experience - that kind of receptivity signals potential chaos and novelty. When that is threatened, a fear mechanism is kicked into gear which signals some threat, the worst of which is the "unknown." This is a biological response to novelty or "newness" solely to conserve psychic energy and maintain the glucose fuel burn. It would be like an override in your car that slows your car down when you are going at a speed that is using more gas for the speed at which you are accelerating.

At the same time your ego is upset because you might find that the way it is constructed up to this point is somewhat useless, that it does not know how to respond to anything other than the way things are. When you become receptive, the ego has to change, to adapt, and to redesign itself. The ego does not like surprises or redesign. The present model, archaic as it might have become in serving you, is just fine as far your ego is concerned. Vision is not a word that your ego wants you to have in your data bank, much less access.

Think of not being able to increase the speed of your car going up a steep hill. The brain is doing something like that when it is time for a "wider vision." We are comfortable when we are coasting along until it slows us down and doesn't seem work to work as smoothly.

The function of vision is to heal the past and to guide the individual and group "brain" toward the future with eagerness and enthusiasm. Inspiration cannot come, the "how" cannot be created, and the leaders cannot emerge when there is a no vision or a puny vision that really does not move you through a transition in life.

We pay little attention to transitions and we know less about them. But they are the stuff of life. We are enthralled by people who keep reinventing themselves because it is the work of all of us. And it is the work to reinvent, sometimes in whole new ways, the visions that once drove us to greatness. A vision will get you into the transition you should have claimed a long time ago or get you through the one you are resisting at the moment.

There is an enormous abundance of ideas and this is the time to get the billion dollar idea. This is the time to get the idea that will put your organization forward in a way that will speak to a new age with aliveness, vitality and verve. A vision, when it is right, arouses passion and the desire to "belong to it." What is it that makes your heart sing? What are you going to do that will make your heart sing?

Everything you learn here from the Emotional Gym, to Strengths, to VibeCore to FuturePac, the VisioNavigator and MasteRevelation is about this vision that we never get done but that keeps us soooo alive in the living of it.

You should be able to put your vision into a single statement. And that the hallmark of an intact, workable vision is that it gives you a sense of personal significance. In its essence, you are living your life well.

The best research in businesses and organizations that succeed show that they are committed to an identity snugly and soundly based on what is called an emerging "hedgehog." It is a statement of central vision. It is the identification of what they do well and what they want to be.

No hedgehog ever fits snugly into place until the "stop doing" steps have been taken. "Stop doing" means the things that have to go, that take up too much psychic energy for the time put into them. They are no longer a fit, they take too much time, or they take a "little" time and energy when it needs to be invested elsewhere. You know when you are scattered, split, and splintered. And you now what does it, even though you may not be willing to face it. That is part of the "denial" of transition. Transition cannot face all at one time, the things that have to go, that you have to "stop doing."

For your heart to sing, what do you have to "stop doing"? Usually it is more than one thing and usually it includes some way of taking care of someone or something in a way that you have to stop.

Most of the folks at Walgreen's could not picture a store without an ice cream counter because it had become so identified with "going to Walgreen's." Had the company maintained it, they would have folded, rather than unfolding guided by a new vision. It was not until the management in charge understood that they would lose their jobs if the ice cream counters weren't gone in 5 years, that they finally dedicated themselves to building the "new" stores that sit strategically and geographically placed in relationship to each other within each location where Walgreen's decides to expand.

What is your "ice cream counter" - sweet, dear, lovely, approved of by most everyone who proclaims their lives would not be the same without it? They have also never offered to clean it or pay for it. What is "dear" when that is done?

What is your ice cream counter? What do you love that is just so much a part of you, that is so sweet and so much a part of your old identity that you can't see yourself without it? It's got to go, whatever it is or it will divide your "heartedness" toward your vision. Yes, I know, I know, "good feels good" and "bad feels bad." But here's the other part of that: we lie and repress feelings so that we don't have to face their truth. And we lie to ourselves about being in "vibration" but it can only last so long. We are great pretenders, but really.............we know.......we know! Eventually you have to face the "silence" you run from and "know" what you are really feeling again. You have to face the "brutal facts."

What you have to **stop doing** is not necessarily something that is unpleasant. It may be just like that ice cream counter at Walgreen's, a part of the old cherished identity, sweet, delicious, "home-like," and very attention-getting. Count the cost. Count the cost. Count the cost. It may, at first, be something that you can't imagine yourself not doing. You can see it in a flash in other people; they are peddling so hard to sustain an image or an old ideal or idea that "just ain't makin it" anymore. Oftentimes, if joy and anticipation doesn't create the movement in the transition, then self-induced illness or the obstacles of an ongoing always changing Universe will and it's like bumper cars without the fun and just the bumps.

Where are you putting your greatest efforts that are giving you the least return in terms of clarity, order, and enduring satisfaction? What don't you want to face?

Grow up and grow into where life's transitions are taking you into what you deeply know, if you are listening and reading the signs. Do it like your unfolding life depends upon it - because it does.

The hallmark of vision is that it gives you a sense of personal significance and your heart sings.

Promise

12

Your vision will give you a sense of personal significance and meaning that will attract to your life vital sources of revelation and support.

It is easier, perhaps, to live in an UpSpiral of positivity when you think that everything is going well. However, it can seem that everything is going well when it's not, and it can also seem that when everything is not going well that it really, really is headed in the very best direction. How many times has something happened to you that you thought was terrible and awful, only to find out, on down the line, that it was the best thing that could have happened? Whatever it was happened so far ahead of what the ultimate good was that you couldn't begin to see where the next door to great things would be. And in the end, the outcome was just what you wanted but in a different way than you had expected. Hasn't that happened to you over and over and over again?

You are engaged in a process that is elegantly simple and profoundly grounded in research and practice. But that doesn't really matter so much as one word which has become a somewhat forgotten word, and that is "revelation." When we have become so focused on what we are seeing in the latest technological device and watching the world, we get very accustomed to seeing "what is." We look, we watch, we identify, we cheer or not, and we see "what is." Revelation is not "what is." Revelation is what is happening on the level of the unseen but because of the way you are learning to live it is happening to you. Living with an expectation of revelation takes the kind of anticipation that waits with eagerness and anticipation of what is to come. Revelation is so unique that you can't just imagine it, or put it on a vision board, or make it an inner movie; it is always bigger and brighter and more surprising than that. It is always the perfect answer and outcome at the perfect time. It is then that the truth is revealed and more steps of the journey unfold.

Sometimes revelation rides in on a bold horse of what looks like calamity or disaster or uncertainty and takes some time to express itself for the hope that it is. But most of the time, revelation comes in a normal, ordinary way. St. Thomas Aquinas said that grace builds upon nature. For our purposes, that exactly applies. Revelation most often comes in like the fog, or maybe even just the mist. It seems very natural and seems like just the right course of events. It just happens in time, on time, in a perfect kind of way. It sometimes seems so ordinary that it is easy to miss as just simply the natural turn of events in life when you are living as you live. Revelation is easy to miss, often, until you look back and realize that something extraordinary has been happening.

Revelation comes in people, in events, in the weather, in the delay of time and in the loss of time, but it comes. And if you know it will, it will.

But revelation comes in its own timing. The space between knowing and having means that after you know what you want, and you form your goals - then, the real unfolding begins to happen. Your job is to know what you want and to live in the feeling state that you already have it. In other words, we live in the goodness of each day. We learn to see goodness all around us, and no matter how things look, no matter what the externals are we know that a Source that is us, in us, and beyond us is creating and bringing our goodness, our goals and our dreams about.

Faith is not an ethereal whim. It is a force of thinking and feeling that knows that we co-create our futures with a divine force that works through our thinking and feeling.

That force does not work through worry and doubt and fear; it does not know them. Revelation works through gratitude, love, peace, joy and hope - that state of being releases our spiritual energy and the full force of our being to both live fully in the UpSpiral of the present and full of Certitude for the future and the fulfillment of our goals, even though they may change some in the process. The space between knowing and having starts with knowing peace, love, joy, gratitude, and hope today, right now!

Your glass is not half empty.

Neither do we learn here that your glass in half-full - that is empty optimism.

Your glass is full and overflowing. This is where you are, this is your reality. It is your life and as you live this life, revelation comes.

Your glass is always overflowing - how do you get to the place where you see your life like this? Because when you do it just gets better and better and better and it is grounded in eagerness and anticipation that is less a focus on "what is" and more of a focus on the knowing of "what's in the works" and is yet not altogether seen or known.

Consider this: the further away you are from knowing that your glass is full and over-flowing is the best measure of how far you are away from being you and creating the life you want. You cannot be caught up in everything that is happening as "it is" because there is no sense that is open and expectant and knowing that what you want will be revealed. That's the revelatory sense.

There is a story of the fern and the bamboo. The seeds of the fern quickly grew green and covered the forest, but it took the bamboo seed four years to even sprout. Then in the fifth year a tiny sprout emerged from the earth. Compared to the fern it was seemingly small and insignificant. But just 6 months later, the bamboo rose to over 100 feet tall. It had spent the five years growing roots. Those roots made it strong and gave it what it needed to survive. Delay is never denial. It just means revelation has not come to expression. It means that the rest of creation in lining up for you for just the right time.

Every living person desires two fundamental things. They want to have the sense of being understood and they want to have a sense of personal significance. They are closely intertwined. We need to find what it is that makes our heart sing and we need to have the sense the song is heard.

As you have lived these steps, you have experienced this and the revelation that comes. Now, pass it along to others who need you to share your experience. You have participated and lived in the UpSpiraLife sanctuary of positivity; find those who are attracting what you have come to know.

12 NEW STEPS FOR A NEW MILLENNIUM
The UpSpiraLife Group

PART IV

The 52
NeuroPositive
Mind Quick Reads

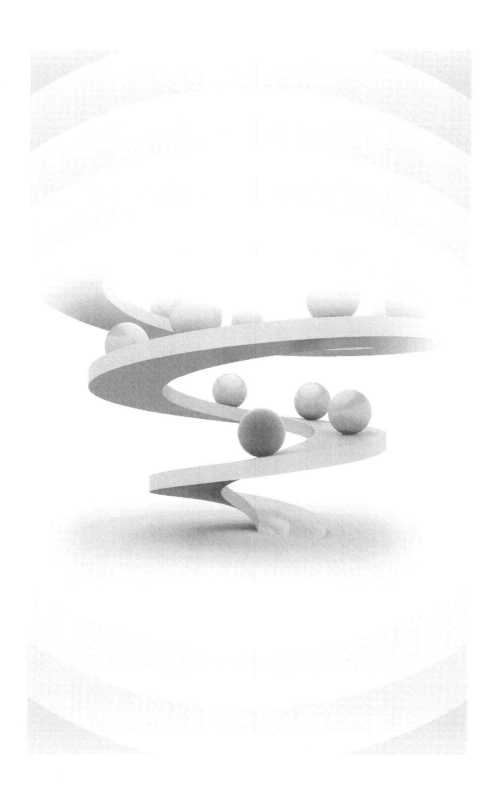

90 Days of Transformation

Here's a life-changing, life-altering exercise for you. First of all, on a scale of 1-10, if "10" is a lot and "1 "is a little, feel the feeling of gratitude at about a "3" or "4." Just a little will work and anybody can drum up just a little, even the most ornery grump or the most doubting mind.

Feeling gratitude, say the following to yourself 30 times a day, while you are in this state of a little bit of gratitude:

I have an abundance of health, wealth, happiness and love. I live in an UpSpiral of love, peace, gratitude and joy. My consciousness of Source, my monetary wealth, and my self-love grow exponentially daily.

And by the way, 30 times a day can be 3 times a day 10 times each time or 30 all at once. Either way, it's less time than you spend in a day grumbling. ;)

See what happens.

911 Emergency Negatives: How Many Really?

In my personal life, I have had only one 911 emotional experience, and it was when I had to rush someone that was having a stroke to the hospital. The stroke happened while driving in my car (and not because of my driving, folks!!!) and I was close to a hospital. That was only one time.

I have often thought that I wanted a phone message like I get from my physician when I call the office. "If this is an emergency, call 911." My recorded response would have to be something like, "If this is an emotional emergency, please call somebody else. If you are in an UpSpiral, press '1' to be connected." Many people think that if they are upset, if they're having an emotional emergency, that I should be the one to listen. Unlike many in our culture of instant accessibility, I have chosen not to be immediately accessible by a cell phone that is joined at my hip.

There may be an end of the emotional scale that is something like a 911 emergency, but they are very few. If we are honest with ourselves, most if any of the negatives in our lives don't need to hijack us into a DownSpiral. Most of our negatives are best served by getting to a higher place, to a better place where we are experiencing positive emotion, and can do our problem-solving from the place of being plugged into our real strengths. That's where we can do our best problem solving.

There is an elegant process of "emotional sobriety" at work here. When you feel negativity or when you are DownSpiraling, go to the Emotional Gym© and start pulsing the positive emotional state that is easiest for you to get to - love, peace, gratitude, joy or hope. Pulse it, feel it, chant it, until you feel some of it. Then it can occur to you to go to your strengths, rather than to their opposites, and use your strengths to begin to develop a strategy, if its only to back off and do the problem solving at a later time.

Let's get some emotional sobriety here!

The "At Ease" State of Mind

At ANI, State of Mind management is very important to our work because we know two significant things.

1.   A State of Mind will grow unless you change it - something on the outside may change it but it will change for only a short time.

2.   We are much more in charge of our State of Mind than we think —it doesn't just happen to us. We create it and it can change with practice.

If you practice an "At Ease" state of mind, feeling it over and over and over and over, even if you can feel just a little of it, the "state" will grow. Set it as the bar of your emotional life, and as the months pass, aim for a higher and higher move toward this bar.

These are the "Olympics of the Mind." You may not be pole-vaulting in Beijing, but you raise the bar of your emotional state just by consistent practice. And you'll feel like you got a Gold Medal.

The AT-EASE State of Mind

Relief (feel a little not a lot)
Peace (move in the direction of peace, just a little peace)
Free (think of a time when you felt free and feel it)
Unburdened (drop your shoulders and breathe)
Casual and more relaxed (walk slower and feel like you feel
when you are more relaxed)
Grateful (focus on something to be grateful for, something lovely)

Put all of these together and call them your "At Ease" State of Mind!

You attract what you get from the direction in which you are moving in your feeling state.

The Universe responds to your feeling state in a positive direction.

Attachment: Do It or Die!

From the time we are first out of the womb till the time we die, attachment is basic to our healthy existence. In a world full of the talk of "letting go and letting God," we are most godlike when we are "attaching." In fact, the letting go always brings another healthier, better attachment, unless we are fighting our own desire. Finding our desire is a process of attaching and letting each attachment teach us about the next and the next.

Our positive emotions and our strengths lived out teach us most about what we want our attachments to be. This means a ready access to positive emotions. The easy access to positive emotions and States of Mind lets this process flow. Our strengths enable the process. Oftentimes "attaching" is like following a trail with ribbons wrapped around trees. There are stopping points along the way that we enjoy that assure us of the right direction but point us forward to the next place on the path. Insecurity wants to stay at the same tree; secure attachment wants to see what's around the bend. Insecurity doesn't like the bend in the road; fear doesn't like the movement of attachment at all. Fear says, "Don't get attached, you'll only have to let go." Fear also says, "Grab what you can and run away from life. Get it while the getting's good, because it's all going to run out."

What attachment knows is that it is creativity, the synergy of your strengths used over and over, and your positive emotions and positive states of emotions felt over and over and over, that are going to spring you to life with the next great idea, the next great break, the next beautiful tree with the next yellow ribbon.

Infants who do not attach wither and refuse to be nourished. So do adults who refuse to attach. Listen to the little "wants" inside of you and lighten up to the inner voice of your own desire. You are not here to make anyone else happy, except from the expression of your own healthy attachments. The capacity to attach is rooted in positive emotion and positive plans.

But, But It Isn't Fixed
Or
I Don't' Have What I Want Yet

Many people live their lives with the idea that if this or that were fixed, then they would be happy or satisfied. That's just backwards. If you can't be happy today, whatever you need fixed tomorrow isn't going to make you happy for any longer a time that it takes you to forget what it was that was so important to your happiness!

I have a client who gets very, very worried about this or that from week to week. We do the work and use his strengths and by the next week, I am anxiously waiting to see how things have worked out for him. He will go an entire session and never mention what was so important and so much in his way the preceding week. He has moved onto another thing that must happen in order for him to feel happy.

Find the ways that you can be happy today, in the day, in the now. Let go and enjoy what you have. Then whatever you want will find its way to you, but not before you have learned to live in happiness and joy TODAY. If you cannot be happy today, or move strongly in the direction of being so, you will never be happy tomorrow.

Can I Have It All?

I was recently asked this question by a young, ambitious, dedicated and devoted business entrepreneur. What would you say? Would you tell her "yes" if she worked very hard, burned the candle at both ends, and was success-driven? We all know that those are not the measures that insure "having it all."

I told her "yes." I know that you can have it all, if you know that you do have it all today.

If you can, today, look around you, proclaim that you have it all, and live in that sense of abundance and gratitude, more will come. If, however, you are discontent, striving from a sense of lack, and driven because you will be happier sometime in the future than you are today, you should go see the movie "Wall Street." It presents this problem very well. And while it does not present the solution nearly so clearly, it is there.

"Having it all" is a state of mind of gratitude. The secret is to live in such gratitude and appreciation of today and its richness that you are open to even greater things. If you live in a sense of lack and discontent and "if only," you will bring more of that into your life.

Gratitude is a word that is used so much that it's hard to grasp its significance. Every positive emotional state - love, peace, joy, and hope, and all others rest in gratitude. Gratitude is a deep knowing of one's own goodness and the richness of life. As soon as we take it in, loving life as it is, it opens its treasures even more abundantly.

Having it "all" is a matter of perception.

Choice

It's very difficult to believe that we have built such strong ideas around the belief that how we are feeling "just happens" to us. It's hard to believe that what we feel is a result of choices we have made over time that have become habits and patterns of feelings.

Feelings are very changeable. You just have to want to change them. Recently something happened to me which seemed very negative and unexpected. It was very hard to believe that even the negative looking thing could become something positive - that it could be transformed to work for the good. It was very hard to start feeling gratitude even at a "1" when "10" is a lot and "1" is a little.

In fact, I just started saying "gratitude, gratitude, gratitude," and it didn't feel like anything happened. It felt like it was all just in my head. I kept thinking of things for which I felt grateful, and picturing them, but I couldn't feel gratitude. I could only think it.

I realized that I was thinking gratitude but I was really feeling fear. Fear and worry, worry and fear - it was like an obsessive cycle that did not want to let go of my mind.

I journaled and said "gratitude, gratitude" and felt oh so little of it.

I prayed and obsessed over fear and worry. God was not to be found.

And then I followed some of my own advice. I put on the new CD for the Emotional Gym and I just kept moving to music, remembering the moves, and moving from one to another. When I finished, I noticed that I did feel a little better. The edge was off, but I was still dulled and not really with it in the same way that I usually am. The feelings were anything but lifted, except perhaps just a little.

And then something happened that totally took my mind off of everything. It was the silliest thing – the recycling man was driving by my house and forgot to pick up my bin of recycled trash. I took off down the street after him and caught him He backed up and he took the trash away. I stood there feeling relieved that the trash was gone! And guess what? The fear and the anxiety largely went away with the trash. Just like that!

I had a few more minor bouts with it the rest of the day, but the cycle was largely broken and gone.

It was my choice. I could remember the day when I would have been depressed and down for a week, isolating and complaining only to the people who were close enough that they had no choice but to listen.

Choice. It's a choice.

Cycling Positive Emotion

All of us know that negative emotions cycle themselves over and over in loop-like processes. What we do know is that positive emotions do the same. Here is an example of the basic cycle of negative emotions and 2 examples of cycles of positive emotions.

Practice these several times each day. Get used to feeling a cycle of feelings. Teach your brain to go through the positive cycle. You can even teach your brain to use the negative signal of "oppression" to start you on a cycle of positive emotion, but like the scales of learning to play the piano, it takes practice and consistency over time.

A great time of year to be considering oppression is the holidays, with all of their activity and expectations. Just the simple expectation of what the holiday "should" be and feel like, over and against its reality, can be oppressing. It is what we make it to be.

This is the cycle that is so easy to get stuck in. Once you get oppressed, you take the whole ride on this coaster.

Oppression (it's on top of me, I'm not in control, it controls me)
Anger or Hostility
The fear of the same anger and hostility expressed toward you
The unconscious rehearsal of lashing out or withdrawing
The actual "acting out" or "acting in" the anger or hostility
The guilt and compromise with life (oh well, that's just how it is)

The ME (Mental Equivalent) Roller Coaster of Positive Emotion

Feeling Good and in control	Appreciative
Excited and Eager	Joyful
Eager and Anticipatory	In Awe and Wonder

Run through a cycle of all of these feelings. The feelings don't have to be large; let them be small- just feel a little bit of them.

The "At Ease" Coaster

Relief	Free	Casual
Peace	Unburdened	Grateful

Delay Is Never Denial

One day I wanted to quit...

I wanted to quit my job, my relationship, my spirituality...

I went to the woods to have a talk with the Universe.

While I know that "why" is never really the question, and that it always diverts me from my strengths, I asked anyway, feeling angry and sorry for myself.

Then I noticed the fern and the bamboo.

Something inside my head went off and said to me, "When these were seeds, the fern grew rapidly and covered the forest, but it took the bamboo seed four years to even sprout."

Then in the fifth year a tiny sprout emerged from the earth. Compared to the fern it was seemingly small and insignificant...

But just 6 months later the bamboo rose to over 100 feet tall.

It had spent the five years growing roots. Those roots made it strong and gave it what it needed to survive.

Delay is never denial. It just means that your UpSpiral, your Strengths, and your VibeCore are growing.

It also means that the rest of creation is lining up for you for just the right time.

Doubt, Doubt! I am Full of Doubt!

There is a tendency to think, or really to be afraid that if you are having "doubts," then you are sabotaging any growth in positive consciousness that you have made. Doubts begin to be a sign that you have missed the mark, and life seen through the lens of this doubt, starts to be filled with anxiety, fear, and dread.

The important thing is to keep the "doubt" in perspective. The "doubt" comes from two places, primarily. The ego (the old self that doesn't work really well anymore) is dying, along with its neuropathways and associations in the brain. Old ways die hard, especially when they belong to the structure of the ego. The other is that the brain is just necessarily made to doubt, to question, to seek more information. The brain, for as long as we live, whether we like it or not, is always scanning for a virus of any kind. A certain kind of doubt is just normal.

This is what is important. Are you predominantly moving, over the days and months, higher in the UpSpiral or are you over a period of time moving into a DownSpiral? That is what most affects your overall vibration. Look at your doubt over a period of months, not from the lens of a day or two of being mired in it. Is the general, gradual move to a more positive mind over time? That is your vibration from which you attract to you what happens in your life. The lean is so gradual that most of the time we don't realize that we are getting better and better at it.

Your vibration is determined by your overall, over time, more whole sense of staying in and moving in the direction of your UpSpiral. A very small amount of movement each day is better than leaps and bounds of temporary enthusiasm that will fade.

Don't make it harder than it is. When you doubt, don't use it as the lens for everything. Keep the doubt in perspective and do something good for yourself that you can enjoy just a little bit. Find just one thing to appreciate and don't work so hard at it.

Growing in consciousness is a downstream journey.

Dwelling... On What?

"Dwelling" is a word that expresses "being with" or spending time immersed in a thing. I can remember a time in my life when I spent a lot of time dwelling on negative things. I just thought that everyone did and that it was natural. If a negative thought or a negative idea came up, I just spent time dwelling on it. I would think about it, I would "think it through." I would muse for a long time thinking about this or that negative thing and I was driven by the question, "why?" I saw myself as a considerate, careful, penetrating thinker, and I was driven by successful "problem solving" and by the goal of always finding a resolution. It was as if I took on not only my issues and problems but also those of everyone else, and I had to find the mental energy devoted to all of it. I would dwell so long on some of these seemingly significant issues that my feelings would quickly follow...into a DownSpiral.

Today I don't ask "why" very often. Especially when it is something negative; I rather ask, "what is the good that can come of this?" I don't often get the answer right away, but I always get the answer just because I've asked. I am no longer resolution-driven because most things don't have a resolution right at this moment. They usually get resolved but not very often by my direction intervention. Things just happen along the way. I am also not problem-driven, but I am interested in finding out how my strengths, applied in an UpSpiral of positivity, give me resilience and bounce-back.

Where your mind dwells is a choice. I choose to dwell on what is positive and good. I choose to dwell on what I really want. Sometime ago, I made a choice to "dwell" on smiling and asking every cashier and service person how they were doing and how their day was going. I started to chat when I was standing in line and I always told the clerks waiting on me to have a great day. When I was dwelling on resolution and problem-solving, I never had time for the clerks or the cashiers. I was too busy dwelling on the larger problems of the world.

The clerks who wait on me are happier, I'm sure. I know that I am. And when I forget to do this, I just go back and start practicing "positive dwelling."

Your mind will dwell on the negative as long as you choose to let it, or it will dwell on the positive if you take little, active steps to go there.

The decisive factor is this: make your day at least 3 times as positive as it is negative and you will flourish.

Ego Attachments: Yes, For Now!

Thanks be for the ego! How else would we move? Except until we learn to move by pleasure and what feels good.

You do not know the "ego attachment" that will open the next door to "flow."

What you are hooked to with your ego, in terms of "got to have it," is just as important as your deepest motivation toward peace, love and wholeness. Never judge anyone who finds "oneness" by sliding their finger across the screen of their iPod and "feels" some of the amazement and delight that will keep them wanting "more." It is all in the wanting "more;" it is never in the "been there, done that" moment.

Being brought to your knees in poverty will open you to cry from your "core" but so will the luxury of an exquisite meal or a rock climb at sunset.

The ego and its attachments to our weaknesses are such a significant driver to the positive side by the contrast they create - if that's the way you need to go. And most folks do.

Or you can just go to your strengths. Strengths tell you everything; where you're not being yourself and where you are going to find "flow." Go to them when the ego gives that indispensable signal of discontent and boredom.

Every Cell Hears

Every cell in your body, recent scientific discoveries have shown, "hears." Not only do your cells "hear" music at the same level of your audible hearing, but your cells also hear what you are feeling and thinking. Every thought, every feeling is heard by your cells, by sound waves and sensory transmissions that are audible to the sensory mechanisms of each of your cells. Stop and consider this for a minute. Every minute of everyday, you are telling your cells how to feel. How do you think that affects their health?

So what your cells assimilate and what they expel, and how they function in healthy or unhealthy ways is fundamentally and radically affected by their environment of sensory information. That information comes from your choices about how you feel and how you think. *Positive emotion is the most power anti-toxin.*

Make the choices for love, peace, gratitude, joy and hope throughout the day. Maybe everything isn't going like you planned or expected. Maybe there is a downer or two, but you can still feel these emotions on some level of 1-10 from just a little to more and more. Can't feel them at all, you say? Then think them. You don't have to deny negative feelings, but you also don't have to stay in them, live in them, or obsess over them. Let negative feelings be a signal to find something to be grateful for and start to pulse a little bit of a thought and a feeling of joy.

You move in the direction in which you intend to go —into an UpSpiral or into a DownSpiral. And your cells are listening to the choice you make. What effect do you suppose this choice to feel toward the "good" has on the health of your always "listening" and sensory receptive cells, to each and every one of them?

Every Conversation Changes The Brain

The brain is a collection of neuropathways that are built based upon the stimulation they receive. A negative conversation, full of gossip and criticism, strengthens negative pathways in the brain. A conversation full of expletives and destructive comments creates and sustains neuropathways of negativity, anxiety, anger, and dread.

We are always creating the structures of our brains in the social interaction we have every day. Yes, you can tell your children - you become the company you most keep. That's just how the socially neuroplastic the brain is - you become what you think and speak and feel.

And once you feel negative and down, getting into an UpSpiral is like losing weight - it's difficult.

Most important is choosing how you want to feel. You want to "feel good." So you put yourself in those situations and with those people who build and sustain the conversations, the ideas, the interchanges, and the feelings that are about "feeling good."

We are, at our essence, five states of being; gratitude, love, peace, joy and hope. You can feel those feelings and be in those states of mind if you choose to be. You will never last in any of them if you don't make the choice. You can always come from one of these places if you discipline and grow the neuropathways in your brain that get you and keep you there.

This week end I made the mistake of going to a movie with a friend upon his recommendation, which I should have checked out. The movie was depressing from the opening scene. Four people were killed in the first 3 minutes and one woman was shot from behind in the head. I should have gotten up and left then, because the movie didn't get better. I am told that the reviews were good, but there is only one review that matters in my choice to "feel good" because I'm the person that's got to do it.

Every conversation, every movie, every interchange, and especially the habitual ones, over time, change our brain toward an UpSpiral or DownSpiral, toward "feeling good" or toward the ill-health of the DownSpiral.

A billion neurons and trillions of interchanges among them are waiting to be formed in the adult brain. How will you build them?

Feeling Good

Developing physical muscle at a gym involves gaining a greater degree of conscious control over the physical body. The Emotional Gym gives you a greater degree of conscious control over your emotions, your emotional state, your moods, and your state of mind. State of Mind Management (SOMM) is what the Emotional Gym is really all about. Remember - you have the power to exert conscious control over your emotions, including the means you employ to gain that control

This week, when your brain wanders here and there, wander it down a more positive path of positive emotions. Say each of the following words 50 times and match them with a little of the emotion. Say "thank-you" 50x, say "gratitude" 50x, say "peace" 50x, say "love" 50x, say "joy" 50x, and then another time during the day do it again. Match the words with a little of the feeling and you will find that the very Center of you will answer back with more of the same state of mind. Do it before you get out of bed and do it before going to sleep. Let go and lose count. Do it when you walk, do it when you hike or bike or exercise. Do it when you're doing nothing. Do it while you drive. Just do it.

You want most deeply, more than anything else, to "feel good." It's a decision, it's a choice, it can happen today and it can happen without anything in your life changing except you. If you learn to feel good now, watch what goodness comes into your world.

How, How, How?

When you are setting goals and dreaming dreams, having hopes and exercising the real, raw courage to own your desires and actually "want" what you "want," "how" is the "stealth tool" which the ego has to cut through, reduce and diminish your dreams. If you knew the "how," what you wanted would already be here. Face it! You don't know the "how" and it isn't even your business. So get your nose of the "how" and get your nose back into your business, which is to own your wants and your desires. Admit that you have them, admit that you want what you want. You say that you are afraid that you will get what you want and find out that it isn't what you really wanted? You're afraid that you'll feel like a failure or a fool? Actually, each wanting builds upon the last. You can't get to where you're going without wanting, and then growing beyond that want to another and another and another.

Give it a break, go ahead and dream and plan, and let the "how" appear as it will, as it always does. It comes from the Source, from God, from Higher Power, from Inspiration, out of the blue, in an instant, from a knock on the door, or a clue in a telephone call you least expected. The "how" is not the problem. You are learning to dream and plan and set goals and keep the "how" out of the way - that is the problem. Everything that you think blocks your way can change in less than a mille-second.

Now put your nose back where it belongs, and want what you want, desire what you desire, plan what you love, ask to find your passion. "Life, liberty and the pursuit of happiness" - do you think Thomas Jefferson knew "how" that would happen when he wrote it down? No, he didn't. I asked him.

I am Angry, I AM ANGRY

And I am not angry at one thing. I am angry at two and three and four things that have been happening for a while over time and it has just gotten to me. I want to lash out, I want to scream at someone, or at least talk loudly. I'm angry.

Here I am on this UpSpiral journey of positive emotion and I'm angry. Or at least I was on this UpSpiral of love, peace, gratitude, and joy and now I'm angry. Good things have been happening to me all week, and I was delirious with joy and hope. Now one week later, to the day, I am angry. Why?

Why? No one really cares about your "why" and neither do you. Anger is a learned response. It's a habitual reaction to frustration. It usually occurs, not over a single thing, but over a series of cumulative, one-after-the-other annoyances that are in and of themselves not so significant. Even that is a part of the frustration. Usually, we are angry because we've gotten angry and it just builds from there and it feels like something is controlling us rather than us controlling our own emotions. That's the big rub.

What is the strength that you have that most addresses the anger? Have a chat with the strength as though it were another person or another voice and see what it tells you to do. It will not tell you why you are angry, but it will tell you what to do to break the cycle.

The whole world gets caught up in this cycle of anger, individually and collectively. Do your part and make a choice. Stay in anger or go to a strength. Create more hostility in the world or bring yourself to peace.

Hint: Do something lovely. It doesn't have to be a great thing for yourself and something thoughtful and lovely for someone else. Just a little thing. And then give yourself a little time and space. Kiss yourself in the mirror and say, "I love you." Go on, kiss yourself in the mirror, leave a mark on the mirror and actually have to wipe it off (or leave it there for a while as a reminder).

Anger is a learned habit and can become an addiction without the exercise of good choices to manage it. You have the perfect strength to deal with it.

I Want To Simplify My Life - Beware!

If you want to simplify your life to more deeply immerse yourself in something that gives you pleasure or something that you love, then go for it. But if you want to simplify your life because you want to retreat or escape what you perceive to be the pressures of life, watch out! If you want to simplify your life because you feel oppressed or overwhelmed, watch out! First of all, life is not simple; it is highly diverse and complex. Look at nature and all of creation; you are greeted with great complexity. It is the nature of the Universe. You are a part of the diversity that is intended to express a part of God as the unique person you are.

Simplify your life for the wrong reasons and you will find yourself taking care of a partner who becomes ill or involved in a family feud or caught up in things you never imagined could fill your time.

You are designed to be involved in life. You are as innocent and beautiful and in need of stimulation as an infant in the eyes of Source. You are designed for experience, savoring life, and deepening meaning, and joy - all of your life.

The retreat from life that is isolation and disinterest, a slow "unplugging" from the stimulation of "aliveness," is not how you are made. You are just not created that way.

Complexity that is creative, diverse and novel - new stimulation - is something the brain and your Spirit need all the days of your life.

Too often the desire to "simplify" is an escape from using your strengths to live life in "aliveness." The hole you create from the motives of escape, withdrawal, and fear will be filled by a tumor, by depression, by becoming ornery and crabby, or by someone else's problems which you feel compelled to get involved in.

It Only Takes 20 Seconds...

...to engage a neuron with a thought or feeling and to begin to build or continue to strengthen a neuropathway. Every thought you think and every feeling you feel "designs" the nature of your brain and the neuropathways that affect every mood, decision, and move. Every conversation you have and the music you listen to, the movies you attend, and the anger or resentment you won't let go of affect the activation of neurons.

While this sounds like an exaggeration, it is exactly this approach that is being used to treat Obsessive Compulsive Disorder. Patients are taught to do something that will both change their thinking and their feeling. In place of exercising the old neuropathways of their OCD behavior, clients are taught to do something totally different that causes them to refocus on some else, like gardening.

Your focus will create in your brain the object of your focus. Try to change the focus of your "feeling" experience. Your feelings will change your thoughts. It is also true that strong focused thoughts will change feelings, but you can't ignore feelings and their power. Decide on a feeling that you want to feel this week - love, peace, gratitude, joy or hope, and then for a week, go to that feeling and feel it over and over again. Let every negative feeling be a cue to go to the positive.

Many people are obsessive about what they feel. They don't feel positive feelings because they've been too obsessed with negative ones. Tend to your emotional garden and grow some stronger, more stable positive feelings.

Knowing What You Want

Everything starts with knowing what you want. We have all been given messages about wanting too much, about the greed of our wanting, about how holy it is not to want. My parents used to tell me that I had a "champagne taste on a beer budget." Nothing has changed. I still do. Only the budget is better and what I want is still more expensive. In life we often get the message that we will get what we need but not necessarily what we want. Or someone may have told you, "All you do is want, want, want; you're never satisfied with what you have." That's right. While I am deeply grateful everyday for everything I have, I am never satisfied.

Many people were told to save their money for a rainy day. I was interested to observe that the rainy day always came to take what they had saved.

We have to get clear about what we are wanting because the mind and the brain are always creating whatever that wanting might be. If the wanting is on a subjective level, we are creating it. The Mind as a creative force is unimaginable. Scientists have tried to recreate models of the power of the right hemisphere of the brain and have simply given up. There is no way to quantify its power to produce, to store, to calculate, and to create.

If you want to get out of this life, if you've decided that you're tired of it and that your life is basically over, there is an illness that will cooperate and help you do that. If you're lying to yourself about the level of your happiness and you're really just treading water, and you'd simply like to escape, you're a perfect vibration for some dramatic thing, usually an accident or an illness. We powerfully create our worlds.

I want health, wealth, happiness and love and I want to live in an UpSpiral of love, peace, gratitude and joy. I want to learn and share, in an elegantly simple way, means of growth that move others to higher levels of happiness and joy. I want to add to making the planet a happier and more harmonious place. I want to see thousands and thousands and thousands of UpSpiraLife Groups all over the world and I want to see thousands of NeuroPositive coaches, teaching all over the world, the simple message that there is a vision of passion for every life.

I want you to feel totally free to want what you want, regardless of what it is. So long as it harms no one else, want what you want. Oh yes, I also want a red Porsche and a black Toyota truck with an extended cab and I'd like the plastic liner to already be in the truck bed. AND I would really get a kick out of getting all of this in these troubled economic times... so filled with abundance!

Limiting Beliefs

All of us have beliefs that limit our experience of joy, that keep us from flourishing.

Limiting beliefs are not necessarily negative thoughts, but they are beliefs about something that we want or would like, but that we think is out of reach.

What do you want, which, if you could have it, you would want even more forcefully?

What do you want, which, if you didn't have to figure out how to get it, you would still clearly want very much?

What seems impossible-- so much so-- that you just don't think about it much?

The "how" doesn't come until you are clear about the "what."

What is it that you want, with no-holds-barred in giving the answers? Own them, write them down, claim them and make them your five year goals. Go ahead... you can change them along the way.

Meaning and Personal Significance: Define and Redefine It Or Die!

Goals are the outward manifestation of our inward meaning-making system. They are expressions of our own sense of personal significance. They are signposts of personal development. What we are wanting and desiring is directly linked to how we are "making meaning." Structures of reasoning, that are more highly developed expressions of consciousness, emerge as we are specific and intentional about our lives - at least they emerge much more quickly. Every want and desire, every goal, fits a transition, a movement from a stage or a settling in to a new one. It can also represent the deepening of a present one. It is this business of desiring and attaching that moves us on and allows the developmental structures of reasoning to unfold. The most exciting structures of reasoning aren't even possible until after age 45 or 50.

The Developmental Stages after 50 are not yet understood or really delineated. But they have to do with broadening or perception. We are designed to get the bigger picture in such a way that the depth at which we experience and appreciate life is greater, more expansive and more satisfying. Life is simply just richer because of our history and our story. The great gift of aging is that it lets us apprehend life at a deeper level of appreciation and awe. Getting the bigger picture, which is really akin to wisdom, is the source of a great deal of peace and inner contentment and the key to a capacity to more greatly enjoy one's own life. But if we stop wanting and desiring, stop setting goals, and stop experiencing this broader and deeper learning, we interfere with the unfolding structure of the brain or the unfolding structures of "knowing." The extent of suffering and decline in the aging process is really a battle against greater and greater aliveness and a "sell out" to some idea that age means decline. How many of the maladies in the second half of life are simply energy and aliveness that has nowhere to go except to create some illness or difficulty rather than continuing to grow?

We are living in an age that is reinventing the second half of life and growing beyond the fear of losing youth, but fear is always difficult to look in the eye in order to watch it wither.

What is giving you your meaning? What is the source of your sense of personal significance?

Milk The Problem

Problems occur for everyone. A friend of mine has fibromyalgia. It is an elusive problem that science is beginning to understand and medical solutions have been slow in coming. But regardless, the fibromyalgia is really is a symptom of a lack of wholeness, of a lack of some inner alignment of vibration. In some way the human system is "off" in terms of its alignment.

So I asked my friend to have a conversation with her fibromyalgia. I asked her to see fibromyalgia as her friend, to befriend it rather than resist it and push it away. Rather than swimming upstream against it, I asked her to go downstream and learn from the condition. I said, "talk to it." And so she did. She asked fibromyalgia what it had to teach her. She was stunned at the answer. She said, "what I got in my head was that it was here to show me how I am loved and adored by Source."

She knew that the answer was correct and that she needed to look deeper. She began to realize that she had been very over-controlling, worried about the future, always fretting, judging, and assessing and never just relaxing and letting go. She realized that the only time she really "let go" was when she played cards and gambled--which was also something of a problem for her.

Oftentimes, we get the messages of what is wrong with us in many ways before it appears as a physical disease. She started to change her life. She slowed down. She got massages, particularly of the head. She learned to meditate. She radically changed her life style and tried not to "over think," "overplay," and "over analyze" everything. She gave up some control.

Problems have lessons to reveal to us. They are teachers form which we can learn. Don't let any problem get away without learning all of its lessons. Milk it for everything it has to teach you.

Very often, the problem disappears when the lessons it has brought are learned.

Pulsing To Oneness

There is within us this search for unity, wholeness, and oneness. We are always being drawn to it, and the more separated we are from ourselves and others and from this ultimate source of unity, the more discontented and out of our own skins we are. We are drawn, as if to a magnet to Oneness and Unity. But how to get there?

As simple as it is, our state of mind can take us there by plugging us in to this sense of unity. When you practice the Emotional Gym, especially the exercise of pulsing, you are going to be headed in that direction. Even in the beginning, when it seems that you can't even feel the feelings of love, peace, gratitude and joy and you can only think them, the contrast of that experience causes you to look at how your thinking or your behavior needs to change, usually just a little at a time. By no means do we have to be in a perfect place to feel any of these emotions. They will come just by wanting them and they will increase over time. You do not have to be whole or well or complete to get them. These feelings are at your finger tips and they are there for you all the time, even in the midst of loss and difficulty. They are present and possible even in pain.

Positive emotions like joy and love lead to a sense of unity. In the face of anything, you can have them. In the midst of suffering, you may be only able to think them, but by wanting them, they come. Begin by pulsing them on a scale of 1-10. "1" is a little bit of them and "10" is a great amount. It is not great amounts of them that matter. It is small amounts of them over time that matter.

100 pulses of love, peace, joy, hope and gratitude a day will do more for you than one or two very big experiences of these emotions in a month. Just pulse a little of them each day, over and over and over until they become the ambient sound track in the back of your mind. They will begin to play like a song that you can't get out of your mind.

Zorba, in the midst of deep grief over the loss of his son, chose to dance. Dance with these emotions that are also states of mind, and your intention to feel them will grow, and they will answer you back and grow within you.

Rocking With Worry

Whether or not you use all of your brain doesn't really matter so much as where you spend each day's allotment of your psychic energy. You only have a certain amount. Use it well or you get tired during the day and burn-out over the long-term. Believe it or not, your brain runs best on happiness. This is "brain synchrony." Your brain runs best on "feeling good." In an UpSpiral, the top is gratitude and joy, the bottom is despair and despondency.

Worry, which is negative thinking about the future, most depletes the psychic energy that produces brain synchrony. Once you get the hang of maintaining brain synchrony, you have the potential of raising your consciousness, which over time could look like this:

Feeling Good

Joy

Flow

Zone

Bliss

Ecstasy

We work at just getting people to "feeling good." The biggest block is worry. My grandmother used to say that she was ruminating. She would sit in a big rocker and rock in a consistent rhythm, with a far away look of concern, and ruminate. What she was doing was worrying. One day, when I was very young, I asked her why she was "rocking to worry" and she responded by saying that it was the only thing she could do about certain situations.

The only way I could distract her was by getting into something that I should get into or by doing something that I shouldn't be doing. That would rouse her and the day would go on. What a model that has become for many of us today. Worry until we create some actual problem that demands our immediate attention and shakes us from our worry.

Worry is a waste of psychic energy. It is a waste of the brain synchrony that really does cause us to feel good, and in higher stages of brain synchrony, move us to joy and even to bliss. It's entirely possible.

90% of what we worry about never happens. The 10% that happens does so in a way that we never would have expected with solutions we couldn't have imagined. Worry is a waste and it is also a choice.

Worry is a habit and it is a character defect. It is also a choice. Let the "rocking" you do be to the feelings of gratitude, peace, joy, love and hope. Instead of worry, lean gently in the direction of the positive. And do something. Move a muscle, change a thought.

Roving Gangs Of Thought

Street gangs in our cities concern us. Gangs form around poverty and powerlessness as a form of support, especially among young people. Negative support and hate seem better than no support at all. The idea of roving gangs creating havoc and violence and gaining power from their numbers is something we abhor. To increase their sense of size and power, oversized jeans, big thick belts, metal piercing flared nostrils, facial tattoos, T-shirts and jackets sized larger than the person exaggerate and give an impression of working very, very hard on dominating and creating respect from fear. And the death toll from young people on the streets just keeps rising.

We just don't like the idea of roving gangs on our streets.

We don't like them at all.

Add to that loud, in-your-face rap music, vulgarity and pornographic lyrics, and we fear what in the world may come next.

The gangs on our streets are a perfect symbol of negativity. And we hate them.

What a perfect image they are for what goes on in our own heads. The lyrics and power-driven pagan drum beats are a perfect image for our own self-talk and our negativity. When our negative thoughts gang up and when they put on "clothes" larger than they are, when their rhythmic beat is a drum in our heads, we wreak a greater violence on our own sense of self than roving street gangs of kids could ever do. If anyone else beat up on us like we do, we would want them shot.

Street gangs mirror, on the outside, the "gangs of negativity" on the inside of our own heads.

When negative thoughts gang up on us, what they tattoo on the brain is a greater violence than anything roving our streets. Our culture has created on the streets, the negative gangs that rove in our brains.

There are gangs of negative thoughts that "rove" the streets of our brains, sometimes with great, great freedom. Sometimes, we haven't done a thing to stop them.

There is another gang in town, another gang on the streets of our brains and it is the louder and louder sweet pulsing beat of:

Gratitude, love, peace, joy and hope.

The pulse of these emotions grows in size when they increasingly take over the streets of our brains and return freedom to one's self-image.

There is a war in the streets of our cities and there is a war in our brains. Let's heal the streets of our cities by healing the negative gangs of thought roving in our own minds.

Can you imagine a world where everyone belonged to an UpSpiraLife Group and worked together on increasing their UpSpiral Score? I really cannot imagine it on my own. My consciousness just can't wrap itself around that. But I can, with all of you holding it in your consciousness as well. When we capture our thoughts and turn them to gratitude, love, peace, joy and hope, there will be no gangs in our heads or on our streets.

SES: The Simply Elegant Solution

Elegance is in simplicity. And so it is when we are "down spiraling" into a more negative place than we are used to being. It happens to everyone when we get the first intimations of being oppressed or less free, by some burden or set of burdens that accumulate.

The solution to burden is an elegant one. In fact, it's simply elegant.

But elegant may not be easy at the start of this until you get the "UpSpiral ball" rolling.

1. Start to pulse the feeling of love, peace, gratitude, joy or hope-whichever one is easiest for you at the time. If you can't feel it, think it. Right in the face of the burden and the down spiraling, keep chanting one of these feeling states.

2. When you get a little bit of a handle on one of these feelings, just an edge, begin thinking about your strengths. Isn't it funny that when you down spiral, you forget what these strengths are? Each of your strengths should be attached to a hero that embodies that strength for you. What would your hero say about how to use this strength in this situation? Keep pulsing the feeling of gratitude (or whatever you have chosen) and think about how to use this strength.

3. Then consider 2 or 3 more of your strengths and begin to fabricate a simple plan that can be done in this 24 hour period. What is the next right step? Just do that, no more.

    Everyday your glass is not half empty, it is not half full. It is fully full and overflowing with everything you need and abundantly more. It will be empty if you focus on the problem and down spiral in worry, dread, and a sense of oppression.

4. Finally, call or email someone and give them a boost for the day.

Results, guaranteed, every single time.

Shame or Vision?
Growing Shame-free Neuropathways

Shame is an ingrained reality in all of us. We have all been embarrassed into shame or shamed at some point in our lives and it exists in us as a very raw, dark place. We very seldom ever see or confront our shame for very long. And it isn't necessary that we do.

We do, however, experience shame in its leakage into an underlying, almost abiding state of guilt. We touch these dynamics when we are in a DownSpiral. The further down you get in a DownSpiral the greater the vacuum that is created. This vacuum gets filled by some kind of guilt, anxiety and doubt.

We like to believe that "digging it out" and facing it will heal this shame and guilt. It won't. Some soul-wrenching admissions of shame may be temporarily relieving, but it is more of the same old focusing on the "dark side," the "shadow side," as way of finding some kind of permission and to have paid a sufficient price to be able to happy, rich, abundant, full of joy. We have been brainwashed to believe that to be a "light chaser" we had better have sweat bullets over our shame, guilt, and dark side. Baloney.

While shame and its seepage of guilt occur in the DownSpiral and not the UpSpiral, it is only in being in an UpSpiral that we really "attach" to our longings, desires, and truest "wantings." Take these deep desires and wantings, along with the permission to be imprecise about them for a while, and form them into goals. Then from a collection of goals, formed over time, start to define and name your vision for your life. The goals and vision are always malleable. As you name that vision, it will navigate you to your passion and to higher and higher levels of "wanting" for greater and greater good.

Your personal vision heals shame by establishing and growing new neuropathways in the brain and letting the old ones, fed too much by too many retreats and too much attention given to negative core beliefs and "darkness," die the slow death they will surely die.

The Zeno Factor from quantum physics shows that we create what we focus on. The very molecules of our neuropathways become fixed by our focus. Focus on shame and guilt and you grow it. Focus on your goals of passion and growth and grow them into your own personal vision of what you have to live and give and your shame will heal. It's a promise.

Shed The Skins Of The Past

You shed the skins of the past by moving forward with positive plans, positive hopes, and positive intentions. You could leave a lot of baggage behind just by getting on with your life.

We give much too much attention to what is wrong rather than what is right. We focus much too much light on problems and negative feelings and not nearly enough on getting on with it. We are made to be resilient and to bounce back. And the process of healing depends on the forward moving process of growth to bring strength, resilience and "bounce back."

Strengths: Flowering or Thwarted?

Why do you think it is that those who bother us most are those who thwart the growth of their strengths?

How you regard your strengths and what you are willing to do with them is like the decision to eat or not eat good food. You can get by on the junk food of your weaknesses, but what builds your sense of self and very directly the happiness you experience, is your decision to flex the muscles of your strengths, to use them more and more and to put yourself in situations where they are used. At work you start by looking at them and finding a few places during the day or each week where you can use them.

Consider this. Your strengths are Spirit manifesting through you. From quantum physics, they represent the Zeno Effect in your personality. They are fixing the elements of the molecular structure of your brain so you move, by the nature of your focus on them, in the direction of strengths or in the directions of weakness and deterioration. You can't get any more clear than that. Strengths move you toward life and aliveness; playing to weaknesses moves you toward deterioration. It starts with feeling disconnected and moves to feeling disengaged, disenchanted, unappreciated, unseen, unnoticed. Feeling unappreciated appears as the State of Mind of loneliness. That's usually the place where we start looking for someone else to fill the absence of ourselves that we have created.

Wouldn't it be just a lot easier to look at these strengths that are you? Flex them, use them, learn more about them. Use every cue of boredom or frustration as a cue that is a gift to go to a strength and learn more about it. One of the most interesting things about strengths is that they usually mean reaching out to the world around us.

You were using these same strengths when you were four years old and they have just continued on trying to develop within you, flowering or thwarted. Where they flower we know more happiness. Where we thwart them, we know more uneasiness and lack of satisfaction.

Swear Words! Damn!!

Swear words are both expressions of negative emotions and inroads to experiencing negative emotions. Swear words, used to be descriptive or as emphasis in speech, are oftentimes an expression of some level of personal hostility for one's self. Can't you just swear because you just want to make a point or for emphasis or color?

Sure, sometimes a swear word says it like nothing else can, with exactly the same emphasis and good feeling. But you have to be good at it and you have to know when to use it. Ask any comedian. It bears repeating: swear words are swear words because they express hostility, usually grounded in hostility towards one's own self.

In studies done at Harvard University in neuroscience, we know that whenever a person uses a swear word, it arouses the amygdala of the old brain, the place of strong negative emotions. When we read a swear word it arouses the basal ganglia, which among other things establishes our habits.

Our swear words make up a good deal of our own inner self-talk. We most use our swear words inside our own heads about ourselves. If anyone on the outside talked to us like we talk to ourselves, we would battle with them. We would be angry with them. We'd probably not talk to them, if they talk to us like we talk to ourselves inside our heads.

I am fascinated by the swear words people use and identify with because usually, they are the same words they use when they are angry or disappointed with themselves. We say horrible things to ourselves inside our heads.

Talk to yourself like you would like others to talk to you. Talk to yourself in the kindest, most gentle and forgiving way you talk to others.

"I am a good and loving person, I care, and I love myself. Or (your name) I thank you, (your name) I respect you, (your name) I love you."

Do it over and over and over and over and your amygdala (that place of negative emotion in your brain) will shrink because it's less active!

The Crucial Deciding Point in the Law of Attraction

Today there are agitations in me that are rubbing against my sense of contentment and satisfaction. I am feeling the initial oppressors of agitation and discontentment. And everywhere I look, I can begin to see things that aren't right, that upset me, that are not as I would have them be. I couldn't tell you exactly what is bothering me. I can't put my finger on what the unrest is. And I want to know WHY. I want to go there. I just do.

I realize that I can do one of two things. I can ask, "Why do I feel this way?" and I can run a search of several events that might have "caused" this feeling state. There is no proof, other than my discontent about each one of them, and that they are sort of just adding up. I so badly want to go to "why" I feel like this. I so badly want to x-ray my discontent. Shall I analyze each one, give thought to each one, play over each situation in my mind and articulate what I don't like? I could really get into the mud of the "why" and just be a pig in it. Let me roll in it and get it all over me and just exist in it.

The more I think about why I'm discontent and ill-at-ease, the more agitated I become and I border on anger. It is just under the surface. I don't like the idea that this Law of Attraction thing works to bring the good I dwell on AND the bad I dwell on, because today I want to chew the rag of what's bothering me, rather than just leave it be and go on with my otherwise wonderful, positive life.

All of this is the roller coaster on the way up to oppression. There is a choice. The feelings of oppression or the feelings of the "At Ease" state of mind or the "Mental Equivalent" state of mind. Or to pulse positive emotions. But this means that I have to decide to go there and I have to decide to run through the process of these emotions a few times.

I'll do this process of feeling these feelings and then maybe I could feel like getting to a list of writing down what are the positive aspects of my life at this point.

But the choice is clear. Oppression or freedom? Which will it be?

The Emotional Gym

Make a decision to start the Emotional Gym and embrace and incorporate it every day for thirty days.

Feel the emotions of gratitude, love, peace, hope, and joy 10 times a day. On a scale of 1-10, if "1" is a little and "10" is a lot, feel the emotions at a "3" or a "4." Feel each emotion for about 5-10 seconds each time. You are "pulsing" the emotion 20 times at a low level of feeling. Don't try to make the emotion last longer and don't try to make it more intense. Work for a series of ten pulses of gratitude for about 10 seconds over and over until you have ten. Then do the same thing with the other primary emotions of love, peace, hope, and joy. This purpose is to learn to get to the feeling of each of these emotions instantly, on call.

These emotions can become the ambient emotional sound-track of your life. You are building emotional "muscle" and you are starting to work on mood predisposition.

The FuturePac
Is It A "Fit," Is There A Click?

One sign of the success of having done this work is knowing that you have a sense of direction. It is that sense of "now I know where I'm going." Armed with the creative power of the UpSpiral, the knowledge of your strengths and how they work for you, and having understood that your "flow" in life is really defined by your VibeCore, now we get to the nitty-gritty of what you want to do with all of this.

You could say that learning to be in an UpSpiral is enough, or that learning your strengths was a big revelation that allows you "to be." However, "being" is always becoming because you are all about what you desire, what you enjoy, and the goodness that you create in the process.

When your goals are right and in place, even though they are always malleable, with experience, there is this sense of things "clicking" into place. They become a center for making decisions.

You will have 5-8 goals. How do they feel? How on the mark are they for you? How clearly do they seem to be a fit and define for you the direction in which you want to move?

These goals, if they are real for you, are already mapping your brain and giving it direction, let alone a sense of inspired purpose and direction!

What is your experience with your goals? What impact are they having on your life, even as you begin to "want" them? That is where it starts. Never mind the "how" right now! What is the impact of beginning to "want" and "desire" them?

The "How" That Binds

One of the biggest problems in moving forward with confidence, trust, and hope is that you cannot see the "how." But think about it. If you knew the "how," you'd probably already be there. The "how" is the part that blocks what enables it - the visioning, the believing, the faith that knows that the real "hows" that are exciting and enriching and life-giving, only unfold in the process. It is in that process that we are most alive to life and most discovering ourselves, if we let it be so. Life is a process of creation and anything thing you do or anyway in which you're living that has even a slice of adventure has an exciting "how" that's unknown, just waiting to be revealed.

That is when the greatest creativity, the greatest learning and the greatest sense of "aliveness" can occur. We live in a time where large "HOWS" are unknown, and that makes them also unknown in our lives. NASA didn't know how, Edison didn't know how, and in the plans you make all the time, including all the things that you want, you stop wanting them if you always have to know the "how" beforehand.

Your job is to ignite your desires with the power of your thought, and it is the job of the Universe to reveal the "how." The space between "wanting" and getting the "how" is the space that most requires you to be the fullness of who you are. Then, and only then, are you able to receive the "how." Let go, enjoy, live in the UpSpiral with the glory and beauty of today and the "how" will emerge.

The Music Of Your Mind

Several stressors accumulate, or maybe a big one, or what "feels" like a big one, and we start the experience of emotions that is like a roller coaster. The emotions which are the result of feeling oppressed or "it's on top of me" are the core of the emotional pattern that is at the root of every addiction. When the feeling of oppression starts in, however it is experienced, projection begins and we start to distort our perceptions of ourselves. How do you clean up a projection?

This business of oppression is a signal at the beginning of a pattern of emotions to which we are addicted, and the consequent escapes (some of which are pleasurable for a while, but don't last) are the biggest blocks to the coaching process.

When they get in the way, they seem to bring down the whole UpSpiral to a DownSpiral, and there is a loss of the sense or use of one's strengths. That's the downside and it's the problem side we work with while we are changing the "lean" toward positive emotions. None of this behavior makes you "neurotic," none of it sets you up for a clinical diagnosis or a DSM IV number to describe your mental state. But it can get worse and worse until disorder becomes the case. This pattern of emotions to which we are addicted is something common to everyone: oppression, the loss of our sense of power and giving it away to something that seems "bigger than us" and "beyond us." Usually the cumulative stress of the small stuff is what does it. It usually isn't the big stuff that gets us down.

However, this isn't where it's at. We just have to know it exists. You don't learn to play a piano by first learning not to play the wrong notes. You learn to play the right ones first.

To make beautiful music, you start with the right notes and you practice and practice the scales. The same is true with the positive UpSpiral life. You have to learn to play the positive scales. The best way to unlearn playing the wrong notes is to learn to play the right ones instead. It's a choice.

But just to make the point, here is the "yukky" side of this made even clearer. The negative scale of emotion that I described above starts with the feeling of "oppression," however that feels for you. It then moves to anger or hostility, then to the fear of anger and hostility. It then moves to feelings of protecting one's self, of running away or lashing out. Then it moves like a roller coaster, picking up speed and out of control, to acting out either the anger or the hostility, then to guilt and shame, and then to feeling half-alive, to rationalization to "not caring" and shutting off feelings. And then, after a while it starts all over again. That's the addictive emotional cycle.

It looks like this
Oppression
Anger/Hostility
Fear of anger and hostility toward you from others
Protecting one's self (isolating, running away or lashing out)
Acting out, actually withdrawing or lashing out
Guilt/Shame
The Compromise of rationalization "Oh, that's just the way life is" or "That's just the way I am."

It's a roller coaster, it's the foundation of addiction because it is the emotional pattern that underlies all addictive and negative habitual behavior. All of it, no exceptions!

They are the wrong notes in the music of life. They don't' work. It isn't a pretty sound scale of music. These are the scales of emotion that are characterized by disharmony and cacophony. They sound and feel awful.

The Positive Scales

So just like you would practice scales to learn to play a concerto, these are the scales of emotion that are important to practice everyday.

Learn them. Memorize them. Practice putting your emotions through these scales that are the opposite of oppression and projection. They are scales of feelings you play to get to a high UpSpiral. You can play these scales at will. Get better and better at feeling them and you will play them very quickly, very skillfully, very well.

You can get so good at playing these scales that you can be in a very uncomfortable situation, at the start of an argument, ready to go on stage, faced with conflict and you can make the choice to run through one of these scales.

These scales are billion dollar "ideas." They are worth everything in life to be able to play and experience the music they can make in your life.

Get really good at them and they will keep you in the "flow" of life. Get exceptionally good and they can keep you in a "zone" of life.

These are two of the scales that can make your life a concerto.

Feel the feelings, one right after the other, over and over just like you were practicing the piano. Make this the music of your mind.

Scale I (The **At Ease State** of Mind)
  Relief
  Peace
  Free
  Unburdened
  Casual
  Grateful

Scale II (The ME or **Mental Equivalent** State of Mind)
  In Control (feeling good)
  Excited and Eager
  Eager and Anticipatory
  Appreciative
  Joyful
  Awe and Wonder

Roll smoothly from one feeling to another and let them build. This doesn't have to be "great" feeling. Just teach the brain this new scale or "roller coaster" of positive emotions. Like the piano, it just takes practice.

Here are the rewards;
Your blood pressure will go down.
Your negative moods will change more quickly.
Stress will decrease.

Your shoulders will drop.

Your breathing will deepen and become more even.

Your attitude will change.

You will like yourself and others better.

Your brain will be in greater synchrony, use less psychic energy, and
 you will have greater access to your strengths.

The world will look brighter and better.

On a scale of 1-10 you do not have to feel a lot of emotion. If "10"
is feeling an enormous positive state of mind, and "1" is a little, play the
scales of feelings through your mind and brain at a "1" or a "2" or a "3."
All you need is a little to teach the brain that it is learning a new "song."

The Rate Of Your Vibe

All of us have a vibe, or a vibration. Some would say that we are a vibration. We think that our genes have so much to do with what we have become, but actually, it is the switches, actual on/off switches that either turn a gene on or turn it off and at a particular time, that determines the nature of our DNA.

Consider this. Bacteria have signals that they turn on to signal each other when enough of a particular kind have amassed to accomplish their purpose. Their signaling is directly affected by what you are thinking and feeling, and they will turn on the "go" sign when you are in a DownSpiral.

And now consider this. They are all responsive to vibration - to the subtle nature of mood and feelings and thought. The rate of your vibration is the ratio between your positive and negative thoughts and feelings. It is controlled more by that than anything else. And it is a much more conscious than unconscious process. You control the rate of your vibration by seeing what is good, praising what is good, lifting it up in yourself and others, and living for what is good. You can be sure of this: what you really want is good and you find it in your UpSpiral of positivity.

The Thank-You Man, The Thank-You Woman

Meister Eckhart was an extremely intellectual, mystic man of prayer. But his advice was acutely simple. He believed that if we never prayed any prayer or did any meditation, that the only practice that was really necessary, that would cover all the bases, was to say "thank-you."

I'm very interested in how important this is in the long term picture of sustaining an UpSpiral. All you really need is "thank-you." Gratitude will always keep you in the UpSpiral. But what of those times when you don't "feel" grateful, that you can't find the "thank-you?" And even if the thought is there, the feeling seems a million miles a way, never mind a state of mind that is joyful and grateful.

It really doesn't matter what you're feeling or what you're thinking. There is a magic in the Universe about this. Just start saying "thank-you" to yourself, over and over and over again. When you wake up, make up your mind to be a "thank-you Man" or "thank-you Woman," and before your feet hit the floor, start the "thank-you." Let the chorus of "thank-you" grow and grow.

The amazing thing that you will find is that the Universe will meet you with this experience, this feeling, and will respond with the state of mind of thankfulness. You just have to start the chant, "thank-you, thank-you, thank-you, thank-you, thank-you."

There are times when I am driving down the highway and my brain has decided to take a detour into thinking about some unpleasant past memory, or the traffic begins to slow, or someone honks a horn and startles me. It is easy to feel like I am "nowhere," going "nowhere," with nothing happening and everything seeming flat, maybe even stale, and I go "thank-you, thank-you, thank-you, thank-you."

I keep it going until my frame of mind changes, which usually doesn't take very long at all.

Thank-you, thank-you, thank-you, thank-you, thank-you

I am a "thank-you man."

The Upset Between Wanting and Knowing

One of the most uncomfortable places of all can be in the formulation of what we want. Most people don't really know what they want, so getting to "knowing" that it's happening is full of anxiety, unrest, doubt and even dread. A lot of people solve this by detaching themselves from their wanting. Whole religions are based upon killing your desires and stamping out your attachments. Instead of flogging the flesh we can flog our wanting and desiring in an attempt to become "empty" or "purified." No thanks. Been there, done that, got the scars.

The formulation of wanting has to emerge in one way or another because it is creation moving forward through you. You have to want what you want even if it changes. But once you want, the space between wanting something and knowing you have it can be full of unrest. This is the secret of getting your vibration aligned with the absolute good of God (or Source, or Essence, Mother Earth, Allah, Buddha, or Jesus.)

Live right now in the feelings of what you would feel like if you had what you want.

HOW CAN THAT BE? How can we do that? What we really want ultimately is love, peace, gratitude, joy, and hope. Learn to live in such a way that everyday you experience the UpSpiral of these feelings and the thinking that accompanies them. In this way, you will close the gap between wanting and knowing that you have it already, that it's on its way in one form or another. Try it, you'll like it. And you'll get what you want.

The Zeno Effect

The Zeno effect proves to us that on a molecular level, what you focus on is what you create. Where is your focus? What is the ambient, background soundtrack of your brain?

When you are not paying attention to it, what is your brain thinking? The brain is always thinking, always working - that's its job. But a lot of time our brains are taking us where we don't necessarily want or choose to go. We live in some default setting that we really haven't even taken the time to define for ourselves; it truly is by default. For a lot of people their default setting is grumpy, cranky, critical, uneasy, worried, anxious, "on guard." Yours doesn't have to be.

We would need fewer medications in this world if we chose to manage more of our thinking and feeling and decided to feel good and to feel happy, and decided to look for what was positive. For example, rather than simply react in fear to the current "new crisis," what if we began to tell a story like we wanted it to be? Like this:

We have gone through crises before of a similar nature. I always have what I need and most of the time I have what I want or I'm moving in that direction. Always in my life, where one door has closed, another door has opened. I wonder what new doors will open, I wonder what will be the good that will come of all this shifting the culture all over the world? One door closes, another door opens, ALWAYS, if you expect that it will. It's the Zeno effect.

Then try this: For each day of my life, for today I will not worry.

Tipping The Scale:
The Management of Mood

How much conscious control do we have over emotions and feelings and consequent mood? The figures vary, but there is one interesting observation in all the research. The more consideration we give to states of mind and happiness, the more the research shows that we have more and more control over emotions than we would ever have thought. A common belief, and it is only a belief, combined with some scattered and speculative research, is that we have 40% control over our emotional state. The remaining 60% is genetic.

Let's just say, for speculation, that the figure is 40%.

You have 40% of your own will that is working with 60% of a genetic predisposition. Of the 60% genetic predisposition, all of that is not "sour" or negative. No one was born with a totally "sour" disposition, although there are some people who are trying to win the title. About 20%, at the very least, of your 60% "genetic predisposition" is positive or toward the positive range of emotion. If you take that 20% and your own 40% of choice, that's 60% and that's enough to keep you in the upward elevation of mood and emotion all of the time. It is a matter of **choice**.

However you cut it, there is an amazing space of choice in emotion. Most of negative emotional patterns are learned. There are some, in a small percentage, that are inherited, but most are learned. And even in inherited, chemical mood issues, there is still a larger range of choice than we believe, that aids in healing and balance.

Here is what is important to know. You can learn and develop a pattern that is like a default setting of the emotions of gratitude, love, peace, hope, and joy. The amount of time your mind just wanders is the amount of time you can choose to lean toward a positive emotion. Consistent positive emotion at a low grade, like a "1" or "2" or "3" on a scale of 1-10, is more effective in maintaining happiness that one big event of happiness once a month.

The best way to manage mood and to elevate mood is consistent practice of positive emotion over time. Consistent means daily. Tip the scales of your life strongly in the direction of positive emotion and you will feel better and be healthier.

It just takes remembering and practice, and those are the hardest things to do. But you can tip the scale in the direction of positive feelings. You know that there are those, who by their own choice, have tipped their scale in the direction of the negative. Why not make a choice to tip it in the other direction?

TouchStones

Each of us has "TouchStones" stored in our brains that affect our energy level. TouchStones are memories which are big, significant reference points for our thoughts and feelings.

A TouchStone can be a positive or negative anchor in our brains. We tend to make much more use of negative TouchStones in our lives than we do of positive ones. The left hemisphere of your brain will remember a "touchstone," particularly a negative one, in a factual way that fits how you use it. Your right hemisphere recalls a memory within a much larger context and transforms negative energy into positive, open, and attachment oriented energy.

How do you get a negative "TouchStone" of a memory that makes you angry or upset over into the right hemisphere so the memory can be healed?

First, make a list of the "TouchStone" memories in your life that you consider negative or that still feel negative. Then ask one, solitary important question that you are willing to give some time to answering: "What was the good that came of this? What is the good that can come of this?" Then allow your right hemisphere, which is connected to the "oneness" of your nature, and to the Universe, to give you the answers. There are always benefits to negative TouchStones, if we are willing to allow the answers to emerge rather than to nurse old wounds.

Give as much energy and emotional play to these answers as you need to move them from the left hemisphere negative list of psychic energy-wasters to your right hemisphere integrator of experience.

This is the benefit. You open your energy, you unblock your psychic energy and you become freer and much more able to be in an UpSpiral where you learn faster, are more creative, and "feel good." This increase in positive energy is a "lubricant" that allows your brain to function with greater ease and integrity.

Transition and Consciousness

If you "attach" easily in healthy ways based upon knowing and using your strengths and staying in an UpSpiral, transition usually appears as a new light over on the horizon of a new potential adventure of learning and experience. If you "hold on" a little too much to where you are, the light appears as a little bit of "itch" where you are - the itch of some low-level discontent. From there the contrast of either way just gets greater. You feel more drawn or feel more of an itch. And then it just grows a little more and more and more.

Our capacity to notice a new light on the horizon depends upon on our aliveness. "Aliveness" is the peculiar trait which describes humans when they are at their best.

Aliveness is noticing this and that, like a giraffe which has a tall reach and notices what is in the distance. The antennae of personal aliveness pick up the signals of what is pulling us forward toward more aliveness and more satisfaction.

We prize being finally getting "settled." Good luck! You get it for awhile, but if you're alive, being "settled" becomes "unsettling" because there is this thing in you which always wants to express and experience novelty. It's hard for a youth-oriented culture to believe what happens at 80 when the only models of aliveness on television are all under 30. It's also hard when those who are 80 have sold out and also act like the only reality in aging is decline.

But it actually happens more at 80, if you let it, because you have more experienced neurons in your brain propping up your consciousness. Have you noticed how people under 30 just really keep doing the same crazy things over and over? Monet was painting his greatest paintings after he was 80 with specially designed glasses, because he could no longer see the whole spectrum of light without them. Imagine that! Painting the "light" at 80! That is what made him great. He painted the effect of the light on an object and not the object itself.

Where is the light appearing on the horizon for you, the faint light that you have to be alive to see?

Vanity Isn't So Fair

Vanity Fair. What a great example of hearing something so often, as a part of our culture, that it never is really questioned. Tongue-in-cheek and clever intellectualizing from another era matters little. It's dangerous when it comes to strengths. Real vanity is the opposite of your strengths, so long as you have been tested for your strengths and you know what they really are.

Vanity is essentially "playing it" to the outside world. It's a mask to create an impression and get a reaction more related to status, power, and where we want to be in the pecking order. Everybody has it and does it, just like everybody has strengths and forgets to use them. Here's the challenge. Use your strengths as much as you use your eye shadow. Use your strengths as much as you do whatever those things you do that get people who notice you to like you better.

Pure vanity plays to the unique opposite of all of your strengths. You have an opposite to every strength. Addiction groups call it your character defect and pray to God for God to remove it, if it is God's will. What a "god!" You need your character defects as a signal to you that you are not playing to their opposite: your character strengths. Yes, the opposite of your character strengths are your character defects and they are, for each strength, unique to every person. Once you know your strengths, you can identify your defects and vice versa.

But here's the most important and significant insight without getting tripped up in your vanity. The evidence is, from all research in the area, that the more you use your strengths the happier you will be. The more you don't, the more you hope that vanity will be fair.

VibeCore: Your Brain on Flow

Your brain in flow is revitalizing and renewing. It represents a state in which it operates most like its natural state - in a high degree of synchrony. This flow is meditation in motion; it is contemplation on the move. Many people who are not good at passive, emptying meditation practices will find that flow is a welcome, much more easily attained state of meditation and a relief from the daily spiritual practices they don't do and feel guilty about missing.

What is meditation? It is a state of becoming "one with." It is unifying in such a way that we transcend the usual patterns of thinking about this or that and focus on a single reality so that, not just our thinking, but time itself slows down. That's what happens in flow. It is perfectly possible to meditate and dance, to meditate and run, to meditate and do a task. This secret is in the "just this" experience.

The experience of the brain on flow is an increase in "psychological capital." What that means is that you are reducing the amount of psychic energy used to do a task and adding to the scope of the connectedness of your neurons. Things are knitting together in new ways in your brain. When they continue to knit together in new ways, (interneuronal association) intelligence increases. You are increasing the positive reserves of the brain on every level when you experience flow.

When One Door Closes, Another Door Opens

This is a remarkable example of a concept we use widely in our work here at ANI. If you go back through your life, wherever one door closed, another door opened. Let me give you a very short-term approach to long, endless, needless, psychoanalysis and psychotherapy. Make a list of every door that closed in your life in one column and then next to it, make a list of the doors that subsequently opened. Perhaps they didn't open right away, perhaps you spent a little time, or what seemed like a very long time, getting ready for the next door to open, but it always opened. The next door always opens when you expect that it will.

Feel sorry for yourself forever, act and feel like a victim, moan, groan and complain and that door will take longer to open. We believe at ANI that Spirit is everything, that Spirit is all there is. If that is true, and it is, then the more attention you pay to the door that is closed, the longer it takes to find the door that will open.

When We Have It All, The Rest Just Keeps Coming

There is something about living on the tightrope of realizing that you have it all, and also knowing that everything you want, in one way or another, is coming. It is not just about living in the now, although that's a part of it. It is also having enough aliveness and interest in life that you are attached to ongoing discovery. The happiest people in the world have a strong interest and curiosity about life and the world, but they also express excitement about the future, with plans, desires, wants, and goals that are just a part of their life.

An Italian researcher studying aging found that the most significant aspect of a declining aging process was getting to be good at what you were doing. You get a job, you learn skills, and over time, you can do it in your sleep, almost automatically. There are almost no surprises, and you begin to use less and less of your brain as you get better and better at doing what you already do. Maybe what you do gets boring, stale and uninteresting, or maybe not, but the essential feature is that you are challenged less and less to do more and more with the associational and integrative learning tasks in the brain.

This narrowing actually has a name. It's called Parsimony and it means the narrowing of the range of diversity and challenge in and to the brain.

Having stability should give a greater appetite for living, not an opportunity or excuse to stop thinking and not use your strengths. That's when you start a process of decline, no matter what your age.

There is a trail of discovery, a journey to the next portal of learning and experience that is running through your life. You can miss the trail, become ornery, fixed, and pretend you are content by not wanting to be bothered by anything.

Find the trail of learning and discovering and flourishing living. It's there and you're either on it or you're not. When you're on that trail, you know that you have it all and you will be amazed at the abundance that just comes to you from all around you.

Where Do You Spend Your Mind...

...and to what does your brain retreat? Our most precious resource is psychic energy. That's the "mental energy" we have in a 24 hour period to do everything we do with our mind and brain. The Mind is the larger master of how the brain thinks, feels, perceives, and does its work. The Mind directs the brain...or it does not. Mindlessness is a lack of consciousness about where we are spending our psychic energy. It's like writing checks without ever looking at the balance in the account.

Mindlessness is what advertisers depend upon. Mindlessness is what people who don't want us to think depend upon. The Mind just wanders from this to that. Think a negative or angry thought and see where your brain goes when you send it mindlessly down that road. Mindlessness just gets the errands of the day done.

There is a principle in psychology called the Zeigarten effect, that states that we have a 9:2 bias in our tendency to notice, to lean, and to remember in a negative direction. It's considered an evolutionary tendency.

If you could quantify the time your brain spends on the positive and the negative, focused on what is beautiful or whining about what you don't have yet, what is right in your world vs. what's wrong, where would you come out?

What would be your ratio of the good in your world, as compared to the negative that draws you in like a fly caught in a web? What is your ratio of positive to negative thinking?

Here is what the significant research of Losada and Fredrickson shows us. To flourish, you need an average of 3 positives to every negative, in whatever way you want to weight them. We need an average ratio of 3:1, positive to negative events, to FLOURISH. For some folks, it's 5:1. Others may only need 2:1. These may be thoughts, conversations, or events.

Mindlessness is the enemy of flourishing in your life. Flourishing takes mindfulness of the world within you and the world around you.

Mindfulness is being awake to yourself. It is attention, it is savoring, it is aliveness. It is what it takes to stay in an UpSpiral. It is not just going along negatively reacting to the weather, to politics, or putting your focus on what is wrong. Mindfulness is your disciplined focus on where the popcorn is popping, and not on the kernels that didn't.

Will Your Brain Decline? Your Choice!

What about the declining aging brain? The brain ages, but, like fine wine, it does not have to decline. The brain develops throughout all of life. Supposed short term memory loss is a myth. It isn't a loss. It is the reorganization and emerging "second half of life brain" which is developmentally changing from smaller thinking to getting the bigger picture. The brain has the developmental task in the second half of life to transfer the psychic energy of short-term memory into wisdom and "getting the larger picture." Positive emotion is the anti-oxidant of the brain - it cleans up narrow and negative thinking that causes negative aging. This negative and rigid thinking is also related, we are finding, to Alzheimer's.

Neuroplasticity proves to us that the brain can always change.

We are increasingly finding the greater and greater degree to which it can change.

How do you want to change your brain?

What thoughts and patterns of feelings do you recognize that take you down the road to negativity and personal rigidity?

You are learning to create a State of Mind (SOM) called Certitude. Tell us how you are doing it and what it's like!

You Attract What You Largely Feel

Feelings are the great revealers of truth. That is why we spend so much time sitting on them and hiding them and betraying them. That's why we dump drugs and alcohol on them, so we don't have to feel them and listen to the messages they want to give us. They tell us what we are thinking or how our thinking and perception are conflicted.

It is not that our little, everyday feelings are magnets that bring everything to us that is just like them. It is the patterns of emotions and the predominant emotions that get conditioned in over time that attract to our lives what our experiences are. You get what you largely feel because you are in the process, in your way, of creating it.

The most predominant emotional state that gets us in trouble is feeling "oppressed." It is the feeling of being powerless or the threat of powerlessness in some way. It is that point at which we feel that things are happening to us over which we have no control and that we are victims. It happens in those times when it just feels like it's getting to be "too much." Our tolerance level has been reached and we begin to feel a little or a lot "overwhelmed."

But here is the truth. Feeling overwhelmed and powerless is learned. You learn it over time. Because there is always an escape from feeling overwhelmed, disgusted, over-it, powerless, or fed up, and that escape is always in the form of some kind of reward. The reward is whatever you do that is not dealing with the problem directly; it's how you avoid the real issue and just "get away." Maybe it's food, maybe it's booze, maybe it's sex, maybe it's religion, maybe it's depression, maybe it's raging and scaring people away. Maybe it's isolating and shutting out the world.

Feelings of powerlessness and being "fed up" didn't just start today. They've become a larger way of feeling over time. They are a larger way of avoiding and "dealing" with what isn't working. These feelings of oppression are largely a way of feeling sorry for yourself, angry that you are, and they are directed back at you in the form of feeling "powerless."

When something doesn't feel good it's telling you to ask what you want. What do you really, really want?

However, there is something you can do that can help. When you feel largely in a negative way, go to a positive place. Use the Emotional Gym and go to a feeling of love, peace, gratitude, hope and joy that is not an escape from the problem but a place that is easier for you to observe it. You can't use the Emotional Gym to hide from negative feelings, but you can use it to better look at why they are there. Practicing positive feelings will give you a buffer of a better place to observe what you let get you down. Go to a higher place and look at what feeling "oppressed" or "powerless" is telling you. How much of it is a habit that needs to change? What do you need to stay away from? What needs to be different? If you can't figure it out, talk it out with someone.

When you largely feel "oppressed" or "powerless" you attract more of the same. When you make a decision to move in another direction and realize that you can feel a little gratitude or a little peace or a little love, you start to shake loose from feeling overwhelmed and oppressed.

Much of the time we are just too easily oppressed and overwhelmed, and feeling like a victim is an excuse for not taking action, for not being direct, and for not being clear with yourself about what you want.

Your Ego is A Smoke Detector

The smoke detector in your home is very sensitive. It lets off a loud squawking alarm at even the faintest detection of the odors that signal a fire. A little smoke from a meal, burnt toast, or a fireplace can set off an alarm that is startling. So it often is with the Ego. The Ego, as it is used here, is the person you are when you are playing to your weaknesses rather than your strengths. Play to your weaknesses and your Ego goes off; play to your strengths and your "real self" moves into play.

The more positive you become, the greater you grow into an UpSpiral, using your strengths, the more sensitive is your detector, the Ego, that you're moving in the wrong direction - one of weakness that is the opposite of your strengths. The more you come from your Inner Being, the real strengths that you have, the harder it is for the Ego not to give itself away. It does so through anxiety, fear, the feeling of being out of sync with yourself, and just plain discord - all signs that you are moving away from your strengths.

You would never want to get rid of a smoke detector or disconnect it. So it is with the Ego. It is a part of a whole - a warning system that lets you know that you are not coming from your strengths. And the more you come from your strengths, the more you get used to playing to them, the more your Ego will make noise because you will be more sensitive to its sounds and warnings that you are getting off track.

Your Strengths Are Impeccable

There is not a situation in your life that your strengths can't address. You have a perfect set of them. Some of you who are reading this know what they are. You've been through our testing process and you can name your strengths and you have grown by using them. Instead of concentrating on your weaknesses and trying to change them and getting nowhere, you have learned that by growing your strengths, your weaknesses fall within your ability to manage them effectively.

Weaknesses are merely the other end of our strengths. In fact, they point in the direction of what our strengths really are. But from the first red check marks on our school papers, or even before, we have learned what is **wrong** with us much better than we have learned what is good about us. Whenever I test a group of people and ask them to write down their strengths, they can usually only list one or two that are actually accurate; they are much better at listing their weaknesses.

Going to a strength, playing to a strength, thinking from a strength is foreign behavior for most people. When we are troubled, stressed and worried or frustrated for very long, it is easy to go to our weaknesses and to play from the opposite end of our strengths.

You never become a well-balanced or a "whole" person, whatever in the world that might be, by trying to correct your weaknesses. You become more of who you authentically are by playing to your strengths and letting them guide you to your own inner brilliance.

Bibliography

Amen, Daniel G.. *Change your brain, change your life: The breakthrough program for conquering anxiety, depression, obsessiveness, anger, and impulsiveness.* New York: Times Books, 2000.

Aspinwall, Lisa G., and Ursula M. Staudinger. *A psychology of human strengths: fundamental questions and future directions for a positive psychology.* Washington, DC: American Psychological Association, 2003.

Begley, Sharon. *Train your mind, change your brain: How a new science reveals our extraordinary potential to transform ourselves.* New York: Ballantine Books, 2007.

Bradberry, Travis, and Jean Greaves. *Emotional intelligence 2.0.* San Diego, Calif.: TalentSmart, 2009.

Brizendine, Louann. *The female brain.* New York: Morgan Road Books, 2006.

Brizendine, Louann. *The male brain.* New York: Broadway Books, 2010.

Brooks, David. *The social animal: A story of love, character, and achievement.* New York: Random House, 2011.

Bryant, Fred Boyd, and Joseph Veroff. *Savoring: A new model of positive experience.* Mahwah, N.J.: Lawrence Erlbaum Associates, Publishers, 2007.

Buckingham, Marcus, and Donald O. Clifton. *Now, discover your strengths.* New York: Free Press, 2001.

Buettner, Dan. *Thrive: Finding happiness the blue zones way.* Washington: National Geographic Soc, 2011.

Cloninger, C. Robert. *Feeling good: The science of well-being.* Oxford: Oxford University Press, 2004.

Cooperrider, David L., Diana Kaplin Whitney, and Jacqueline M. Stavros. *Appreciative inquiry handbook for leaders of change.* 2nd ed. Brunswick, OH: Crown Custom Pub., 2008.

Csikszentmihalyi, Mihaly. *Flow: The psychology of optimal experience.* New York: Harper & Row, 1990.

Damasio, Albert. *The feeling of what happens, body and emotion in the making of consciousness.* Orlando, Fl, Hartcourt, 1999, Hartcourt Press, Orlando FL.

Diener, Ed., and Robert Diener. *Happiness: Unlocking the mysteries of psychological wealth.* Malden, MA: Blackwell Pub., 2008.

Doidge, Norman. *The brain that changes itself: Stories of personal triumph from the frontiers of brain science.* New York: Viking, 2007.

Frankl, Viktor E. *Man's search for meaning: An introduction to logotherapy.* 3rd ed. New York: Simon & Schuster, 1984.

Fredrickson, Barbara. *Positivity.* New York: Crown Publishers, 2009.

Gilbert, Daniel Todd. *Stumbling on happiness.* 1. ed. New York: Vintage books, 2007.

Glasser, William. *Choice theory: A new psychology of personal freedom.* New York: HarperPerennial, 1999.

Goldberg, Elkhonon. *The wisdom paradox: How your mind can grow stronger as your brain grows older.* New York: Gotham Books, 2005.

Goldberg, Elkhonon. *The new executive brain: Frontal lobes in a complex world.* Oxford: Oxford University Press, 2009.

Haidt, Jonathan. *The happiness hypothesis: Finding modern truth in ancient wisdom.* New York: Basic Books, 2006.

Langer, Ellen J. *Counter clockwise: Mindful health and the power of possibility.* New York: Ballantine Books, 2009.

Larkin, Dr. William K. *Growing The Positive Mind.* Rancho Mirage, CA: Applied Neuroscience Press, 2008.

Larkin, Dr. William K., and Dr. Donald B. Johnson. *Plans to The Universe and The Answers Back.* Rancho Mirage, CA: Applied Neuroscience Press, 2009.

Ledoux, Joseph, *The mysterious underpinnings of emotional life.* New York: Simon and Schuster, 1996.

Linley, P. Alex, and Stephen Joseph. *Positive psychology in practice.* Hoboken, N.J.: Wiley, 2004.

Lipton, Bruce H.. *The biology of belief: Unleashing the power of consciousness, matter and miracles.* Santa Rosa, CA: Mountain of Love/ Elite Books, 2005.

Lyubomirsky, Sonja. *The how of happiness: A scientific approach to getting the life you want.* New York: Penguin Press, 2008.

McGonigal, Jane. *Reality is broken: Why games make us better and how they can change the world.* New York: Penguin Press, 2011.

Newberg, Andrew B., and Mark Robert Waldman. *How God changes your brain: Breakthrough findings from a leading neuroscientist.* New York: Ballantine Books, 2009.

Pert, Candace B. *Molecules of emotion: Why you feel the way you feel.* New York, NY: Scribner, 1997.

Peterson, Christopher, and Martin E. P. Seligman. *Character strengths and virtues: A handbook and classification.* Washington, DC: American Psychological Association, 2004.

Peterson, Christopher. *A primer in positive psychology.* Oxford: Oxford University Press, 2006.

Rath, Tom. *Vital friends: the people you can't afford to live without.* New York, NY: Gallup Press, 2006.

Rath, Tom. Strengths finder 2.0. New York: Gallup Press, 2007.

Reivich, Karen, and Andrew Shatte, *The resilience factor: 7 essential skills for overcoming life's inevitable obstacles.* New York: Broadway Books, 2002.

Schwartz, Jeffrey, and Sharon Begley. *The mind and the brain: Neuroplasticity and the power of mental force.* New York: Regan Books/ HarperCollins Publ., 2002.

Seligman, Martin E. P. *Learned optimism.* New York: A.A. Knopf, 1991.

Seligman, Martin E. P. *Authentic happiness: Using the new positive psychology to realize your potential for lasting fulfillment.* New York: Free Press, 2002.

Seligman, Martin E. P. *Flourish: A visionary new understanding of happiness and well-being.* New York, NY: Free Press, 2011.

Siegel, Daniel J. *The mindful brain: Reflection and attunement in the cultivation of well-being.* New York: W.W. Norton, 2007.

Siegel, Daniel J. *The mindful therapist: A clinician's guide to mindsight and neural integration.* New York: W.W. Norton & Co., 2010.

Snyder, C. R., and Shane J. Lopez. *Handbook of positive psychology.* Oxford England: Oxford University Press, 2002.

Taylor, Jill Bolte. *My stroke of insight: A brain scientist's personal journey.* New York: Viking, 2008.

Vaillant, George E. *Aging Well: Surprising guideposts to a happier life from the landmark Harvard study of adult development.* Boston: Little, Brown, 2002.

Vaillant, George E. *Spiritual evolution: A scientific defense of faith.* New York: Broadway Books, 2008.

Appendix A

The Strengths Portrait

"Where Are You Playing?" Assessment

1. List your strengths in the right hand column. (an abbreviated notation)

2. List your weaknesses, <u>what you consider</u> to be the opposite of that strength for you, in the left hand column. (an abbreviated notation)

3. Score from 1-10 how much you are using a strength and then score how much you are allowing the opposite of the strength to function.

"10" means that you are using a great deal of a strength. "1" means that you are hardly using it at all, at least in a conscious way. It is similar for what you consider to be the opposite of your strength. "1" is not really using the weakness at all, and "10" is letting the opposite of the strength "play" strongly in your life.

It's Opposite	**Strengths**
(What you consider to be the opposite of your strength)	(List your **VIA** first and then your **SF** Strengths)
10-9-8-7-6-5-4-3-2-1 _____	_____ 1-2-3-4-5-6-7-8-9-10
10-9-8-7-6-5-4-3-2-1 _____	_____ 1-2-3-4-5-6-7-8-9-10
10-9-8-7-6-5-4-3-2-1 _____	_____ 1-2-3-4-5-6-7-8-9-10
10-9-8-7-6-5-4-3-2-1 _____	_____ 1-2-3-4-5-6-7-8-9-10
10-9-8-7-6-5-4-3-2-1 _____	_____ 1-2-3-4-5-6-7-8-9-10
10-9-8-7-6-5-4-3-2-1 _____	_____ 1-2-3-4-5-6-7-8-9-10
10-9-8-7-6-5-4-3-2-1 _____	_____ 1-2-3-4-5-6-7-8-9-10
10-9-8-7-6-5-4-3-2-1 _____	_____ 1-2-3-4-5-6-7-8-9-10
10-9-8-7-6-5-4-3-2-1 _____	_____ 1-2-3-4-5-6-7-8-9-10
10-9-8-7-6-5-4-3-2-1 _____	_____ 1-2-3-4-5-6-7-8-9-10
Total -B _____	_____ Total-A

Subtract B from A. The total is your PTYS Score. _____

What does your PTYS (Playing To Your Strengths) score mean? You can best answer that question by considering the result. If your strengths score is higher, you will be playing to your strengths more, you'll be higher in your UpSpiral Score, you'll be happier and you'll feel "on top it", feel good, and feel free. If you score is higher in playing to your weaknesses (Column B), the more you are in a DownSpiral or inclined to be there, the more oppressed and less in charge you will feel, with decreased creativity and limited options. Overall, you'll feel more like "it's on top of you." You will feel less good and less free. If your score is more even, as in "B" cancelling out "A," you are undermining your strengths, your progress and your UpSpiral, and your life is most likely experienced as mediocre or frustrating. The results are not absolute, but they give you an indication, a "red flag" of when you are not using and living in your strengths.

Copyright 2011 Dr. William K. Larkin